I'm Not Drunk, Honest!

Don Gresswell Ltd., L   J

Works by the same author

A novel
Exiled in Paradise
(To be published in late 1994)

Plays

I'm Not Drunk, Honest!

The Death of Jack the Lad

I'M NOT DRUNK, HONEST!

an autobiography

by

Hal Lever

Cover designed
by
Hal Lever

Lever Book Press
September 1994

British Library Cataloguing in Publication Data

Lever, H.
  I'm Not Drunk, Honest!
  1. An Autobiography
  1. Title

ISBN 0 9524154 0 2

Printed in Great Britain by Eaton Press
Westfield Rd., Wallasey,
Merseyside L44 7JB

Published by Lever Book Press
P.O. Box 53
Liverpool L69 4NP

iv

Foreword

This is a story which must be read!

It is an inspiring account of a man's refusal to be destroyed by an accident which shattered his body, distorted his sight, blanked his memory and all but obliterated his capacity for speech. But it is more than that. It is also the story of a man's self-belief and persistence in the face of constant misunderstanding, humiliation, and even insult. It reveals how insensitive many of us can be to the problems of the disabled: some of the passages in which Hal Lever records reactions to his attempts to speak normally are almost unbearably moving. Nor is the insensitivity and impercipience confined to the lay public. I suspect some of the medical profession have cause to feel deeply ashamed about their response to their patient's pain. The writer's exposure of their limitations is the more powerful because it is presented without malice or bitterness.

And running beneath the story of what must be seen as an almost miraculous recovery is another just as poignant - Hal Lever's desire to become a writer. The autobiography, written without the aid of 'ghosts,' is neither his only nor his first struggle to pin meanings and feelings with words. There is a novel in manuscript and numerous attempts at plays; there is undoubtedly more work to come.

Because this story is Hal Lever's own and not some 'as told to' version of a life, it has, rough edges not withstanding, authenticity and pace and also allows the man himself to come across strongly in all his admirable individuality - quirky; stubborn; often irritating in his persistence; irrepressible; endlessly optimistic; unflaggingly brave and, in the end, lovable. Here is the stuff of the island's survival in the Second World War. Here is the heroism of the ordinary person - too seldom sung, too seldom celebrated. Here is the victim who refused to be a victim and who defeated the corrosiveness of self-pity by will and wit. Here is hope for us all.

David Evans
University of Liverpool.

Dedicated to
my
Mother

Special Thanks To:

Emma Thompson.
Esther Rantzen and the "That's Life!" team
P's & Q's Design.
Jacqui King, Sidmouth, Devon.
Shell Chemicals U.K. Ltd.
Eaton Press, Westfield Rd., Wallasey, Merseyside L44 7JB.

Acknowledgements

Although I wrote, typeset, designed and published this book entirely
myself, I would like to thank the following people, companies and
organisations for their advice and encouragement. I must surely have
been a thorn in their sides at times, but, despite my pestering, the
individuals mentioned have all remained good friends.

David Evans, lecturer, University of Liverpool.
Graham Chan, Computer Laboratory, University of Liverpool.
Dept. of Continued Education, University of Liverpool.
Alf Greene, Larry Neild and Sue Critchley - "Liverpool Echo. "
Sue Lee and Claire Stokes - "Liverpool Daily Post."
Rex and Peter, P.A.C.T. Bootle, Department of Employment.
The late Bill Rawlinson, senior lecturer at Millbrook College,
Liverpool.
A.G. Fountain and Alan Loughrain, lecturers also at the above.
Margaret Clark, lecturer, University of Cambridge.

CONTENTS

Chapter 1

A New Dawn

Suddenly I hear a noise! I do not know what it is or where it is coming from. My eyes open but instantly shut again - the bright obscurity above me is too dazzling. Hesitantly, my eyes flicker open and gradually adjust to the light. My vision is a blur - all I can make out are reddish-brown blotches that seem to be swimming against a creamish-coloured background.

Lying there, face upwards on the mattress, I am feeling very weak, as if all my energy has been sapped from me. My head is throbbing, my face is burning, and I can hear the blood pulsating in my ears. I try to swallow but an excruciating pain in the upper half of my chest prevents me from doing so. I want to clear my throat but cannot - it is as if I am trying to blow up a paper bag that has a hole in it.

I stare blankly upwards into the blurred unknown. The air smells pungently clinical in my nostrils, and I can hear a slight humming sound in my ears.

As my eyes adjust to the light, I am able to see more clearly - the edges of the reddish-brown blotches are better defined.

No thoughts are passing through my mind - it is as if I am suspended in a vacuum, while the rest of the world is carrying on unaware of my existence - it seems I am restricted to viewing my own world purely objectively. Everything appears so very strange - as if I have suddenly been plunged into a world so lonely and alien to me that I am unable to relate to anything I can see, hear, feel, taste or smell. I do not try to move - I do not know how to or even if I can. I just lie there, alone in an unknown world.

I become fearful as I suddenly hear footsteps to my left. As they grow louder my eyes focus towards the bottom of the bed, not knowing what to expect. I feel terrified - the thudding in my chest beats louder.

Out of the corner of my eye, I can see the material of the screen around my bed move as a figure brushes by it. I hear people speaking, but their words mean nothing to me. Suddenly, the speaking stops. I can see the screen move again and hear that dreaded sound - the sound of footsteps. As they fade away, my fear diminishes but the echoes still linger in my ears.

My eyes begin to wander. To the left of my bed is a machine, which is making the humming noise I heard earlier. It has numerous dials and switches, as well as a red light flashing on its top surface. Many wires dangle from the back of it, but I cannot see to what they are attached. I move my head, ever so slowly, around to the left while straining my eyes to follow in their direction. My left eye begins to water, so I blink and the machine appears to move to and fro.

Suddenly, I become fearful again for as I move my head so too do the wires. Nothing detrimental happens to me however, so I begin to relax again - my instinct made me apprehensive, but my natural inquisitiveness soon prevailed. I slowly turn my head and again the wires move. It is amusing at first but, as I am unable to understand why it is happening, I soon tire of it. Behind the machine are two tall stands that tower above me. Two bottles are attached to the top of each stand, and from each bottle hangs what appears to be two tubes - both their ends are attached to both my left hands. As I lower my eyes, the two tubes appear to get closer together, until, at head height, they finally seem to merge into one. My eyes continue to move downwards and they become two again.

Slowly, I move my head around to my right to see two different machines and two trolleys stacked with bottles. A tall black metal container stands in the corner - it has white lettering on it, but each letter seems to jump about when I stare at it - it is blurred and I cannot decipher the words. Dangling from the container are two breathing masks. In the background is another screen.

Suddenly, I can hear those dreaded sounds of footsteps again. As the noise grows louder, my apprehension increases and the thudding in my chest becomes faster.

My eyes are fixed towards the bottom of the bed. I can see my four feet and notice there is an opening in the screen beyond them. Suddenly, I see two figures, dressed in green and white, go walking past. They continue walking and the sound of their footsteps eventually fades away.

I feel feverish and my ears are burning. I am sweating profusely, even though one of the machines is blowing cool air directly onto my body. I continue to stare blankly towards the bottom of the bed. All that is covering me is a narrow white sheet around my midriff.

Slowly, my head turns to the right. I can see that both of my right wrists and forearms are bound in plaster cast. A thumb and four fingers protrude from each of them.

My eyes suddenly dart towards the gap in the screen at the bottom of my bed. I am immediately terror-stricken: two blurred figures, dressed in green and white, are standing there. Their images are dim, but I can see that their mouths are ajar.

Terrified, I stare at them, not knowing who or what they are. I can hear my heart racing, as it continues to thump against my chest.

Without warning, the two figures rush away - moments later, I hear voices coming from behind the screen.

Four blurred figures, two dressed in blue, and two dressed in green and white, suddenly appear at the foot of my bed. The two in blue speak to the other pair, who then disappear behind the screen.

The two blue figures walk in step around to my left side. I am powerless to do anything, and, as they approach, their images seem to merge to become one blur.

The figure looks down at me and says something. I do not understand her, but her voice is gentle and comforting.

As I look fixedly up at her, my eyes become better focused. I can still feel my heart thudding against my chest.

She speaks to me while taking hold of my left wrist and goes on to take my pulse. Occasionally, she glances back and smiles warmly at me.

I am still terrified. I do not know who or what she is or why she is there. I just continue to stare up at her. Everything seems so strange to me, for my mind is filled with incoherent thoughts.

Again she speaks to me - this time in a more pronounced and slower fashion. Her words eventually do begin to take on some meaning, although I am unable to fully comprehend what she is saying.

She continues speaking but the more she says to me, the more mixed up I become. Although she is trying to make herself understood by leaving long pauses between each sentence, she is still talking too fast for her words to register in my brain.

I feel a sudden twinge in my throat. Instinctively, I grimace and attempt to swallow. I try desperately but find myself coughing painfully instead. Suddenly, a red and green blob of blood and mucus shoots upwards from a valve in my throat to spatter against the creamish-coloured ceiling.

She leans over me and examines my throat. I can smell her hair - it is so refreshing and so different to the pungent, clinical smells around me.

I hear a sudden gurgling sound being emitted from within my throat. I brace myself instinctively, awaiting another fit of coughing but nothing happens.

She speaks to me again, but I continue to stare up at her, unable to understand what she is saying or why she is standing over me.

As she leans across and puts my hand in hers, I immediately realize that her skin is warm and soft. I feel less vulnerable and much safer.

She is distracted by the appearance of four larger figures, dressed in white, standing at the bottom of my bed. Letting go of my hand, she looks at them, while they are speaking to her. She turns to smile warmly at me before saying something and moving away from my side.

I sense she is abandoning me all of a sudden, and I want to stop her from leaving. I try to speak but can only squeal.

She appears to sense my feelings and turns back. Smiling, she squeezes my hand gently and says something, as if to reassure me. I

4

respond to the caring tone in her voice, and I begin to relax once more.

Again she speaks to the figures in white and then disappears behind the screen.

As the four blurred figures approach, they gradually merge into two. However, this does not bother me; I simply accept it without question.

One of the figures says something to me. His voice is much deeper than the voice of the figure in blue.

I do not understand what he is saying or know how to respond - I merely stare at him.

He begins to examine my eyes using a bright light while the other observes and takes notes. They then speak to each other, but the pace of their speech is too fast for me to understand. The first one picks up an eye-patch from the trolley and proceeds, extremely carefully, to put it over my head. He then positions it across my right eye.

My vision immediately improves. I can see things much more distinctly by only using one eye.

The figure taking notes suddenly puts his pen and note pad down on the trolley before taking hold of my left hand and leaning over to speak to me. "Hal, we are doctors. You have been in a car accident," he says, in a slow and very pronounced manner. "If you understand what I'm saying, I want you to squeeze my hand."

I continue to look fixedly at him, trying to make out what he has said. Slowly, his words take on meaning and I begin to understand him, but I cannot squeeze his hand - my mind is far too incoherent to try to exert any control over my body.

He moves away from my bedside and has another discussion with his colleague. He then returns and, again, leans over me. "Hal, you have been unconscious," he says very slowly. "Squeeze my hand if you understand."

I eventually understand what he has said and realize that this is why I am in hospital. However, it is difficult to move my hand in response, so I flicker my eyelid instead.

Seeing this movement of my eyelid, he suddenly steps back and says something to his colleague. I do not know what he says, but I can tell by the tone of his voice he is delighted.

He approaches and smiles at me. "You are safe, do not worry," he says, deliberately and slowly. "If you understand what I am saying to you, please blink your eye."

It takes quite some time for me to understand what he has said, but I eventually blink my eyelid.

I am going to have a look at your throat - we had to put a special valve into it," he says slowly.

My upper chest and throat feel very sore and tender, as he carefully examines the tracheotomy valve.

His prodding and probing make it difficult for me to breathe. I suddenly grimace and the doctor steps back quickly as I cough deeply from my chest and heave violently. I suddenly see another blob of blood and mucus shooting forcefully upwards from the valve in my throat to spatter against the ceiling. I begin to breathe more easily.

After completing their examination of my throat they leave. I can hear them talking to somebody behind the screen, but they are speaking far too fast for it to be comprehensible to me. The talking stops and all I can hear are the sounds of footsteps fading away.

As time passes, my mind becomes a little clearer and I begin to think about what the doctor said to me. I do not question what he told me - I just accept it as fact. My thoughts are still confused, however, and I am unable to concentrate for very long.

Suddenly, two figures, dressed in green and white, appear at the foot of my bed. This time, one goes to my left while the other moves to my right.

I am not as frightened by them as I was before, although I continue to stare at them.

The woman dressed in blue returns and again takes hold of my left hand. "I'm Sister Malloy and these are two of my nurses," she says slowly. "If you can understand me, I want you to blink your eye."

She waits patiently, looking down at me and smiling encouragingly.

I eventually blink my eyelid.

6

She smiles with delight and then speaks to the two nurses, who answer her. I listen to what they are saying, but I still cannot understand their words.

The two nurses come nearer and very carefully lift my head and shoulders off the bed. The Sister then tilts the headrest into an inclined position and places half a dozen pillows behind me.

"You should feel more comfortable sitting up," says the Sister slowly, as the two nurses lower me gently back against the pillows.

I continue to stare at her, while she makes my bed more comfortable for me.

She turns and says something to the two nurses, who immediately leave and disappear behind the screen.

Taking hold of my left hand, she squeezes it gently before putting a pen in it. It immediately falls to the floor, since my hands are very weak and I cannot control them. The movement of the muscles in my body lacks co-ordination, and I cannot remember what a pen is, anyway. My eyes follow her while she bends down to pick up the pen and puts it in the breast pocket of her uniform. She looks back at me and takes hold of my hand. "Don't worry, you're going to be all right - time is a great healer," she says slowly, as she looks down and smiles at me.

I continue to stare strangely at her. My mind is working erratically and is still very confused. I want to ask her if I am still alive on Earth or dead in Heaven. I try to form the words but cannot. As I try to speak, I realize it is too much of an effort for me to open my mouth and move my tongue; they feel as though they are glued together and my fears surface again.

A deep gurgling sound is emitted from the valve in my throat, and I quickly glance down at my chest but nothing happens. When I look back up at her, she smiles compassionately.

"Your Mother is here," she says slowly. "She can only see you for a minute, though."

I continue to stare at her, as I try to grasp the meaning of what she has said. However, I have no notion of what a "mother" might be exactly, so I do not blink my eyes.

She lets go of my hand and smiles, as she looks straight at me and slowly shakes her head. "You're a miracle," she says before turning and walking away to disappear behind the screen.

Now that I am sitting up in bed, I begin to feel a little better although my mind is still deranged. I am however less apprehensive. I try desperately to think of the meaning of the word "mother." Although I vaguely grasp the sense of the word, my mind is still too mixed up to relate it to myself.

A figure, wearing spectacles and dressed in brown, appears at the end of the bed. As she approaches my side, her bloodshot eyes focus on mine. Holding a crumpled handkerchief to her drawn and tired face, she smiles down at me.

I simply stare at the stranger by my side, not recognising her at all. I wonder why she is here.

She sits down on the chair and takes hold of my hand. "Hello, Hal, thank God you've pulled through," she says very slowly while wiping her eyes with the handkerchief. "You've been in a car accident. They've all been in to see you - Gordon flew from Canada, but he had to go back after a week," she says, carefully pronouncing her words.

Her voice is gentle but I merely continue to gaze at her.

When I eventually understand what she has said, I become even more perplexed. What does she mean by the words "they've all been in to see you?" And who is Gordon and what is he doing in Canada? I have no idea what she is talking about - I can vaguely understand the words, but I still cannot connect them to myself.

She looks down at me, as if she is expecting me to acknowledge her somehow.

I continue to stare at her, unable to recognize her at all. "Who is this person and what is she doing here?" I wonder, trying to unravel the mystery.

"Me and your Dad will be coming in tonight. The doctors told me that I must only stay a minute, so I should be going," she says slowly, while smiling and gently squeezing my hand in hers.

I continue to stare at her as she bends down and kisses my hand before leaving my side.

Reaching the bottom of the bed, she stops, turns towards me, and takes out her handkerchief again. She wipes away the tears of joy that have welled in her eyes and then returns to my side. Taking hold of my hand again, she kisses it and looks upwards. "Thank you, God," she says. Putting my hand back on the bed, she smiles again before turning and walking away. Moments later, she disappears behind the screen.

As soon as she has left, the two doctors return. Later, more doctors come while a series of rigorous examinations is carried out on me.

Throughout that day, many different doctors came to my bedside. Some would examine me, while others would merely look at me and talk amongst themselves.

My mind slowly becomes more active although it is still far from fully conscious. My head still feels heavy and the muscles at the back of my neck are tense. I am feeling extremely tired after the many examinations I have undergone, although my mind is curious about this new world and refuses to allow my eyelids to close.

I desperately try to remember if I have previously met the stranger with the bloodshot eyes. I can recall what she said to me, but she does not exist in my memory. I try to remember who Gordon is, with the same result.

As my natural inquisitiveness increases, I find it more difficult to concentrate. My mind soon tires and my attention flits about looking at the numerous mysterious machines and equipment around my bed.

The Sister allows only my parents to see me that evening. I recognize my mother, with the bloodshot eyes, but only because I have seen her at my bedside hours earlier. To the best of my knowledge, I have never previously seen her before that day, nor the man at her side.

They seem very content to see that I am merely staring at them and do not try to ask me any questions. They mention the names "Madeline, Angela, Jennifer, Gordon, Brenda, Linda, Colin and Janet," but they are just names to me. I do not realize that they are talking about my brothers and sisters.

It has been a very strange and tiring day and my eyelids are beginning to grow heavier. Before visiting time ends, my weariness gets the better of me, and I cannot hold my eyes open any longer. They close and I fall asleep.

Chapter 2

The Next Day

The next day, I woke up feeling a little better. My head felt as if it was supporting a heavy weight and I was still tired and weak. I was a little less apprehensive but felt very alien and lonely in my new world. Despite the events of the previous day, I still felt as if I was suspended in some strange limbo. I still wanted to know whether I was alive on Earth or not - but how was I to find out?

A nurse, dressed in blue, approached me, carrying a feeding cup. "Good morning, Hal, how are you this morning?" she asked slowly.

I merely stared at her and wondered if I had seen her the day before.

"Let's make you nice and comfy," she said, before lifting my head and shoulders carefully and arranging my pillows.

"There, now that feels better, doesn't it?"

I did not respond.

"I've to put your eye-patch over your other eye, today," she said, looking down and smiling at me. Very carefully, she removed the patch over my right eye, adjusted the elastic, and positioned it across the other one.

I knew she was not the Sister I met yesterday; her hair smelled differently.

"I'm Sister Lloyd," she said slowly, as she gently squeezed my hand in hers, "I'm going to feed you some warm milk." She put her left arm around my shoulders and lifted the feeding cup to my lips with her right hand.

It was my first drink since regaining consciousness and it tasted good. I could not get it down properly because it was difficult for me to swallow. My mouth and especially my tongue felt numb.

"Take it easy - don't be in so much of a hurry," she said, as I attempted to gulp it as fast as I could.

Suddenly, I winced and began coughing. The Sister had to pat me on my back for what seemed like a lifetime so I did not choke. My eyes had begun to water and mucus was dribbling down my nose as I gasped for air.

Later that morning, many doctors examined me. So many of them had come to see me the day before that I was unable to remember all their faces. Some of them would have an entourage of junior and student doctors in tow. They would look studiously down at me while discussing different aspects of my condition. It was difficult for me to understand English even when spoken slowly to me, so I had no chance of comprehending their medical jargon.

Shortly before lunch, three radiographers wheeled in a portable x-ray machine. I was subjected to numerous x-rays, since it was considered too dangerous to take me from my bed.

During the next few days, there was little change in either my condition or the treatment I received. The most important thing was that I was becoming more aware and responsive to my surroundings. I was beginning to feel less tired and my brain was becoming a little more active, although I was suffering from amnesia and many other injuries.

Four or five days after regaining consciousness, my parents brought the family's photograph album into the hospital. They showed me snaps of each of my six sisters and two brothers, but I still showed no positive reaction.

I did not recognize anybody. I was able to identify my parents, since they were by my side, but I could not remember anything at all about my past life, come to that. They showed me a photograph in a newspaper article. Although the face did look familiar, I was in no fit mental state to know that it was a photograph of myself. My mother told me that, after finding £27 in a lost handbag at the age of twelve, my photograph had appeared in the newspaper. Nor did I recognize any of the photographs taken of me when I was away at sea. It was surprising to discover that I used to be a Cadet Officer in the Merchant Navy. In particular, my parents seemed surprised that I did not remember the photograph taken inside the ward of a Japanese hospital. They told me that when my ship was docked in Sakata, Japan, I had developed appendicitis during the night and had to be rushed to hospital. Later that day, after the operation had been performed on me, the ship had sailed for Brazil. I had remained in the hospital for a fortnight, before I was flown home. They showed me many other photographs taken when I was at school and when a student at Hull Nautical College, but I could not relate to any of them.

Each day, a variety of doctors would examine me many times. They would usually have a hoard of eager students trailing after them. Apart from the usual genial greetings they would never address me directly,

Later, the physiotherapists would come to give me many exercises to do. It was hard work and I dreaded it. Even though they would always give me plenty of encouragement, it was too exhausting to enjoy. They attempted to strengthen the grip of my left hand by giving me a sponge ball to squeeze. I could not use my right hand, as my broken wrist was still in plaster. After a few days, I was able to use my left hand and arm - but not effectively, since my limbs were still weak and badly lacking co-ordination.

A week later, although I was still on the "Critical List," they did allow more of my visitors to see me. I would never attempt to smile at them; they were strangers to me. I would just lie in bed with my head swaddled in pillows, and stare at them.

I did eventually get used to hospital life and continued to show signs of improvement. My brain had begun to function better, albeit at a very much slower pace than normal. Nevertheless, the strange stare on my face did make it difficult for others to tell how I was feeling.

I began to recognize more of the words that I heard, and I was able to understand them far more quickly. Whenever I came across a "new" word, I would say it repeatedly in my head to fix it firmly in my brain.

However, it would soon become boring, since it was difficult to sustain my concentration for a long period.

During the next few days, I made more progress and even tried to communicate with my parents. They were overjoyed, even though I could only manage a babble, which they could not understand at first.

In attempting to rediscover my lost past, I would try to force myself to remember my mother and father, as well as the other people I had seen on the photographs in the album. But it was difficult. How could I consciously make an effort to remember something that seemed to have gone from my mind altogether?

The tracheotomy valve was still lodged in my throat and made it even more difficult for me to communicate with others. It took a great deal of effort just to make the strange sound come out of the valve in my throat. It was very painful. The nurses told me that I would be able to talk if I put my hand over the valve. I tried this but it did not make much difference - I was still unable to speak. However, this action did allow me to make noises. The doctors and nurses reassured me that everything would be all right, once I had been down to the theatre to have the valve removed.

When the day arrived for the valve to be taken out, everybody seemed to be in a joyous mood. I did not fully understand the intricacies involved in the operation, but I looked forward to the time when I would be able to breathe through my nose and speak properly again.

However, things do not always turn out as expected. When I came around from the effects of the anaesthetic, I was still unable to speak and barely able to move my mouth or my tongue. It was difficult to breath properly, and this inevitably affected my speech. When I did eventually manage to speak, my words were so slurred that they were completely unintelligible. I spoke frustratingly slowly and was barely able to utter one word for every breath I took, and, even then, it took an experienced ear to understand what I was trying to say.

I did not realise this at first, and, because people were so understanding and caring, they would not tell me that my speech was badly impaired. It may seem odd that I was not aware of the problem, but there are many times when a drunken man does not realise he sounds slurred.

The best way of describing my speech is to say it was a drawn-out babble. I sounded like a voice on a record that is played at a much slower speed. It was as if I was speaking extremely slowly and yawning at the same time.

Now that I was more aware of my breathing and swallowing problems and could take care in the way I swallowed, I was allowed to eat semi-solid food. While I was unconscious, I had been fed intravenously and had lost a couple of stone in weight. To remedy this, I was fed on "Complan," as well as other semi-solid foods.

I was still unable to carry out the simplest of tasks due to the lack of co-ordination in my limbs. The nurses had to feed me, since I could not hold any cutlery in my hand. The lack of co-ordination affected most of my body movements and meant I had to relearn to control and synchronize the movement of my limbs. This became apparent when I tried to feed myself; for instance, when attempting to put food into my mouth, I would usually misdirect it and end up putting it in my ear.

Since my right wrist was still in plaster, I could only use my left hand. I also had a nervous twitch, which seemed to occur at the most untimely moments; for instance, when I tried to drink from a beaker. I would suddenly twitch and the beaker would go flying out of my hand, hitting the wall on the other side of the ward - the top of the beaker would come off and the contents would be emptied over the floor.

The lack of control over my bodily movements also meant that I was unable to walk, not that I was anywhere near well enough to be out of bed.

Nonetheless, the staff of the Infirmary treated me as if I was somebody special. Nothing they did for me was ever too much trouble for them, and there would often be a nurse sitting close at hand to help me whenever I required assistance.

The plaster on my right wrist did not cause me too much discomfort, since I was in no condition to use my hand. When the plaster was removed, my wrist appeared to have healed successfully. It began to ache later but I did not inform the doctors or nurses. I was so grateful to them for having saved my life that I did not want to put them to any further inconvenience.

Ten days after I had regained consciousness, the doctors decided that it was safe enough to dry shampoo my hair. My scalp was caked in dried blood, and, as a result, my hair was a mass of curls. Later, they combed it, before letting me look at myself in a mirror. I had been looking forward to seeing myself, hoping the sight of my face would help awake my dormant memory. When I looked in the mirror, my face did seem familiar, but I was still unable to remember anything of my past. I was bitterly disappointed.

As I grew more aware of other people's reactions to my defective speech, I began to wonder why some people would look at me, their faces screwed up in confusion whenever I spoke. Eventually, I realized I did not speak properly. Since nobody had mentioned this fact to me, I did not worry too much about it.

One afternoon, a dozen men of about my age came to see me. They told me they were my work mates, and that I worked as a Trainee Chemical Plant Operator at Shell Chemicals' Carrington plant, near Manchester. I did not recognize any of them; I merely stared at them, but they did not seem to mind. It was such a strange situation, since they all seemed to know me well. I was embarrassed because they were very friendly, but I did not feel any particular warmth towards them. They even told me about my twenty-first birthday party I had celebrated with them three months earlier, but all of this was news to me. A nurse overheard one of my work mates mentioning my car accident and informed the Sister, who immediately summoned them to her office. When they returned they changed the subject.

She must have told them about my speech problem as well as the difficulty I had in understanding others speaking because they spoke extremely slowly and did not give me the chance to reply. Most of the time they told jokes and talked about people who had sent me their regards. They brought me a large bunch of flowers and a basket of fruit from Shell. The other patients and the nurses thought they were great fun, but all I could do was lie there and stare.

16

People would always tell me how lucky I had been to have survived and that I was a miracle for doing so. I only vaguely grasped what they were talking about to begin with. Eventually, it slowly began to dawn on me that I must have been involved in some sort of accident.

I was revelling in the attention the staff were paying me; it was so encouraging. I wanted to show people that I was not going to allow my injuries to get the better of me. I decided that the more I spoke, the better my speech would become. Regardless of who was around, I made up my mind never to be ashamed of the way I spoke. I would often ask people how I sounded, and, if they understood me, they would usually say "Fine" or "Well, I can understand you." However, if I insisted on being told the truth, they would usually admit that I spoke slowly. I therefore decided to try to speak faster, but it was difficult and my speech would sound much worse - if that was possible.

One afternoon, a professor, with a crowd of student doctors trailing behind him, came to see how I was recovering. They all stood around my bed discussing various aspects of my case while not bothering to talk to me. I felt bored and wanted to speak to them. Although I had made a pledge earlier never to be ashamed of my speech, I soon felt like going back on my word. The doctor and students before me were strangers, so I was not sure how they would react to my babble.

Eventually, I began to tell them a joke that a nurse had told me. With the decorum typical of their profession, they patiently stood looking down at me, while I laboriously continued to tell them the joke. However, I did not realize that they could not understand a word I was saying. They must have thought I was well and truly insane, especially at the end of the joke. I remember telling them the punch line and suddenly bursting into laughter, while they stood looking down at me, absolutely straight faced. I had not had much opportunity to use my stomach muscles in hospital, so they were weak and far from taut. When I began to laugh I found it difficult to stop. I was doubled up in bed, desperately trying to get a grip on my stomach muscles. While I struggled to keep my mirth under control, I kept glancing up and saw an assortment of bewildered faces looking down at me, which provoked another bellow of laughter. I managed eventually to stop, but this was only because my stomach muscles were aching. I suppose it was my fault for laughing at my own joke. Nevertheless, this outburst of merriment did exercise my facial muscles and I lost my strange stare.

Six weeks after the accident, time seemed to be passing more rapidly. Both my mental and physical health were slowly improving, and I had progressed to eating some solids, although body building liquids were still an important part of my diet.

The Sister told me I would be going to another hospital. She said something about "specialist treatment," and that I would be able to recover more quickly there, but I did not fully grasp what she was saying.

Chapter 3

Welcome to Winwick!

I vividly remember the day I was transferred from Warrington Infirmary to Winwick Psychiatric Hospital. It was a cold afternoon in February. The weak wintry sun was barely visible through the morbid greyness above. A peppering of frost was still present on the window sills. The wind was not strong, although its gust was enough to make me grit my teeth.

The weather did not bother me. Swaddled in a shawl, I was wheeled out of the Infirmary. Many of the nurses I knew were standing on the steps of the hospital, as they braved the weather to wave farewell to me. Some of them were blowing kisses to me, while the ambulance man wheeled me out to the awaiting vehicle.

I was sad to be leaving. It felt as if I was leaving part of me behind. Because my amnesia was so bad the only people I could recognize were those I had met since regaining consciousness. It was therefore natural that I should have formed a certain attachment to the place. My mind was still not functioning well enough for me to realize that I would probably not have regained consciousness if it had not been for the care and attention I had received from the Infirmary's staff.

Sister Malloy had told me I was going to Winwick Psychiatric Hospital, where there would be more staff better qualified to care for a patient with my particular injuries. I never questioned the decision to transfer me, since I had no idea what the word "psychiatric" meant at the time.

The ambulance men lifted me out of the wheelchair and carried me into the ambulance, as a nurse carried my bag.

I managed to smile at the nurses on the hospital steps as they finally waved and wished me well. I tried in vain to raise my hands in farewell, but the lack of co-ordination prevented me doing so.

The nurse accompanying me was wearing her navy blue serge cloak. Sitting next to me, she held my hand as we moved away from the kerb. Her hands were warm and soft and her manner relaxing. I felt safe with her I found the ambulance man sitting opposite me very cheerful and amusing at first. He spoke very slowly so I was able to understand him. However, I began to tire of his sense of humour after a short while. At that particular moment, I wanted to think about what was happening to me. It was all the more frustrating because as soon as I attempted to formulate a question in my mind, I would usually forget what I wanted to ask, or something else would distract me from my thoughts.

As we made our way through the busy streets of Warrington, I had a feeling of *déjà vu*. The sounds of activity and the pungent smells of the town seemed to strike a chord within me.

From my position, I could see a view of the town through the shaded window opposite me. Shop signs could be seen and the noises of the traffic could be heard, as we moved through the town centre. The sound of a car horn reverberated in my ears, and the pungent smell of diesel abused my nostrils. As we continued through the traffic, the shop signs became less frequent, the barrage of noise lessened and the smells became fresher. Eventually, the road became quieter and we were soon travelling in the open country. The ambulance reduced speed suddenly and turned off the main road.

Glancing up, I noticed we were passing through a gateway with large sandstone posts and wrought-iron gates. As we pressed on, I could see a column of white smoke rising out of a chimney on the gatehouse roof. The sky was overcast. I could see the tops of many large trees.

I looked at the nurse again.

She smiled and sat down. "Trees," she said, squeezing my hand.

As the ambulance turned, I could see a large building with ivy growing up its facade. There were bars on the windows, but I did not wonder why.

The ambulance stopped and the driver got out. He came around to the back to open the door, so his colleague could join him. They both went inside the building, while the nurse remained behind in the ambulance holding my hand.

I did not understand what was going on and began to feel afraid. I looked anxiously at my companion.

Sensing my fear, she put her arm around me and enveloped me with her cloak. As my head rested on her breast, her heartbeat was soothing to my ears, and I continued to stare out at the red-bricked building.

Suddenly, a woman appeared from behind the opened door of the ambulance. She was tall and her head was bald, except for a few short black hairs that seemed to stand defiantly erect. She grinned at me and I could see that her upper and lower front teeth were missing. The black duffle coat she wore was frayed at the edges and hung loosely about her frame. On her feet was a pair of dirty plimsolls that had no laces. Her large bulging eyes were blank as she stared at me.

"Are you here on holiday, as well?" she asked, as she grinned and put her hands behind her back while swaying to and fro. "The doctor said I can go home next year."

My apprehension grew as I looked mystified at the strange woman. In response, the nurse looked down and held me closer to her.

At that moment, one of the ambulance men came back with a wheelchair. "Hello, Jean, are you having a nice holiday?" he asked the woman, while winking at the nurse.

The woman burst out laughing and suddenly ran inside the hospital. The ambulance men carried me out and put me into the wheelchair. As I sat there, the nurse took hold of my hand and squeezed it, obviously expecting me to look up and smile.

I stared at the ground, since my feelings of isolation had surfaced. I felt as if I was being abandoned. My thoughts went back to when they told me of my transfer to Winwick for "special treatment." I had wondered at first what that meant exactly, and the meaning of the word "psychiatric" soon began to dawn on me.

Some mistake had been made, surely. I was perplexed and even wondered if the reason for sending me to Winwick was that somebody had labelled me as insane without my knowledge. "Am I mad?" I asked myself. I certainly sounded strange but surely I was not insane - but how was I to prove it?

The nurse let go of my hand as the ambulance man wheeled me into the hospital. We went through a labyrinth of eerie corridors, which were painted bright green and yellow, but they still appeared dismal to me. We continued along what seemed to be a never-ending maze of passages, before we eventually entered a large hall.

A thick-set man was standing in the far corner, near the door of the Intensive Care Unit. He was in his forties and was wearing a grey serge suit that had seen better days. Down the front of his jacket were the remnants of some of his meals. His hair was cropped short and his face was fat and unshaven. On his feet he wore a large pair of black boots, which were scuffed and in need of polishing.

As we approached, I could see that he was picking his nose. When he saw us looking at him, he looked away quickly but continued his activity.

"We're going to meet your Charge Nurse now," said the nurse.

I looked up at her, puzzled.

"A Charge Nurse is in charge of a ward - like a sister only a man," she added, upon seeing my bewilderment.

I did not fully grasp what she meant. From her words, I conjured up an image of a man in a female nurse's uniform.

The nurse rang the bell and we waited.

Suddenly, the man standing in the corner turned and looked at me; his eyes were blank and his face expressionless.

I was apprehensive and looked up at the nurse, wondering what was going to happen next. She looked down at me and squeezed my hand in response.

"Don't worry," she said slowly, as she turned to look at the man, "he won't harm you."

Suddenly, I heard the sound of a key rattling in the lock.

The Charge Nurse opened the door and stood before me. Much to my surprise, he was not wearing a female nurse's uniform. He wore black trousers, a white shirt and a black tie. Brushing his black wavy hair back with his fingers, he smiled at the nurse before looking down and giving me what appeared to be a wry smile, as he welcomed us inside.

He wheeled me across the ward and, with the help of the nurse, lifted me into a bed. He spoke to the nurse, and they shook hands. Without saying a word to me, he left my bedside and then walked half the length of the ward and went into his office. I felt uneasy. I wanted to return to the security of the Infirmary.

Before the nurse left on her return journey, she looked down at me in the bed. "Don't look so worried - you'll soon get better in here," she said, leaning across and kissing me on the cheek. She said something else as she was walking away but I was not listening - the softness of her lips on my cheek mesmerized me. She waved as she left the ward.

I felt sad and nervous, more so since I did not like the look of the hospital. To make matters worse, I did not like the look of the Charge Nurse. In particular, I did not like the smug way he had smiled at the nurse and then at me. I sensed somehow that he disliked me.

Again I began to think about my mental state and wondered whether people were mistakenly assuming I was insane, or whether I was crazy but did not realize it. How was I to tell? How could they tell?

As I sat up in my bed, I was able to see the Charge Nurse putting on his black blazer. He left his office and walked in my direction.

He was not at all as I had imagined a Charge Nurse to be. Deep down I felt a bit peeved at his lady-killer looks and arrogant manner. I did not know what it was exactly, but I did not like the first impression I had of him. I had the feeling that I should not trust him.

After pulling a chair closer to my bedside, he looked at me and smiled. "Hello, Hal, my name is Tommy Malloy - you can call me Tommy," he said in a slow and friendly sort of way. "I'm the Charge Nurse on this ward.

Although his amicable manner surprised me, I simply smiled back and nodded to show him I had understood.

Recognising a familiar sound, I remembered that one of the

Sisters at the Infirmary was also called "Malloy." My first reaction was to tell him this, but then I began to wonder if all senior nurses in charge of hospital wards were called "Malloy." Fortunately, I remembered that I had never heard anyone use the name "Malloy" to address Sister Lloyd.

I was eager to tell him of this coincidence. Unfortunately, in my excited state, I attempted to speak as fast as possible with the result that my speech came out even more babbled than before.

I saw the puzzled look on his face and realized he had not understood me. It was tiring to speak since it meant having to pause for breath every word or so. I felt frustrated and down-hearted.

"Look, Hal, try to slow down," he said compassionately. "Parts of your throat, mouth and tongue have been paralysed due to the shock of the accident. You have been through a hell of an ordeal, but you must not get upset about your speech"

Feeling better, I began to relax for the first time since arriving in the place. I realized Tommy was much more understanding than I had first thought.

"I know a lot more about you than you think," he said, smiling.

Surprised at his words, I gave him a puzzled look.

"Sister Malloy in the Infirmary is my wife," he said slowly. He raised his eyebrows and went on. "You're all she's been talking about for the past six weeks."

Once I had understood what he was getting at, I felt very relieved. A great burden had been lifted from my shoulders. I realized that he knew I was not mad and that I could trust him as a friend.

From then onwards, I got on well with Charge Nurse Malloy, who insisted I call him "Tommy." He turned out to be really genuine and a first class nurse - which only goes to show that you should not judge a book by its binding.

A man in his early twenties occupied the bed to my right. His name was David. He was grossly overweight and his black hair was cropped short. He did not look at me but continued to stare at the pictures in the comic that lay opened before him.

To my left was an old man, whose name was Amos. His ruddy

cheeks contrasted against his pure white beard and silvery white hair. He was senile and appeared to be contentedly living in a world of his own.

Later that day as I lay in my bed, I closed my eyes and tried desperately to will myself to recover some memory of my past life. I began by thinking about the people identified as my parents, but it seemed that my memory was a blank. It was futile - the more I tried, the more my mind would wander. The only coherent recollections in my mind were the events that had taken place since waking up and finding myself in a hospital bed. My frustration grew to such an extent that I began to doubt if I had a past at all.

I was startled out of my fruitless quest by a male nurse, who told me that the doctor was coming to examine me. He helped me to sit up in readiness for the examination before going about his duties.

Shortly after, the door opened and in walked a fine figure of a man. He was wearing a smart tweed suit and sported a dark-brown beard.

"Hello, Mr. Lever, I'm Doctor Kelly," he said, as he drew up a chair to my bedside.

He had a deeper voice than anybody else I had met. Although he had a friendly bedside manner he did not say a great deal, or even ask many questions. Those questions he did ask merely required a nod or a shake of the head in response. He did not stay long but excused himself, saying that he had to attend an urgent matter elsewhere in the hospital.

After he had left, a nurse informed me that the evening meal would soon be ready.

I was hungry and was looking forward to getting some food into my stomach. I had missed the afternoon tea-break while travelling from the Infirmary, and the fresh air must have whetted my appetite.

A nurse came to feed me, but I could not eat all of the meal. Despite my hunger, it was too revolting to choke down. The soup was so diluted that I could not discern its flavour - mind you, it was hot - so hot that it almost scalded my tongue, which is all the more dangerous when parts of the throat and mouth are paralysed. As for the rest of the meal, I merely nibbled at it. The meat, which I think was brawn, was sliced so thinly that it seemed to melt in my mouth, before I had the time

25

to taste it. The potatoes, still with their many eyes intact, were cold and not cooked properly, and the peas were as hard as peanuts. There was a choice of either sago or rice for dessert. I did not like the look of either, so I finished with a cup of strongly stewed tea and some digestive biscuits that the nurses at the Infirmary had given me.

That evening my mother and father came in to see me. The nurses at the Infirmary had warned them that the food in Winwick was not very appealing, so they brought me a pile of ham sandwiches, two packets of digestive biscuits and a couple of bars of chocolate. I ate the sandwiches and, even though my mother fed me, it took me over an hour since I had to be careful swallowing my food.

When my parents saw Amos, they said he reminded them of Archie, a tramp who used to roam the streets around where we lived in Kirkdale when I was a boy. My mother told me that when I was seven, I had befriended Archie. She went on to tell me how one afternoon, I had taken him home and given him something to eat while she was out shopping. The story amused me, although I found it difficult to believe.

After the Night Charge Nurse had locked up for the night and switched out the main lights, one of the patients started screaming and shouting. His constant raving annoyed the other patients. Eventually, the male night-nurse had to telephone for more help, which came in the form of two burly-looking members of the hospital staff, who soon sorted him out. They held him down, while the male nurse gave him an injection to make him sleep. He never bothered anybody again that night.

The ward was soon quiet once more. As I lay there, I began to think about how different life in the Infirmary was to that in Winwick.

Suddenly, Amos let out an almighty scream. I turned in surprise and could see that the light from the bathroom was shining on his face. He was fast asleep.

My eyes closed and I began to think of him. Although this old man appeared to be happy in his isolated world, I still felt sorry for him.

I did not get much rest that night. As soon as I started to doze off, somebody else would start screaming or shouting in his sleep. In the end, the Nurse suggested I take a sleeping tablet. Reluctantly, I accepted.

The next day, I settled back in bed and attempted to remember my past but was distracted by a scraping sound low down to the left of my bed. Mystified, I looked down to see what was making such a racket.

It was Amos. He was sitting on the floor with a shopping basket by his side. The floor was paved with yellow tiles, apart from one coloured black every so often to break the monotony. As I watched him, he was trying to pick up a black tile near my bed. Although he failed to pick it up, he imagined he had done so and went on to put it into his basket. He then unconcernedly moved away to the next black tile, where he repeated his actions. Without a care in the world, he continued around the ward, until a male nurse took away his basket and put him to bed.

After almost a month in Winwick, I had grown used to the daily routine, which mainly consisted of lying in bed and doing nothing but thinking. It was just as well I had lost my memory and had nothing with which to compare my present existence, because the boredom would surely have affected my sanity. However, I was able to recognize my family, although I was unable to recall clearly any history of events in my life. The only lucid memories I held were of my life in a hospital bed, either in the Infirmary or in Winwick.

My life was very isolated. The nurses would awake me at six thirty in the morning to give me a beaker of warm tea. Later, they would wash and shave me before giving me my breakfast. Afterwards, there would be little for me to do. I would long to see the food trolley coming, not because I was necessarily hungry, but because it would mean a break in the monotony. Tommy would have a good talk with me every few days to see how I was progressing. I was largely left to my own devices.

Life only seemed to liven up at visiting time, when I would enjoy the company of my family. Although I could still not remember much about my past, most of my earlier doubts and fears about my relatives no longer possessed me, and I had come to accept them as my kin. Nevertheless, my identity continued to haunt me.

Because I was part of a large family, I was never short of visitors.

It was an ordeal for me to sort out their names at first. Nevertheless, I had a great advantage over the other patients. At visiting time, I would usually have at least four visitors to cheer me up and to bring me a gift of some sort. Only occasionally would a visitor come to see one of the other patients. Most of them did not have any relatives, or had been disowned by them. It was a sorry state of affairs.

Since regaining consciousness, I had always taken twelve vitamins tablets each day. Upon my arrival at Winwick, however, I began taking a sleeping tablet every night, because the ward was often too noisy to get a good night's sleep. I did not like the idea of taking one at first. I was afraid of not waking up again, and the pill would make me feel drowsy the following morning. Apart from throat lozenges, I did not receive any other medication or treatment.

Even though the food at Winwick was not at all appetizing to look at, I began to eat more of it. Whether this was the need to satisfy my hunger or simply to give me something to do is debatable. When I first arrived at Winwick, I was always the first patient to be fed by the nurses. However, as time wore on and my co-ordination slowly improved, they began to leave me unaided until they had fed the other patients. I would always be amongst the first to be served my meal, but they would usually leave me waiting, knowing that I would eventually begin to feed myself.

Their ploy worked, even though it was frustrating for me at first. I would often drop my knife, fork, or spoon on the floor and have to wait for a nurse to pick it up for me. My co-ordination was still far from perfect, and I would often spill bits of food into my bed, as well as get it over my face, in my ear or in my hair. I often had to have a wash and my sheets changed afterwards. Nevertheless, as the days went by, my co-ordination was slowly improving and I was becoming much more independent and aware of my circumstances.

After six weeks in Winwick, I was able to think more clearly, although my mental awareness and responses were still much slower than those of the average person. On the only occasion I saw the doctor, he decided that I should no longer wear the patch over my eye. My double-vision had not improved significantly but he felt my eyes would benefit if I persevered without the patch.

Chapter 4

The Beauty of Nature

Since my accident, I had been almost entirely confined to a hospital environment, apart from the brief ambulance ride from the Infirmary to Winwick. I had come to regard Winwick as my natural home, simply because I had no memory of any other life-style. Homesickness never bothered me, since I had never seriously thought about life outside a hospital ward. In that respect, I had become institutionalized.

One glorious day in early April, Tommy and a nurse put me in a wheelchair and took me to the solarium, built onto the ward. They left me sitting in the bright sunlight by an opened window.

I could feel the sun's rays gently caressing my face, as I sat in the wheelchair, surrounded by different species of potted plants. Suddenly, I became aware of the flowers, the grass, the trees, and could hear the birds singing. The natural beauty surrounding me was intoxicating. A glorious feeling of tranquillity was overwhelming and had a dramatic effect on me. I sensed a dormant part of me was suddenly awakening. I felt wholesome and thankful to be alive.

This experience seemed to trigger off a new awareness in me. Instead of continuing to lie back in my bed, I made up my mind to actively think about my circumstances. Taking a long look at my situation, I compared it with that of my fellow patients. It did not take long for me to realize that I was not only lucky to be alive and, apart from my memory, was still able to retain full control over my mental faculties, unlike the other patients. It was true that my reactions were a lot slower than those of an average person, my speech was incomprehensible, I was unable to walk due to the lack of co-ordination in my legs, and my right wrist was too tender to be used properly, as well as having many other disabilities besides, but these seemed irrelevant to me now. The important thing was that I was alive and had the essential ability to think. The other patients did not have this gift and were doomed to live in institutions for the rest of their lives. My prospects were much brighter for I still retained the potential to try, at least, to change my own predicament.

That day greatly changed my life and brought a new dimension to the way I viewed myself. It would have been easy for me to say that I had hated all the sympathy relatives and hospital staff had freely given me, but to be honest, I used to love it. People would tell me how courageous I was to have survived the accident. They always seemed to compliment me for never feeling sorry for myself, but I had lost my memory and therefore could not remember what my life had been like before the accident. Consequently, I had nothing to feel sorry about.

I could have remained an invalid and had others looking after me for the rest of my life. However, it occurred to me that, rather than lie there like a stuffed dummy, I needed to do something positive to speed up my recovery. I took the decision on the spur of the moment to try to walk.

The door to the bathroom was to my left between Amos's bed and my own. I decided to get out of bed on the right and walk around to the other side, while holding on to the bed for support. Once there, I would lean over and grab hold of the toilet door, leaving me with no option but to walk. Why I chose to get out of bed on the right and take the long way around is a mystery to me - I just did not give myself time to think straight.

As I have already stated, things do not always turn out as planned. Getting out of the bed on the right, I managed to make my way around to the other side. Due to my lack of co-ordination, I had to drag myself along with my upper body supported by the bed. It was hard work and I was sweating profusely.

I took my time with the next phase of my plan. My intention was to grab hold of the door handle and then support myself by holding on to it, until I could transfer my weight onto my feet. My excitement grew and after a short rest, I took a deep breath and went ahead.

I grabbed hold of the bedpost and pulled myself up into a standing position, so I could lean across the door to grab hold of the doorknob - it was at this point my plan went wrong. As I grabbed for the it, I immediately realized my mistake: although there was a handle, it was a swing door that could be opened from either side. I fell forward against the door, and it swung open away from me. I tried to turn around in an attempt to grab hold of the doorway but lost my balance, falling flat on my back and banging my head on the stone tiles. I immediately began screaming for help, while I lay helplessly kicking my feet in the air, as a young baby often does.

Tommy heard my screams and came running in, very anxious. He made me lie still and asked me many questions while examining me. After checking to see I had not sustained any serious injury, he called for another nurse to help him. They carried me back to my bed.

As I lay looking up at him, I could see he was annoyed with me, and he told me so in no uncertain terms. I did not have time to understand the words he used, but, judging from the expression on his face, I understood his gist. When he finally calmed down, he told me never to be so foolish again. He also added that he would be the one to decide when I was ready to begin walking.

After he had left me, I looked across the ward to see Amos on the floor with his basket by his side.

Smiling to myself, I lay back closing my eyes and began thinking about the antics of this adorable old man.

As I did so a recurring vision of another old man came into my mind. His face seemed familiar. I tried to remember who it was, but, once again, it seemed that the more I tried to remember, the harder it became. My mind began to wander.

Suddenly, I saw the face of the old man again, but this time I could recognize him - it was Archie the tramp. My memory had started to come back.

I was able to remember the first time I met him. He was sitting on the pavement begging outside the "Banjo" pub, near our house in Oriel

Road. I was only seven at the time and felt sorry for him, since he was hungry and had no money to buy food. I decided to take him home to get him something to eat. My mother had just gone shopping and nobody else was in the house. Since she always put visitors in the parlour, I showed Archie in there and told him to wait, while I went into the kitchen to make him something to eat. I made him a cup of tea and a stack of jam butties, which I wrapped up in a brown paper bag.

As I was about to go back into the parlour to give Archie his food, I suddenly remembered that my mother had baked some scones that morning. I rushed over to the oven and there, sure enough, were two trays, each containing twelve freshly-made scones. I took four from the first tray and buttered them before calling out to Archie in the parlour. His face lit up as I gave him the feast. He was full of gratitude and gulped the tea down in one go, while clutching onto the scones and jam butties. Before going out of the front door, he turned and tapped me on the head. "Yer a good lad," he said, "God bless yer, Son!"

Later, I was sorry he had not said "God help you, Son!" because one of our neighbours had seen Archie going into our house with me and had told my mother when she was returning from the shops. As soon as she walked through the front door, my mother called my name. She sounded more anxious than vexed and wanted to know if Archie had been inside the house. I lied, telling her he had only stood in the hall, while I gave him a drink of water and a jam butty. She was not too annoyed but remarked that he would probably always come to us whenever he was hungry. She told me never to do it again.

I thought I had got away with it, but, as I was going out of the kitchen, she spotted the crumbs from the scones and immediately looked in the oven. She called me back and asked what had happened to the four missing scones. I had to think quickly so I said that I had eaten them. She was dubious at first but I managed to convince her. Nothing more was said until she noticed that the four missing scones were from the first tray - the tray containing the scones baked with currants. She knew very well that I detested currants and would never have eaten them. What could I say? I could not deny it. I apologized for lying and pleaded with her not to tell my father what I had done. She said she would not but gave me a good ticking off before sending me up to my room.

However, that was not the end of the matter! I had not been in my room for long, when she shouted for me to go downstairs. "Uh, oh, what have I done now," I said to myself. I went down and found her in the parlour. She glared at me angrily and pointed to the new pale-green carpet that had only been laid the week before. I looked down and was horrified - Archie had left his dirty footprints on the new carpet.

I was sent up to my bedroom again, and when my father came home from work he gave me a good spanking.

The sound of breaking glass suddenly distracted me from my thoughts. I opened my eyes to find myself in Winwick. I looked about and saw that Amos was in trouble again. He had knocked an aluminium vase off the table in the centre of the ward. Without a care in the world, he babbled happily to himself, as he stamped his feet in the large pool of water on the floor. It was only when he looked around the ward, smiling and babbling to himself, that I realized my parents were right - he did look similar to Archie the tramp.

It suddenly dawned on me that a fraction of my memory had surfaced. I became excited and screamed with joy, which immediately brought Tommy and another nurse rushing towards me.

In my excitement, I forgot my speech and babbled so fast that Tommy had to tell me to slow down. By the time I managed to explain about my memory, my poor jaw was aching with use. He smiled broadly saying that it would probably only be a matter of time and patience before my memory was fully restored.

It certainly was a day to remember. If it were not for this flashback, I would have continued to have doubts about my true origin. Although there was no reason to disbelieve anything my parents had told me, it was much more satisfying to be able to recall the past myself.

I must have spent the whole of that morning lying on my bed running through that event many times in my mind. Once again however, the more I tried to induce my memory to return, the more the probability of it returning seemed to recede.

My father learned about my new ability to remember when he visited me later that afternoon. He was almost as pleased as I was. Although I told him about it, I did not remind him of Archie's footprints on the new carpet nor of the good hiding he had given me.

A couple of days later, Tommy walked up to my bed smiling broadly. He was carrying a metal frame-like contraption.

Looking at him in amazement, I wondered what he was going to do with it.

"Well, how's our kamikaze pilot today? Have you tried any more amazing suicide stunts lately?" he asked, facetiously referring to the fall I had taken two days earlier.

My embarrassment must have been obvious as I smiled sheepishly and then looked down.

"I've arranged for you to have some physiotherapy treatment, next week - they'll be around to see you."

"Oh, good, anything to break the boredom," I babbled.

"In a few weeks we're going to begin teaching you how to walk again - only this time, you'll be under supervision and will be using one of these," he said.

"What is it?" I asked, taking a deep breath and pointing to the contraption he was holding.

"A walking aid - look, I'll show you how to use it."

I watched him eagerly, as he went on with the demonstration.

"It looks easy." I jabbered, in my excitement.

"Well, it depends - as long as you take one step at a time and don't try to rush things."

"Great, can I have a go now?" I said, as clearly as I could.

"No, you can't!" he said abruptly, before smiling broadly. "First, you've to strengthen the muscles in your legs, and then, you will have to show me you can keep your balance when you're standing."

"But my legs are strong enough," I protested.

"Look, you've been in bed for more than three months, they're bound to be weak - I should know, shouldn't I?" he asserted.

"I know, but ,Tommy, my legs are strong. I bet you I can walk!"

"You won't listen to me, will you," he said, laughing to himself, as he shook his head and looked down at the floor. "There's a lot more to walking than you think!"

"Look, I'll show you!" I said, full of enthusiasm, as I pushed back the blankets.

"You stay right there!" he said authoritatively, before softening his voice and smiling. "Who do you think you are - Superman?"

"Superman?" I asked.

"Oh, you don't know, the comic ..." he said, before quickly putting his hand over his mouth. "Sorry, I forgot your memory."

"Well, can I have a go, then?" I enquired.

He shook his head and laughed to himself again.

"Oh, go on Tommy."

He crossed his arms and thought for a moment. "Look, so that you don't attempt to go for walkies by yourself again, I'm going to let you prove to yourself that your legs aren't strong enough to support your weight. If you can't walk, then, in future, you must do exactly what I say. Is that a deal?"

"All right," I jabbered, as I threw the bedclothes off and tried to put my legs over the side of the bed.

"Hold on a minute while I get some more help," he said, waving for a nurse to assist him.

Tommy stood on my right side, while the nurse hurried over and stood by my left.

I suddenly looked at the nurse again. I had not seen her before, since it was her first day on the ward. Most of the other nurses in Winwick were male, and the only females I had seen were middle-aged. This nurse was about nineteen and attractive.

"Right, Pauline, I want you to witness this," said Tommy, as he looked at me and grinned broadly. "Hal here, thinks he can just stand up and walk. He seems to forget the time he's been lying in bed - not to mention that he's lost the co-ordination in his legs. I've told him it's not as easy as he thinks, but he won't have it, so we've had a bet. If he loses he has promised not try to walk without my permission."

"All right," she said, smiling encouragingly at me.

"Right, I'm ready," I babbled, as I sat on the edge of the bed.

"Go on, then, let's see you," said Tommy, as he and Pauline helped me into a sitting position. They stood at my side, ready to catch me if I should fall.

It felt strange having my feet on a solid surface again, even though I was still sitting on the bed. I tried with all my might to stand up but could not. I attempted to lift myself up by pressing down on the mattress with my arms at my sides but to no effect.

This revelation frightened me and badly dented my confidence. I just stared ahead, oblivious of everything around me. I had been convinced that I could walk but I could not even stand up. It was a weird and daunting situation. It terrified me merely to think about the possibility that I might not walk again.

"Are you all right?" asked the nurse, looking down at me and touching my shoulder.

I looked up in surprise. I could smell the sweet cologne she was wearing. It was so refreshing to me that I suddenly realized just how attractive she was. I had not really looked at her when she had first come over but now her face appeared stunning.

Suddenly, the problem with my legs did not seem half as important as it had moments earlier. Her presence alone seemed to give me much more encouragement, so that I became even more determined to show Tommy I could walk.

"Well," asked Tommy, smugly, "are you satisfied?"

"So maybe I'm unable to get up off the bed and stand up, but it doesn't mean I can't walk!"

"All right, Pauline," Tommy said, shaking his head and glancing at the ceiling. "We'll lift our hero off the bed to see if he can walk. Then we might be able to get a bit of peace around here!"

They lifted me into a standing position and supported me.

It felt strange to be standing up, and I immediately began to feel dizzy. I was trying to keep my balance, but my head felt as if it was made of lead. My stomach began to churn and I felt as if I was going to vomit.

Pauline and Tommy sensed this and let me sit back on the bed.

"There you are," he said. "Now, do you believe there's a lot more to walking than you think? Come on, Pauline, let's put him back to bed."

"That's not fair!" I babbled affirmatively, "you haven't given me time to get used to being out of bed." I was short of breath, and my jaw was aching because of my protestations. "I'll be O.K. in a minute!"

"All right, I'll give you one last chance. We won't get any peace if we don't!" said Tommy, before shaking his head again and smiling to himself.

They waited patiently while I sat on the edge of the bed. Occasionally, I shook my head and knitted my eyebrows together, in an attempt to clear my mind. "I am going to walk," I continued to tell myself, attempting to build up my confidence. I was determined.

When I was ready I nodded my head.

"All right," said Tommy, looking at Pauline. They both lifted me to my feet and continued to support me.

I gritted my teeth, determined to prove Tommy wrong. I looked down at my feet. "Move, you beggars, move, will you!" I continued to tell my legs. I mustered all the energy I could to will them to move, but it was futile - they would not budge. The problem was that my legs felt lifeless.

Tommy and Pauline put me back into bed, and I finally admitted to myself that I was unable to walk. It was a great shock. I could feel my confidence ebbing away.

"Look, Hal," said Tommy, "if you still want to try to walk, you must listen to what I tell you! And remember no more heroics - you could seriously injure yourself, do you hear me?"

I looked up and nodded, almost in a state of oblivion.

"Well, the physios will be coming around to see you later - they want to assess the strength in your legs. Don't worry about not being able to walk at the moment. There's a lot of hard work to do before that time arrives. First, you'll have to build up your leg muscles and then you'll have to teach your legs to move correctly."

His words immediately enlivened me, although I did not take in fully what he was telling me. Puzzled, I looked up at him.

"Look, at the moment, your brain isn't sending the correct messages to your leg muscles."

"What do you mean?" I babbled.

Tommy looked at the floor and scratched his chin. "Well, let's just pretend you are in the Army, and the Sergeant gives you the order to march. Ordinarily, your brain would instruct your right leg to move forward, as it instructs your left arm to swing back. Then your left leg will receive the message to move forward while your right arm swings back. At the moment, your brain is telling both of your legs to move in the same direction at the same time - which is impossible for anybody to do. That's why you can't walk. Let's face it, if the soldier tried to put both legs forward at the same time, he would not be able to move forward - he would stay in the one spot."

"Well, why is my brain sending the wrong message?"

"Your head took such a bang in the crash that all the messages from the brain got mixed up. And don't forget, you haven't used your legs for quite a long time. Now, your brain has to learn to send the correct messages again."

" I thought you were going to say I wouldn't be able to walk again."

"Well, a lot depends on you! I know you've got a lot of determination, but you've also got to go about things in the right way. Take that stupid trick you did the other day - you were lucky you didn't kill yourself!"

"I know - I'm sorry."

"I can understand your eagerness to walk, but you must take it one step at a time."

"Don't worry, I will!"

"Yes, well make sure you do! You could easily have injured yourself and got me into serious trouble."

"Sorry, Tommy, it won't happen again."

"All right, I won't mention it again, as long as you tell me first, before you try to break your neck."

I nodded, feeling a little ashamed.

Chapter 5

One Step at a Time

The following week, I realized that my condition was improving, since I was feeling much better, both physically and mentally. My mind was becoming much clearer, although I was still nowhere near lucid enough to wonder what life was like beyond the walls of the ward. I never questioned where my visitors were going after they had seen me and just took it for granted that the hospital was my home.

Although I was only able to remember a small part of my past, it was enough to give me hope that I would soon be able to remember more. Each night, I would lie in bed and try to will my memory to return. The next morning, it would always be disappointing to discover that I could recall nothing more of my past. My efforts were futile but I never stopped trying. However, there were times when I would suddenly find myself thinking of situations that I was unable to recognize. I would spend hours trying to recall the tantalizing images but it was all in vain.

The fact that Tommy believed I would be able to walk again gave a great boost to my confidence. In the back of my mind, however, I still remembered how wrong the doctors had been about my speech. They had told me that as soon as they had removed the tracheotomy valve from my throat, I would be able to speak normally again. Was it possible that Tommy would also be wrong about my ability to walk again? This doubt eventually turned to worry, since I dreaded even the thought of spending the rest of my life in a wheelchair. I tried to dismiss such notions from my mind - it was far from easy.

One morning, I was lying in bed with my eyes closed, attempting once again to will my memory to return. I was not having much success but I continued trying.

"Hal Lever?" said a voice that startled me out of my reverie.

I opened my eyes to find a rotund bearded gentleman standing over me.

"Yes," I managed to splutter, in surprise.

"I'm Mr. Forbes, the physiotherapist. I've come to examine your legs. I've got to know exactly what exercises to give you when you come to the department tomorrow."

He examined my legs thoroughly, while his chubby little fingers poked and prodded my leg muscles. He made me lie in many positions, as I pushed and pulled my limbs against his powerful arms.

"Well, your muscles need building up first, and then we'll have to teach your legs to move correctly. We'll help you as much as we can, but after that it will be up to you."

"How long will it take me to walk?" I managed to yawn out.

"It depends how your muscles react - how quickly you are able to train your legs to move correctly. Most of it will depend on your will to succeed, but it won't be easy."

Greatly inspired by what he had said, I began telling myself that I would soon be able to walk. I was determined, even though I had to do it Tommy's way and not my own. I could not contemplate spending the rest of my life in a wheelchair and knew that if it was merely a matter of will power, then I would be able to do it.

The following morning, a nurse put me in a wheelchair to take me to the Physiotherapy Department. We left the ward, and, after passing through the hall, we continued along the corridor painted bright green and yellow. It surprised me to see how pleasing to the eye the colours now appeared - so different to the first time I had seen them.

I was left sitting in the corridor, while the nurse went inside the Physiotherapy Department to report my arrival. Shortly afterwards, she came out and returned to the ward. Moments later, a woman, dressed in a white overall, came out and smiled at me.

She was in her late thirties and of average build. Her short black wavy hair and black-rimmed glasses made her look severe. "Hello, Hal, I'm Mrs. Forbes - you met my husband yesterday. How are you feeling this morning?" she said cheerfully, not sounding at all severe.

I breathed deeply and smiled. "Very well, thank you." I said, trying my best to sound intelligible.

"We'll soon build up your muscles," she said, as she wheeled me into the Physiotherapy Department.

The size of the room surprised me. I had imagined it would have been built on a much bigger scale. The room was small and cluttered with unused equipment. On the wall opposite was a set of wall-bars that appeared to be brand new, since the lacquer on the bars was still intact and had not lost any of its gloss. A filing cabinet and a table positioned at the base of the wall-bar meant that it could not be used. On the wall to my left was a series of pulleys that had no rope. A large chart, illustrating the muscles of the body, decorated the wall on my right.

Suddenly, the door opened and in walked Mr. Forbes. "Good morning, Hal," he said cheerfully.

"Good morning," I babbled nervously, unsure of how I should react to him.

"I've got you a new wheelchair - come and have a look," he said, as he walked out of the room.

Mrs. Forbes wheeled me out into the corridor, where I found a sparkling new wheelchair. They carefully lifted me into it before taking me back along the corridor to the hall.

"Right, Hal, we'll show you how to use it, and then we'll leave you with it for a few weeks. You will be able to build up the muscles in your arms" said Mr. Forbes, in a slow and purposeful manner. "After that, we'll start building up your leg muscles and improving your balance before trying you out on a walking aid. It'll be hard work."

I looked excitedly at him, but found he was glaring at me. He suddenly began to wag his finger.

"Charge Nurse Malloy warned us that you'll probably want to do things your way," he said, looking right into my face and continuing to wag his finger. "Now, let's get one thing straight before we start - either you do things my way, or you don't do them at all - O.K?"

I nodded sheepishly at him.

"Right, well, it's all right for you to use it in the hall and in your ward," he said, pointing down at the wheelchair, "but on no condition must you go anywhere else! Do you understand?"

I nodded eagerly.

"One last bit of advice - take it easy, especially for the first few days. Don't forget, you've not used your arms for quite some time - they'll soon get tired."

I nodded as I moved away from them. They watched as I slowly made my way around the hall, before they returned to their department.

Using the wheelchair was very strenuous and boring work at first, and I was often short of breath. I soon got tired but remembered what Mr. Forbes had said about straining my muscles. Not wishing to disobey him, I decided to take it easy for the first couple of days.

The following week, Tommy told me to report to the Physiotherapy Department. He had noticed that I was working hard at my exercises and not straining myself, so he had remarked on it to Mr. Forbes. Consequently, Tommy allowed me to go to Physio without an escort. I appreciated his trust and did not want to let him down.

Mr. Forbes lifted me out of my wheelchair and set me on a chair to do leg exercises. He began by chalking a square on the floor in front of me and then put a number of bean-bags inside it. The object of the exercise was to lift my left foot off the floor and then to push each bag out of the square. Having accomplished this, I was to grip each bag with my toes, lift it and place it back inside the square. Once accomplished I was to do the same with my other foot.

It appeared simple enough and I was confident I would have no trouble doing it. Sitting on the chair, I had to will my legs to move - it was frustrating as my limbs seemed to have a will of their own. When I moved one foot, the other one would move in the same direction. To prevent both my legs moving in unison, Mr. Forbes simply tied one of my feet to the leg of the chair. This worked and I did eventually meet with some success, although I still had great difficulty directing my movements. Apparently, the only answer was to do it the hard way - by repetition. For the rest of the morning I had to sit and tell my feet which way to move, until they were each trained to do this task independently. The process was tedious, since it was difficult to maintain my concentration, but I was slowly making progress. Nevertheless, at the end of the session, my feet were just as disobedient as when I began the exercise. It was frustrating and I realized it was going to be a long and difficult process.

That evening, when my parents came to visit, Tommy asked to see my father. This surprised me as he had not mentioned anything to me earlier. I looked at my mother and could tell by the look on her face that she was expecting bad news. Perplexed, I wondered if something had happened that I knew nothing about.

Much to my surprise, my father was grinning like a Cheshire cat when he came out of Tommy's office. Considering my circumstances, it turned out to be the best news, for which I could ever have wished.

"Two more days to go and you'll be going home for the weekend," said my father excitedly. "I'll move your bed and things downstairs, so you won't have to climb any stairs."

The thought of going home for the weekend had never entered my mind. The news came as a wonderful surprise for both my parents and myself.

I was to go home on the Friday afternoon and return on the Sunday evening. Tommy strictly stated that I was not to leave the house or do anything that would be over-tiring. He also made it clear I should not have too much excitement.

It was going to be a big day for me. The doctors were hoping that allowing me to go home would help to restore my memory. I would be back among my family again, see my own home and the mementoes of my past life for the first time since the accident.

When my visitors left, the initial euphoria of my visit began to recede and I became apprehensive. I was anxious about what my former life might reveal about my character. My relatives had told me much about myself, but the more they told me, the more complex my personality seemed to become. It was a bizarre situation.

The following day, I went to the Physiotherapy Department, but I was too busy telling Mr. and Mrs. Forbes the good news to spend much time exercising my legs. In my excitement, I spoke too fast, with the result that they could not understand what I was trying to say. It was exhausting and I soon became tired. After I had managed to get through to them, they suggested I rest on the gym mat - I fell asleep for two hours.

By Friday, my fears had disappeared and my excitement grew with every passing minute. I wanted to get changed into my clothes, but Tommy told me that I would have to wait until the doctor examined me.

The events of that morning are all too vivid in my memory. After having breakfast, I lay on my bed and watched the door in anticipation of the doctor's arrival. The time seemed to drag as I kept watch on the fingers of the clock as they slowly changed position. The doctor had not appeared by ten o'clock nor a quarter past, and by half past, I was almost having palpitations.

At eleven o'clock, I saw Tommy coming out of his office. He had a grim look on his face, as he approached my bed.

"Sorry, Hal, but I've got some bad news," said Tommy, sounding sincere. "The doctor won't be coming to see you today, so you won't be going home this weekend. I spoke to him about you on the phone, but he said he would have to examine you first before allowing you to go for the weekend ..."

I did not want to listen to the rest of what he was saying. I was devastated. The last thing I wanted to hear was an excuse, so I quickly pulled the blankets over my head and lay there full of anger and frustration. I tried to force myself to cry but could not. All I wanted at that moment was to be alone to wallow in my self-pity.

Many of my relatives came to see me that evening - it was as if they had all come to make up for my disappointment. They were very entertaining and I forgot my anger. My father assured me I could definitely go home the following weekend.

Once my visitors had left, my disappointment soon returned although not as acutely as before. At least, they had assured me that I could go home the next weekend.

On the following Monday morning, I attended Physio as arranged. Tommy must have told Mr. and Mrs. Forbes of my disappointment, because they did not mention the matter.

The exercises to strengthen my leg muscles were difficult for me to do at first, but the more I practised the easier they became. The Forbes's often told me they were surprised by my progress, although I realized that this may have been a ploy to give me encouragement.

I decided to continue practising the exercises on my return to the ward. I knew the Forbes's would give me more praise the following day. However, the next morning my legs were stiff and aching all over, so Tommy made me stay in bed.

When I woke up on the following Friday, I was full of anticipation. I was finally going home. Much to my dismay, I had a cold so the doctor declared I was unfit to travel and would not issue me with a weekend pass. Understandably, I was bitterly disappointed and began to wonder if the doctor was trying to stop me from leaving the hospital on purpose. My suspicions did not last long, however; and I eventually realized he had my well-being at heart.

Nevertheless, Tommy said he had a surprise for me that would make up for my disappointment - I was to receive tuition on using a walking aid that morning. He and Mr. Forbes had recently discussed my progress and had agreed that I was now ready to use a walking aid.

Although overjoyed to hear this, I remembered my last attempt to walk when I discovered that there was no sensation in my legs. At the time, it was a great shock for me and my confidence began to ebb. Fortunately, it soon returned - all I had to do was to look at the other patients around me to realize how grateful I should be.

In recent days, I had repeatedly told myself that if the worst came to the worst and I was unable to walk again, it would be best to face facts and to accept the consequences no matter what they were. I was reluctant to do this at first but eventually realized it would be best. After all, I would still be alive. What was more important, I would still be able to think coherently.

However, my mood was very positive that morning, and any fears that I might not walk again did not enter my mind, at first. I was full of confidence and determined to walk.

I was sitting in my wheelchair when Mr. and Mrs. Forbes eventually arrived with two young and attractive nurses. They wheeled me out into the hall, accompanied by Tommy.

Mr. and Mrs. Forbes knelt down on the floor in front of me, while the nurses stood on either side to support me. Mr. Forbes moved my left leg forward, while his wife held my right leg to ensure it did not move. Then, Mr. Forbes held my left foot, as Mrs. Forbes moved my right one forward. The two nurses allowed me, in stages, to support myself, while remaining close at hand in case I toppled over.

Slowly, we made our way around the hall. It was a slow and tiring process, because I would often have to stop to rest to catch my breath. There was plenty of encouragement from the staff, so my confidence did not desert me. Although the atmosphere was serious when we began, it was not long before I was playing the buffoon and had them all laughing their heads off. To a large extent, I felt like an actor playing to an audience.

When my legs had become accustomed to the correct movements, Tommy and Mr. Forbes put me back in the wheelchair. The others were discussing the most effective method of introducing me to the walking aid, while I was having a much-needed rest.

It was a big moment for me - a moment that I had long been waiting for. Nevertheless, my confident attitude began to wane, as the memory of my previous unsuccessful attempt to walk began to haunt me, once more. Eventually, they decided that I should stand holding onto the crossbar of the walking aid. Tommy would stand close to my right side, and Mr. Forbes would stand close to my left, to support my weight if and when required. I would have to lift the aluminium walking aid in front of me, then allow it to take my weight, while I first moved one leg forward and then the other. Mrs. Forbes stood behind me in case I fell back. The two nurses would stand in front to encourage me.

Standing between the two men, I looked at my legs, wondering if they would let me down again. I was becoming increasingly nervous at the thought of failing. My confidence was beginning to ebb again.

At that moment, the nurses began to encourage me verbally. As

I looked up, the girls were looking straight at me, urging me to take a step. My confidence immediately returned.

Looking down again, I concentrated my thoughts on moving my right leg. I gripped the crossbar of the walking-aid and desperately willed my right leg to move - but it would not. After trying again, without success, my anxiety grew.

"Lean over to your left and then try," said Mr. Forbes encouragingly. "Come on, you can do it!"

A chilling silence fell about us. I took a deep breath and repeatedly told myself I was going to walk. I leaned over to my left so that my left foot supported my weight, and my left hand held the crossbar to stop me from overbalancing. My eyes focused on my right foot, as I ground my teeth together and urged my leg to move.

There was no reaction at first, but I soon found that my right foot was beginning to stir. Shortly afterwards, there was a rousing cheer from everybody around me, as I moved my foot forward without too much difficulty.

I had made an important breakthrough. I could feel my face beaming with pride. I do not think I could ever have felt so elated.

Silence prevailed eventually and Mr. Forbes told me to sway to my right and then to move my left foot forward.

I took a deep breath and swayed to my right while looking down at my left foot. I frantically told it to move forward. Eventually, it began to move, but as my right hand took the weight of my body, I felt a sharp pang in my right wrist and immediately let out a loud cry. The pain was so intense that I had little option but to let go of the crossbar. I fell to the right and let out another scream, as my right wrist suddenly smacked against one of the legs of the walking aid. Luckily, Tommy and Mr. Forbes leapt forward and grabbed me to prevent my falling any further.

The event badly shook me. For a few moments, my mind was oblivious to everything, before I suddenly became aware of a stinging sensation in my right wrist. I looked down at the inside of my right wrist and what I saw astonished me. I held it up to show the others.

Tommy was alarmed at what was protruding from my wrist. A

trickle of blood was oozing out of it, and a cube of glass had emerged from beneath my skin. It had been embedded in my skin at the point where my wrist had been broken in the accident. My skin had grown over it, but the fall must have dislodged the glass and brought it to the surface.

The piece of glass, about an eighth of an inch cube, must have come from the windscreen. I was amazed that it had been under my skin for such a length of time without realising it.

A shiver suddenly ran through me, as I realized how badly injured I must have been when arriving at the Infirmary. The doctors and nurses at that time were obviously too concerned about my unconscious state to worry about a broken wrist.

My walking lesson came to an abrupt end. After attending to my injury, they took me back to the ward and immediately put me to bed, where they told me to stay for the rest of the day.

Once I recovered from the shock of the incident, I began to realize that I had almost taken two steps using the walking-aid. I felt euphoric to have overcome the obstacle that was holding back my recovery.

By the early afternoon, I wanted to get up. The wheelchair had given me so much freedom that it now felt as if I were a prisoner.

However, the stinging sensation in my wrist continued to bother me. I got used to it eventually and always positioned my hand so that it did not cause me too much pain.

I convinced Tommy the next day that I was all right, so he allowed me to sit in an armchair next to my bed. I soon became restless and began to pester him to allow me to use the wheelchair again. He was against the idea at first but eventually agreed to my request.

My next walking lesson was to take place on the following Monday, because there was only a skeleton staff on duty at the weekend. On the Monday, I learned to use the walking aid properly and spent every available moment walking around the hall for practise. My progress at first was slow, but, after a few days, I became adept at using the aid.

Chapter 6

At Last!

During the five months that had elapsed since the car accident, it had never crossed my mind that I might be allowed home for a weekend. To my surprise, it was the doctor who had first suggested the idea, in the hope of curing my amnesia. However, he had twice disappointed me by refusing to let me go and I still suspected he was deliberately preventing my leaving the hospital. The desire to see my home had taken on a new urgency, and my only hope was that the doctor would not disappoint me a third time.

On the Friday morning, I was sitting on the bed waiting for the doctor to arrive. All traces of my cold had disappeared, so I could not see any reason why I should not be allowed to spend the weekend at home. Nevertheless, I was still apprehensive and expecting him to find some excuse to prevent my leaving.

He came to the ward on time and was smiling broadly, as he walked up to my bed. I did not return the smile, because I was still angry with him for my earlier disappointments.

I still remember the way he looked at me after examining me that morning. He sat looking at me pensively, as he stroked his beard. "I rang your parents earlier this morning," he declared suddenly, "they're expecting you home later this afternoon." As he was leaving my bedside, he patted me on the shoulder. "Have a nice weekend - you deserve it," he said, smiling down at me.

As soon as he had left, I waved to Tommy, who was in his office. "I can go home for the weekend!" I babbled at the top of my voice. It was difficult to believe that the time had finally arrived.

While waiting for the ambulance to arrive, I sat thinking about my injuries. The problem that haunted me most at that moment was my loss of memory. The doctor was pleased to hear that I could vividly remember one past event - the incident with Archie and the scones. Tommy had expected the rest of my memory to return within a short space of time but it did not.

Recollections of my family life seemed to be growing stronger, although it was difficult to ascertain if I had recalled some of the facts my family had told me and had simply left the rest to my imagination. My amnesia only seemed to apply to my personal past, as I was still able to recall my everyday perceptions and recognize such things as the make of a car. In recent days, however, I was more frequently finding myself thinking for fleeting moments about events in my past, but was unable to make any sense of them. My inability to relate the incidents to a specific time or place was all the more frustrating. In many ways, it was like having a piece of a jig-saw and not knowing where it fitted while at the same time not knowing what the completed puzzle would look like. It was perplexing.

My fractured skull and two broken ribs had mended without a hitch. The only physical injury that was still causing me concern was my right wrist. It was necessary to avoid using my right hand whenever it was possible. I had not reported it to anybody, since I was naively hoping that the niggling ache would eventually go away. I was grateful to the medical staff for all they had done for me and did not want to inconvenience them any further. Although my parents had told me I had been left-handed, it was of little relevance to me now, since the movements of my limbs were still badly lacking co-ordination.

Nevertheless, by this time, I was beginning to show a significant improvement. My co-ordination had improved to such an extent that I was allowed to use a walking aid. I was also able to use my hands more effectively, although only able to feed myself using one hand. However, it was still a slow and frustrating task and I would often misdirect my hand. Instead of putting the food in my mouth, it often ended up on or in different parts of my anatomy. As soon as the co-ordination of my hands had sufficiently improved, I was allowed to sit in an armchair to eat my meals. Eventually, I was permitted to sit alone at the very large dining table, sitting in my wheelchair.

Because of the paralysis to parts of my throat, mouth and tongue, it was still difficult to swallow. Many times, my food would lodge in my throat, and I would have to cough it back out of my mouth. The same thing would happen with liquids.

My double-vision had only improved slightly. It was very tiresome and annoying at times, since my eyes would often deceive me. As the doctor believed my vision would eventually correct itself, he decided that I should discontinue the daily wearing of the eye-patch over alternate eyes. Unfortunately, I had got into the habit of closing one eye and only using the open one. Consequently, the nurses would often have to remind me to use both eyes - a task that was far easier said than done.

Nobody had told me the full details about the accident. At first, it had never even occurred to me to ask about the crash, and I had merely accepted whatever I was told. It was not until I began to think more clearly that I began to question things for myself. Even though my speech made it difficult for me to communicate, whenever I managed to ask my family about the accident the subject was quickly changed. I needed the answers to many questions: if any others had been injured; if I had been a passenger; if I was able to drive or even if I had a car.

The forthcoming weekend soon returned to my thoughts. I wondered what it would be like living at home - a home I could not remember in great detail. Although I had accepted my parents and kin, there were times, even when we were together, that I would still feel terribly alone and inadequate.

Clutching my walking aid, I slowly made my way along the concrete path to the ambulance parked in the hospital driveway. Tommy, Mr. and Mrs. Forbes, and two nurses were standing in the hospital porch, as they waved goodbye to me.

"Have a good weekend," shouted Tommy from behind me, "and don't go trying to walk behind my back!"

It was too difficult to turn around and babble something to him, while I held the aid in front of me. Instead, I merely turned my head sideways and smiled.

A nurse said something, but I did not hear her properly - it must have been a funny remark because they all laughed.

I was feeling both excited and a little apprehensive as the ambulance man carried me inside the vehicle. He put me in the seat next to his own. As he closed the doors, I could still hear the staff shouting words of encouragement and wishing me well. .

"We'll soon have you home," said the driver, in his broad Warrington accent. "Three quarters of an hour and you should be there."

As we pulled away, I could see Tommy and the other staff continuing to wave. They had become my friends, and I deeply appreciated everything they had done for me. My mind thought back to the day I had been transferred from the Infirmary. I had not liked the look of the place nor of Tommy. My assumptions had turned out to be completely wrong; I certainly learned my lesson.

While we were waiting to turn onto the dual carriageway from the hospital entrance, a large petrol tanker hurtled across our path. I shivered suddenly when I imagined it colliding with another vehicle. "Nobody would have much chance of surviving," I said to myself.

I was glad that the driver was not very talkative, for I wanted to get a good view of my surroundings, in the hope that my memory would return.

We crossed the dual carriageway and headed for Liverpool. As we drove through Rainford, Prescot, and other outlying districts of my home town, I was trying to remember if I had ever been there before. Alas, my memory was blank.

Continuing along Queens Drive, we turned into Haggerston Road and then into Walton Village, where I apparently lived. Still nothing seemed familiar.

We pulled up outside a large house, and I saw my father standing at the door of it. When he spotted the ambulance, he rushed out down the garden path, while my mother came to the doorway and waved to me.

The driver got out of the ambulance and carried me out to my father, while a hoard of strangers gathered around and wished me well.

"Hiya, Hal, how long are you home for?" asked a young lad.

"Just for the weekend," I jabbered.

"Hey, he doesn't half speak funny," said another boy, who was standing next to a woman.

"Shut up, Big Mouth!" said the woman, as I stood there, holding on to the walking aid.

"Here you are, I'll carry you in," said my father, as he bent down to lift me up.

"No thanks, Dad," I said, shaking my head frantically, "I can manage." I was keen to show everyone that I could walk, albeit with a walking aid.

"O.K., but let me lift you onto the pavement," he said. "Be careful how you go!"

Once he had lifted me onto the pavement and given me the walking aid, I slowly and proudly walked up the garden path. When I reached the front door, the many well-wishers at the gate applauded.

My father lifted me over the threshold, and, as soon as my feet touched the floor, my mother put her arms around me and hugged me tightly.

"Welcome home, Son," she said, her eyes suddenly filling with tears of joy.

"Good to have you back home, Son," said my father, as he gently patted me on the back. "I've brought the spare bed down from upstairs and put it in the lounge. Come and have a sit down - I bet you're dying for a decent cup of tea."

Smiling, I followed him into the living room. I was immediately attracted to the French windows, which were open and looked out onto the garden, full of flowers, at the back of the house. The sun was bright and I had to squint my eyes to see four tall floodlights in the distance.

"Goodison Park, Everton's ground," said my father, who was now standing behind me. "They didn't have a bad season."

Sitting at the table, I savoured my mother's home-made scones that were allegedly an old favourite of mine. After having endured the food in Winwick, they certainly became my favourite again.

It was strange to be sitting in the living room where I had supposedly sat so many times before. Eager to regain my memory, I asked my parents to remind me of my past, so they spent an hour relating their favourite memories of me. As they were talking, I looked into their eyes and could tell that they were willing me to remember. I simply could not and felt inadequate again. The expectant look on their faces was so touching that I was even tempted to pretend to remember something, but I resisted.

My father pointed to a coffee table and asked if I remembered making it. I looked blankly at him. He told me that I had been a D.I.Y. fanatic and had made furniture and fireplace surrounds for the family and friends.

Eventually, the conversation became too taxing for me, so I asked to see my bedroom. I was eager to look through my old belongings, hoping that they would hold the key to restoring my memory. My parents replied that it would be best to wait until Colin, my younger brother, came home from school, so that he could help my father to lift me upstairs. I insisted that I could crawl up taking one step at a time and just needed somebody to ensure I did not fall backwards.

It was apparent by the looks on their faces that they did not like the idea, but I did not give them time to object. I quickly got on my hands and knees and crawled out of the room to the staircase. I managed to get up the stairs on my own, while my father followed close behind, carrying the walking aid.

Once he had opened the door of my bedroom I asked to be left alone. He understood and told me to knock on the floor if I needed anything. He then left me.

Using the walking aid, I walked into my bedroom and suddenly felt very odd. To some extent, it seemed as if I was trespassing, violating another person's privacy; as if I was trying to relive the life of a stranger.

Covering the walls were pennants from some of the places I had apparently visited when in the Merchant Navy. There was a suitcase under the bed that I managed to pull out by getting down carefully onto the floor. It contained many souvenirs of my travels around the world, ranging from a bus ticket bought in Buenos Aires to a beer mat from a bar in Yokohama. I also found a newspaper cutting from the "Hull Daily Mail," featuring a photograph of me sitting in Hull City's football ground before the match. The article was entitled: "First from Goodison - rides all the way." I was amazed and thought that I must have been a keen Everton supporter to have ridden the 130 mile distance. I then turned my attention to the wardrobe, where my old Merchant Navy uniform was found on a hanger. I tried it on and discovered that it was too big for me. Nevertheless, I stood in front of the full-length mirror trying to imagine myself as a Cadet Navigation Officer on the bridge of a ship. Alas, I could recall nothing.

An hour later, my father took me down for my evening meal and to see my youngest sister, Janet, who had come home from school. I had only seen her once at the Infirmary, as she had not been allowed to visit me in Winwick.

Colin came home soon after. Since he was off for a week's camping holiday with the Scouts that afternoon, I did not see him for long.

I watched television later but could not recall having seen any of the programmes before. Nonetheless, I soon found it boring, since my mind was too active to allow me to sit down and watch.

It had been a tiring day for me, so I went to bed at nine o'clock that evening. I lay there thinking about my situation. I had finally arrived home for the weekend, but I was still left with some feeling of alienation. Although my family had given me a warm welcome, I felt, at times, as if I was imposing on strangers - as if there was no bond to unite me with them. Yet, at other times, I did indeed feel as if I was in my natural abode. It was all very strange for me.

I spent many hours that weekend rummaging through my old belongings, trying to find a key to unlock my past. I came across many surprising souvenirs, both from my school days and from my life at sea. It was difficult to envisage doing some of the things I had evidently done. Consequently, it made my predicament harder to accept.

By the time the ambulance picked me up on Sunday afternoon, I was looking forward to returning to Winwick, even though I had enjoyed the weekend. I felt a little out of place at home - it should have been dear to my heart, but in many ways I found the situation tedious and of little significance to me. Although I was considerably better informed about the past events of my life, I was still unable to recall any of them vividly, apart from the incident of Archie and the scones.

When I returned to Winwick, the doctor told me he was not too surprised my memory had not yet returned. He added that he was not expecting an immediate response, although I sensed he was a little disappointed.

I soon got back into my usual routine and continued to practise using my walking aid. After a further three weeks of walking around the hall all day long using the aid, I had become very adept at it.

When the day finally arrived that I was to try to walk independently I was delighted. Although I had told myself positively that I was going to walk, I distinctly remember having my moments of uncertainty. My first step would be the most difficult, especially since I had to balance correctly. Fortunately, my fears were immediately dispelled when I remembered the plight of my fellow patients.

Tommy pushed me into the hall followed by Mr. and Mrs. Forbes and the two nurses - the same team as before. They all gathered around and I was encouraged to take a step forward. After having spent so much time practising, using the walking aid, it was not long before I took my first step independently. I was delighted, especially when the two nurses gave me a kiss on the cheek.

Once I was able to balance correctly, it did not take long before I was able to walk the length of the room. I was so determined to improve my walking that I spent all my available time walking around the hall.

On one occasion, I remember going out of the hall and getting lost in the maze of corridors. Two male nurses found me and took me back to the I.C.U. Upon my return, Tommy gave me a good lecture. At the time, I did not know why he was so annoyed but remember him saying it was for my own good.

Ever since that fateful day early in April when I was taken into the solarium my progress had been remarkable. The doctor, the Forbes's and Tommy were so impressed that it was decided that I should be transferred to Delph Neurological Hospital, an annexe across the main road from Winwick.

Most of the patients there were being treated for various nervous disorders but were not considered to be as seriously ill as the patients in Winwick. The main reason for my transfer was that they believed hypnotherapy would help to build both my confidence to speak more clearly and to restore my memory.

Nevertheless, it was decided that I should continue to visit the Physiotherapy Department twice a week. I still needed to further improve the co-ordination in my hands, which was still not good enough to write clearly, for instance.

The niggling sensation in my right wrist was continuing to give me much discomfort. It became so severe that I finally reported it to the doctor. It was therefore decided that I should receive heat treatment on my wrist when attending the Physiotherapy Dept.

Chapter 7

Delph Neurological Hospital

I was sorry to be leaving the I.C.U. It had been my home for the past five months, and the staff had shown an exemplary commitment to their work. I had made significant progress in my recovery and had formed a special relationship with Charge Nurse Tommy Malloy and with Mr. and Mrs. Forbes, the Physiotherapists.

As a nurse was taking my travel bag out to the awaiting ambulance, I sat on my bed, looking across to the other side of the ward. As usual, Amos was sitting on the floor, still trying to pick up a black floor tile and put it into his basket. He seemed content to sit there trying to pick up the tile while constantly smiling and babbling to himself. I had become fond of this white-bearded old man with the amusing mannerisms, so I rushed over and sat down on the floor next to him. When I shook his frail white hand I immediately noticed how warm, soft and smooth his skin was. Looking into his empty bright-blue eyes, I desperately tried to catch his attention. I dearly wanted him to recognize me or at least to acknowledge me in some way, but my presence did not seem to make any difference to him. He merely continued to smile and babble to himself. I felt a sudden gush of emotion flow from my heart and wished something could be done to make him well. Alas, he was senile and beyond all help.

Tommy warned me that I had better hurry, so I got quickly to my feet and thanked him for everything he had done for me. He modestly told me he was only doing his job. We shook hands and he told me to come back to see him when I was discharged from Delph. I admired Tommy; he had a big heart and was very understanding.

When I reached the door, I stopped and turned to take one last look at the ward. I thought back to the day I had arrived from the Infirmary and realized how much I had recovered since that time. However, the staff had done all they could do for me at the I.C.U. - it was time for me to move on.

As I got into the ambulance, the driver winked at me and smiled. "You've really come on these last few months, " he said, "I remember seeing you when you arrived."

I nodded and smiled proudly.

We crossed the dual carriageway and continued along a winding lane that was surrounded by open grassland. Ahead of us lay Delph.

It differed from Winwick and the Infirmary, mainly because it was run on similar lines to a convalescence home. Most of the patients there were recovering from a nervous breakdown or other mental disorders. It catered for both male and female.

The majority of patients were introverted and were having difficulty coping with the everyday pressures of this increasingly complex world. Many of them merely needed a break to get some of the frustrations and anxieties out of their system. Others had subconsciously shut out the real world from their minds while attempting to create a sanctuary of their own.

One patient, in particular, was a persistent liar and an extrovert. He was twenty-two and boasted that he had nineteen G.C.E.'s at O level and twelve at A level standard, as well as two B.A. degrees he had gained while studying at Cambridge University. The first time I met him, I was gullible enough to be impressed by his educational attainments. However, I began to take his claims with a pinch of salt, when he told me the following day that he used to play lead guitar with a group and had spent the previous three years touring the "States." I eventually decided to give him a wide berth.

Most of the time, the patients wore everyday clothes and were able to participate in the many activities that took place within the confines of the hospital. Most of them would spend the day watching television, playing cards, or simply walking around the grounds.

After a couple of weeks, I noticed that each of the other patients would be confined to their beds for a day or two every week or so. It seemed odd, at first, until it dawned on me that it usually happened after they had been to Winwick to have "electric shock treatment." I realized that among the patients there was a kind of status award system, whereby the more doses of "shock treatment" a patient received, the more respect he or she would gain from fellow patients. I can even remember wishing that I received such treatment, merely to attain their respect.

Twice a week, I would travel the short distance by ambulance to Winwick to attend the Physiotherapy Department for co-ordination exercises and to receive heat treatment on my wrist. I used to look forward to going as it was a break from the monotony of my life at Delph.

A Trip to Winwick for physiotherapy
(rear) A nurse and Mrs. Forbes (front) Two patients and me

The other days of the week were terribly boring and I often felt as if I was in a world of my own. When the weather was good, I would walk around the grounds, pondering over my predicament. When it was raining, I would lie on my bed and do the same. The only respite from the tedium came when my visitors arrived in the evening.

At the beginning of the third week, the charge nurse told me to go over to Winwick to have my first hypnotherapy session. The idea of being put into a trance fascinated me.

On my arrival at the clinic, the doctor informed me that I would first have to listen to a relaxation record; this was to make my mind more receptive to the treatment. She took me into an adjoining room and left me lying on her couch, listening to the record. It instructed me to relax every part of my body, beginning with my toes, feet, legs and so on, right through to my eyelids. It finally went on to describe the countryside on a peaceful summer's day.

The record was relaxing and I did begin to feel the stress draining out of my body. However, I was only able to listen for a short time before becoming bored. My mind was too active, and I was too intrigued by the process of hypnosis itself to pay much attention to the record.

The doctor came back into the room and told me to sit comfortably in the armchair in front of her desk. She then instructed me to extend my left hand out in front of my eyes and to concentrate my thoughts on my middle finger. She then began the hypnosis ...

"You will stare at your middle finger and let your whole body relax. You will breathe as deeply as you can. You will empty your mind of all your thoughts and just concentrate on nothing else but your middle finger. You are just listening to my voice and are drifting into a very pleasant state of mind. As you stare at your middle finger, you will find that your eyelids are getting heavier and heavier. You are feeling very tired. Your eyelids are beginning to close. They feel so heavy that you can no longer hold them open. Your body will become completely relaxed. Your toes, your feet ... and your face will be totally relaxed, free from strain, tightness, stress and tension ..."

She went on by encouraging me to remember my past and giving me a general pep talk to build up my confidence. According to her, when the session finished she would tell me to wake up and I would I would open my eyes and feel refreshed.

When she told me to open my eyes, it was obvious to me that I had not been anywhere near a state of trance, since I could remember everything she had said to me. In addition, I felt drowsy rather than refreshed. I had only pretended to have been in a trance, because of my gratitude to the medical profession and my reluctance to let the doctors think they were failing in their treatment. As I was leaving the clinic, the doctor smiled at me knowingly, as if she realized that I had only faked the state of hypnosis.

Upon my return to Delph, the Charge Nurse asked me if I would prefer to have my own room, rather than sleeping in the general ward. I jumped at the chance; I needed to be alone.

Although the room was small and basic, with inadequate ventilation, I still felt far more independent and could freely come and go, during the day. At night, the nurse would lock the door, I did not question this practise, but the staff inferred it was for my own good.

The next morning, as an excuse to get away from the hospital for the afternoon, I asked the Charge Nurse if I might have permission to go into Warrington, only a short bus ride away. I had a growing need to get away from Delph, since the boredom was beginning to frustrate me. Although lying by telling him I needed to buy a birthday present, he took my request seriously. Much to my surprise, he went to consult the doctor. I returned to my room to lie on my bed, fully expecting my request to be refused. However, he returned later and gave me permission to go, as long as I did not take any of the other patients with me.

This was good news for me. It made me feel as if the staff were treating me as a normal human being again. Although I had already realized that I differed in many ways from the other patients, this was the first time that I was aware of the staff treating me differently to the other patients.

I spent the afternoon in Warrington, walking around the shops. I had a cup of coffee in a cafe and tried to strike up a conversation with a couple of women. One insulted me and accused me of drunkenness, while her friend simply rebuffed me. I was very upset and wondered how people could be so cruel. I began to feel sorry for myself and caught the bus back to Delph.

When I returned to my room my mood had not changed - that is, until I remembered the predicament of my fellow patients. It soon dawned on me that there were many more people who were worse off than me. I felt guilty and realized that I was one of the luckiest people in the world, not only because I was alive, but because I was also in control of my own mind. Regarding the two women who insulted me, I comforted myself with the notion that it takes all kinds of people to make a world. Although upset, I did not mention the incident to anybody.

I regularly attended the hypnotherapy sessions, but since they continued with no apparent improvement of my memory, I began to think that the whole exercise was a waste of time. I felt sorry for the doctor

However, this situation changed after the fourth session. I could not remember anything after the stage where the doctor said my eyelids are getting heavier and heavier. I also felt refreshed when I was leaving her clinic.

That night, as usual, the Charge Nurse locked my door and switched off the light. I was about to doze off but found myself remembering my past.

Chapter 8

Childhood Pranks

I was born on 17 November 1948 and spent part of my early child hood in Oriel Road, near the boundary of Liverpool and Bootle. I had one brother and four sisters. Being the sixth child, nobody could rightly accuse me of being pampered.

Times were hard for my parents, as they were for most people in those days, but we always got by. My father did not have a trade, so he worked as a fireman or as a security officer. Fortunately, he had a bit of capital in the bank so we rarely went short. My mother was only seven stones but could she work. Mind you, there is good stuff in small parcels, as the saying goes, and she was certainly no exception. She was very house-proud. After leaving school at the age of fourteen, she had gone into service. She was a great cook and always managed to keep us all clean and tidy - that was some feat, considering that there were no "mod-cons" like automatic washing machines - only a scrubbing brush and a "dolly-tub."

I was three when my sister Linda was born. Two years later, I began my education in the infant's section of St. Paul's School, which my elder brother and sisters had also attended.

Every family has a black sheep, and, at an early age, I was given this label. Why I do not know, although it may have originated with my kindness to animals. I thought it was only natural to give Flo, our pet mongrel, a hair cut in the hot weather, and to give her bleach to drink when she was thirsty. Anyway, that name stuck with me for the rest of my early childhood. Gordon and my older sisters were always telling me that I should not be doing this, that or the other. I was convinced that they all had it in for me.

I spent most of my time with Gordon during the school summer holidays. He was four years older and not that much taller. On Sunday mornings, if the weather was good - it usually was in those days - we would often go 'camping' on Waterloo beach. Our tent consisted of two old broom handles that we would stick in the sand to support an old Army and Navy blanket. We would take a stack of jam butties with us and a bottle of lemonade, made from water and lemonade powder. It was quite a walk for me, so I would often lag behind and complain about my poor feet. As soon as our house was out of sight, I would usually begin eating and drinking. By the time we arrived at Waterloo, I would have gobbled all my food, while Gordon still would not have touched his.

We could only spend about an hour on the beach, before we had to set off for home - that was the hardest part. As usual, I would be moaning all the way back and would often stop to rest. Gordon would press on and often left me behind, but I always knew he would be hiding somewhere, waiting for me. We would arrive home starving, exhausted, and longing to go to bed.

When I moved into the junior school, Gordon had passed a scholarship to go to John Hamilton Technical College. He was a child-wonder. Whenever I asked him about anything, he always seemed to know the answer. At the age of eleven, he made a crystal radio set and used to develop and print his own photographs that he had taken with a "Brownie" camera he had saved up to buy from the second-hand shop.

Because he had excelled at Saint Paul's School, the teachers expected me to follow in his footsteps. I detested school and was more interested in having a good time. I always preferred to make my classmates laugh - or at least try - than to take any serious interest in schoolwork. One Christmas, before the Nativity play, the teachers allowed me to perform a sketch on the stage with a few friends. We called ourselves "The Crazy Gang." I organized it and made sure we all knew our lines. We just cracked jokes and acted the goat. After we had told our first few gags, we all seemed to forget our lines and had to make them up as we went along - something that did not go down well. We resorted to doing somersaults over each other and ended up staging a mock battle on the stage. Everybody had a good laugh at us and when we finished we threw a pile of "Gob Stoppers" and "Uncle Joe's Mint Balls" into the audience. We went down a treat - or at least the sweets did.

We all got our pocket-money on Saturday morning. I would receive sixpence, and my parents would always encourage me to save some of it each week. Every Saturday morning, Jennifer, Brenda, Gordon and I would walk along Stanley Road to the Post Office to buy a saving stamp. I would feel as rich as a millionaire when the clerk gave me my Saving Book and threepenny stamp.

The other three would then go to have their weekly piano lesson. I was supposed to go too, but I hated it; I believed the piano was only for girls, so I was excused from going. Hurrying home, I would sit in my room to dote on my recently acquired savings. However, it would not be long before I was rushing back to the Post Office to cash in my threepenny stamp, so that I could go to the Saturday Matinee. I used to go to the "Commodore" or the "Princess" to see Flash Gordon, Batman, Zorro or Roy Rogers. They were the good old days, when all the kids used to cheer when the "goodies" were on the screen and boo when the "baddies" were shown. Afterwards, I would run home pretending to be a cowboy, using my duffle coat as a cloak and slapping my backside, as if to whip a horse.

During the summer holidays, Angela, Brenda and Gordon would go pea-picking on Bill Tyrer's farm in Bickerstaffe. I would always plead to go with them, but they would tell me I was too young. One evening, they got sick of my nagging and agreed to take me the next day. I could barely believe my ears when they told me - I even went to bed early.

The next morning, they got me up at six o'clock. I had a wash and a breakfast of tea and toast, before the four of us set off for Kirkdale Station, where we caught the train to take us to Town Green and Aughton. We met a crowd of other pickers on our arrival and were picked up in a Land Rover by Ted, the Foreman, and Tommy Oliver, a farm labourer, to take us to the field where we were to pick. On the way, I saw a herd of cows in a field. I had never seen farm animals before and thought they were wonderful.

I had to behave myself, especially when Martin, another farm labourer, was about. He was an ogre of an Irishman and just the sight of him terrified me. Most of the time, he would march up and down the drills with his pitchfork, checking that none of the pickers had left any peas on the stalks. His large beady eyes would glare downwards, as he constantly swore under his breath. I would never look in his direction when he was about - I was too afraid. Occasionally, he would have to go elsewhere on the farm and leave us unattended. That was my signal to go in search of adventure.

On one such occasion, I wandered away to a copse of trees surrounding a pond at the bottom of the field. I had never seen anything like it before - I was in heaven. I tried to catch a tiddler, but just as I was about to grab it, I spotted a frog on the side of the bank. Much to my dismay, as I dived to catch it, I slipped and fell into the pond. I panicked and started screaming. Gordon, my two sisters, and most of the other pickers rushed to see what was the matter. By the time they arrived on the scene, I had managed to climb out of the pond and was sitting on the bank crying my eyes out. While the sun dried my clothes, I think everybody in the field told me off. When I arrived home, my father gave me the usual good spanking. For some reason, they would not take me pea-picking again that summer - spoil sports is what I called them.

In August 1957, after many years on the Corporation's Housing list, we left our old house in Oriel Road and moved to a new four-bedroomed Corporation house in Northwood, Kirkby. My mother had just given birth to Colin, my youngest brother, so we needed the space.

Kirkby was a new town and, like most other new towns, had many teething problems. There was a clash of many subcultures, which resulted in there being many arguments and disturbances between neighbours.

I enjoyed living there, but my parents hated it. My mother had a very quiet nature - often too quiet for her own good - and was a great worrier. Her health suffered because of the unrest, and she longed to get as far away from the place as possible. My father felt the same. I was eight and too young to worry about such things as neighbourhood arguments. After living in Kirkby for six months, my parents tried desperately to get an exchange. They advertised repeatedly in the "Liverpool Echo" but were always unsuccessful. Kirkby had acquired a bad name, and the only people willing to move there were from similarly troubled districts of Liverpool.

I was enrolled at Simonswood Junior School, where I must have spent the two most uneventful years of my life. Nothing out of the ordinary seemed to happen to me, except for the time when I took a job after school as a paper-boy. Gordon had been working as one for about a year and put my name forward when a job became vacant. At the time, I was ten, although I told the newsagent I was twelve.

I had a small paper-round and was always on the look-out for new business to increase my earnings. One day, I was particularly pleased when I signed up a new customer. According to her, she previously had her papers delivered by my competitor but his service had not been reliable. She lived in a top maisonette and was really good business for me - or so I thought at first, since she ordered a morning and evening paper, two on a Sunday and two weekly magazines. She paid me on time for the first few weeks and even gave me a tip. However, as time passed, I began to see less of her. Whenever I called on a Thursday or Friday evening for the money, nobody ever seemed to be at home. However, one Friday night when I called for the money, one of her young sons opened a window and shouted down, "Me Mam said she's not in." What was I to do? I did not want to lose her custom, but I had to consider the fact she had not paid me for four weeks. I decided not to deliver any more papers until she had paid the bill.

As luck would have it - if luck is the right word - the following afternoon, I bumped into her in the Town Centre. When I asked her for the money she owed, she replied that her husband was away at sea and that she had been in hospital for three weeks. She added that the doctor had only discharged her that morning. Feeling guilty, I even apologized for having troubled her. She then told me that she had purposely left the money at home for me that morning in case I called for it while she was out. Eager to keep her as a customer, I said that I hoped she was feeling better. She thanked me for my concern and for continuing to deliver her papers. I told her not to worry and that I would call at the house for the money that evening. She then asked me to get her another magazine - she had been reading a serial in it, while she had been in hospital and wanted to read the next instalment. I told her I would deliver it that evening. I felt relieved that she was going to pay the bill and promised to put the magazine through her letter-box that evening with the "Football Echo."

After finishing my deliveries, I called around for the money, as arranged. To my great dismay, nobody would answer when I rang the bell. Annoyed, I stood back from the door and looked up to see her watching me from the living room window above. When she spotted me looking up at her, she quickly moved back behind the curtain. I was furious and realized that the story about having been in hospital was probably untrue. I have never liked being made to look foolish - she must have thought I was stupid, so I decided to teach her a lesson. "Are you listening everybody," I shouted, at the top of my voice, "the woman in number 27a owes four weeks paper money and she won't pay me."

Pleased with myself, I contentedly walked down the path. However, before I had time to open the gate, her front door flew open and out ran a giant of a man, wearing a vest, and a thick leather belt to keep up his trousers. He gave me one crack across the face and threw me over the garden wall and onto the pavement. I was sobbing as I picked myself up and ran away. I thought of telling my father but realized that he would go around to see him and that would have meant more trouble, so I kept quiet about the whole affair. However, from then on I was very wary about whom I accepted as a customer. What is more important, I also learned when to keep my big mouth shut - for a short time, anyway.

After completing my junior education, I began my secondary education at Ruffwood Comprehensive School in September 1960. Some of the school customs seemed strange to me at first, but I soon got used to them. All the teachers wore "cap and gown," and the female members of staff were to be addressed as "madam" and not as "miss."

I enjoyed the time I spent at Ruffwood and will always remember it as the place where I began to grow up - even though during the first year, I received the cane for messing about on many occasions. I was forever in trouble and earned myself a reputation for being a "good fighter." Unfortunately, this followed me right through into the second year. My parents did not know this; if they had known they would certainly have chastised me.

At the beginning of my second year at Ruffwood, I realized the stupidity of fighting, especially without a viable reason - if there is such a thing. What made it worse was that I hardly knew the boy I fought nor had I ever caused any of the fights. Eventually, it dawned on me that my school friends were using me for their own entertainment.

Fortunately, my attitude towards fighting suddenly changed one day. While walking home from a friend's house I saw two men arguing outside the "Molineux" pub. One of them was about six feet tall and built like a block of flats. The other was a midget in comparison and built like a whippet. Despite his size, the smaller man suddenly jumped up and forcefully butted the other one in the face. Blood splattered in all directions, as the big man fell to the ground, and his opponent kicked him repeatedly in the stomach.

It was a barbaric sight that really sickened me. It affected my attitude towards fighting and was an important changing point in my life. I suddenly found that the desire to fight physically no longer formed a part of my nature: I had realized now how futile it was.

The next time a boy came up to me to "offer me out," I tried to reason with him and make him see how pointless fighting was. When I thought I was beginning to get through to him, the onlookers immediately began to urge him to punch me. Eventually, he began to throw punches but I just stood there, trying to avoid his fists. It was not long before my nose was bleeding and my eyes had taken a pounding. My opponent was declared the "winner," since he had given me a good beating.

He may have "won" that fight, but I had never been so content in my life. I enjoyed every minute of it and have never fought physically against another person since that day.

No longer interested in fighting, I had to find some outlet for my excess energy. Playing football was my favourite pastime, although I was never good enough to make the "A" team. Dissatisfied with my position in the "B" team, I turned to rugby. I made the grade and played as a forward in the "A" team. I was not a particularly good player, but would always turn up for practice and whenever we had a match.

The teacher in charge of the rugby team was Leon Morris, an ex-member of the British Lions squad. He arranged for us to play against his former school, Barry Grammar, near Cardiff. We spent the weekend there and stayed in the homes of our opposite numbers in the Barry side. I stayed at the home of a lad called Dai. He was an only child, and his father was a doctor. They lived in a residential area and their wealth and culture overwhelmed me. I nearly got lost in the carpet pile and when their grandfather clock chimed, I almost dropped a cup of tea in surprise. At the rear of the house was a vast orchard and a greenhouse with all kinds of funny-looking tropical plants and fruits.

On the morning of the game, I did not feel very well but did not tell anyone as I wanted to play. We kicked off and were leading 6-5 until just before the final whistle. However, in the middle of a loose scrum, I got my head between the ball and somebody's boot. I had concussion and was walking around the field in a daze. Somehow, I suddenly found myself with the ball in my hands, so since the goal-posts were in front of me, I kicked the ball towards the try-line. Then, holding my head, I collapsed to the ground.

I woke up in hospital later that day, suffering from glandular fever and concussion. Mr. Morris and the team came in to see me later.

"How are you, Hal?" asked Mr. Morris concernedly.

"Oh, I'm all right - a bit of a headache and I feel a bit shivery, but I'm not dead yet," I said.

"That must have been some bang on the head you got," said Les Lewis, a friend, who was built like a tank and, when he had the ball in his hands, was almost as hard to stop.

"Yes, but it was worth it - we won, didn't we?" I said smiling.

An uneasy silence fell about us as the others looked at the floor.

"Well, we did, didn't we?"

"No, I'm afraid they beat us 10-6," said Mr. Morris sadly.

"10-6, but how could they? Do you mean nobody touched the ball down after I'd made that beautiful kick?" I said, feeling let down.

"Actually, it was a beautiful kick - the only thing wrong was that you kicked it towards your own touch-line. They just ran on and scored a try, which they converted!"

I looked up at them - what could I say?

The next day, the team went home while I remained in hospital for a week. An ambulance brought me all the way home from Cardiff. It was exciting and I felt very important. However, I will never live down the fact that it was my fault we lost at Barry.

One day, I found a handbag in a telephone box near where we lived. It became apparent from its weight that there was money inside. I was too afraid to open it in case the owner returned and thought I was going to steal the contents. I waited outside the kiosk for ten minutes hoping that the owner would return to claim it but nobody appeared.

My parents had always gone to great lengths to teach me to respect other people's property, so, after ten minutes had passed, I decided to take it home. My mother opened the bag and looked inside for a name and address. There was no identification but there was a purse that contained £27.

£27! I had never seen so much money before.

"Put your coat on, we'll have to take it to the police station," said my father.

Off we went to the police station. Filled with excitement, I clung on to the handbag.

"What a day," I thought, "finding all that money!" I could hardly believe it. "And now I'm actually going to go inside a police station for the first time in my life. Wait till I get into school on Monday and tell all my mates," I thought, barely believing what was really happening to me.

As we walked up the path to the police station, my father was looking down at me, smiling broadly.

"What happens now?" I asked, apprehensively.

"You found it son, so now it's up to you to report it," he said, as he opened the door.

"But, I don't know what to say," I replied nervously. "They might think I've pinched it - they may even lock me up."

"Don't be daft, they'll be pleased you handed it in - you may even get a medal."

"Honest, Dad, will I get a medal?"

"No, son, you won't get a medal, but you might get a reward."

"A reward! Cor, how much will I get, Dad?"

"Don't know, son. Anyway, you're doing what's right, that's the main thing."

We went inside and I told the duty policeman what I had found. He was delighted and surprised that I had decided to hand it in.

"Well done, Hal!" he said, as he looked down at me from over the counter. "It's a pity there aren't more people like you around here,"

He told me that if nobody claimed the handbag within three months, I would become the rightful owner of it. He also added that if somebody claimed it, they might give me a reward, although that would be up to the owner. He then showed me around the police station.

That was not the end of story. Although the owner claimed the handbag later that evening, she never gave me a penny. Nevertheless, I did get a write-up and my photograph in the "Kirkby Reporter," the local weekly.

One day at the beginning of August 1963, I found the rest of the family waiting for my return home from delivering papers. They excitedly informed me that we were going to exchange houses out of Kirkby. Apparently, somebody had enquired about the advertisement in the "Liverpool Echo," and wanted to exchange with us. I did not know what to think at first, for I had many good friends at school. I was the only one of the entire family who did not mind living in Kirkby, but I had no say in the matter. Where were we going? - Kingston upon Hull, Yorkshire.

Chapter 9

Reaching Adulthood

We arrived in Hull in early September, 1963 and lived on the Anlaby Park Road South Estate. The neighbours were friendly and I settled down very quickly.

Angela and Madeline had remained behind in Liverpool to get married, and Jennifer, who was trying to break into show business, was working in a dancing troupe in Liverpool. Gordon had begun a B.Sc. Honours degree course, reading Physics at Nottingham University, while Brenda began her job as a secretary for a local firm of solicitors. Linda and I were enrolled into Boothferry High School. Colin began at the local primary school, while Janet was too young to attend school.

I was fourteen and placed in the top class of the fourth year, while Linda was similarly graded in the first year. Apart from the vast difference in size, the most obvious difference between Ruffwood and Boothferry was in the level of education. I was ahead of the other pupils in the class, because standards were much higher in my former school.

Since I had already covered all of the topics on the curriculum at Ruffwood, I was popular with all of the teachers, since - according to them - I set a good example to the rest of the class. I was well-liked by my classmates and could not do a thing wrong. My popularity with the boys stemmed from my support for Everton F.C., because they had recently won the First Division Championship. As for the girls, they liked me as soon as they heard I was from Liverpool - the home of the Beatles.

In those days, anyone from Liverpool could do no wrong. "Beatlemania" was alive and well to say the least, boosted by the reputations of other Liverpool groups and show-biz personalities. Since

I came from Liverpool, it may be of no surprise to you that I had a Liverpool accent. I was often asked by the girls to say "Paul, John, George and Ringo," or "Rhythm guitar and mouth organ." My class-mates would also ask me to teach them to speak "Scouse" and on more than one occasion I told them that Gordon, my brother, had gone to school with John Lennon. I am not sure if they all believed my harmless fib but they wanted it to be true, so that was good enough for me.

Hull City's football ground, Boothferry Park, was less than a mile from where we lived. Whenever the "Tigers" were playing at home, my school friends and I would stand at the top of Bunker's Hill and support them. On a few occasions we would travel to watch them when they were playing away. While my friends would always travel by train on the "Football Special," I used to hitch-hike and would always arrive at the away ground long before they did.

By sheer coincidence, on Saturday, 4th January 1965, the "Tigers" were to play at home against Everton in the F.A. Cup. All my friends in Hull were ecstatic, knowing that mighty Everton were coming to play Third Division Hull City at Boothferry Park. After having always been a faithful Everton supporter, there was no question as to which team would have my support. I arrogantly told my friends that Everton would thrash the "Tigers." Of course, they all boasted otherwise and even placed bets with me that Everton would not win.

When the big day arrived, I put on my Royal Blue anorak, track suit bottoms, and Everton cap and scarf. At 10.00 o'clock in the morning, I jumped on my bike and rode the short distance to Boothferry Park. When I arrived at the ground, the only other person standing outside was a newspaper reporter.

"Have you got any souvenir papers, please?" I said proudly in my native Liverpool accent.

"No, son, you're too early. Why, where are you from?" asked the journalist eagerly.

"Liverpool - I'm an Everton supporter!" I proudly replied, holding my head up high.

"What," he asked, almost in disbelief, "do you mean you've ridden all the way from home on your bike!"

"Yes, why not?" I asked, unaware that he was assuming that I had ridden the 130 miles from Liverpool.

Before realizing what was happening I found myself sitting in the best stand, clutching a complimentary ticket I had been given, while a gentleman from the press took my photograph. That evening in the "Hull Daily Mail" my photograph and story was on the front page: "First from Goodison - rides all the way!" The reporter-gave me a free ticket for the best stands, so I certainly was not going to ruin his story by telling him I was living in Hull at the time.

On the following Monday morning at school, my school pals were convinced I had purposely set out to dupe the reporter. They would not believe me, when I tried to tell them otherwise. The truth of the matter was the reporter was so eager to obtain a scoop for the newspaper that I did not have time to explain that my home-was then in Hull.

However, Everton only managed to draw and although they won the replay at Goodison Park, I still lost the wager!

I applied to Hull Nautical College to enrol on a two-year pre-sea course to become a Merchant Navy Cadet Navigating Officer. I attended the interview and was accepted onto the course beginning in the following September.

Aged fifteen, I began at the Nautical College in September 1964, along with six other boys of the same age. I found the course interesting and we studied for the G.C.E. at O level in Mathematics, English Language, Physics with Chemistry, Seamanship, and Navigation and Astronomy.

I was constantly dreaming of going to sea when I was at the Nautical College. I was aware that on rare occasions some shipping companies would allow a relative of their senior personnel to sail on their ships as a supernumerary - a non-paying passenger who is prepared to work as a crew member if required. Alas, I did not know any senior personnel or have any relatives in the Merchant Navy. Nevertheless, I was determined to go to sea during the Christmas 1964 vacation.

The day after the College broke up for the Christmas holiday I visited many shipping companies in Hull asking if I might be allowed to sail as a supernumerary on board one of their ships. I was not having any luck and was on the point of giving up when I came across the offices of the Klondyke Shipping Company. I had never heard of the line before, so I did not rate my chances as good.

Walking confidently into the office, I almost opened the door in the face of a well-dressed gentleman. I apologized, and he smiled and asked if I was from Liverpool - my accent must have given me away. I realized he had some connection with the Company, so I told him of my desire to sail on one of their ships over the Christmas and New Year period.

"Sorry, it's not the Company's policy," he said, before putting his hand across his mouth in an attempt to hide his grin. "I admire your pluck, though!" At this point, I realized from the quality of the suit he was wearing that he must have held a senior position within the Company. I explained that I was attending the Nautical College and intended to go to sea as a Navigation Cadet Officer. I also stressed that I was a good worker.

He grinned again and thought for a moment. "Just wait here a few minutes - I've got to see somebody inside," he said, before disappearing into the office.

My excitement mounted, as I clenched my teeth and tensed the muscles in my neck. "My luck is in," I thought.

The man reappeared five minutes later and, to my great delight, told me that one of their ships, the "M.V. Framptondyke," was leaving Hull the next evening and that I would be allowed to sail on her. All I had to do was to go to the Shipping Federation to collect the necessary papers.

Elated, I joined the ship the following day and sailed to Portis Head, where we discharged our cargo of scrap metal. The next day we proceeded to Port Talbot, where we loaded coal for Rotterdam and Vlardingen. We were only away for two weeks and I enjoyed it tremendously - except when we were crossing the North Sea on New Year's day. The weather was ghastly and I was sea sick. My memories of the trip are particularly vivid, since I spent most of the night on deck, throwing up over the side of the ship. Whenever a crew member passed me on the deck he would look down at me and laugh aloud before saying something facetious like: "Suffering man, suffering!"

The following February, my family moved back to live in Liverpool, and I had to move into lodgings. My parents applied to the Education Committee for help with my expenses. The course at the Nautical College was not classed as Higher Education, so I could only apply for a discretionary grant. This barely paid for my uniform and books, leaving my parents to pay for my lodgings, bus fares, and everything else I needed. It was quite a sacrifice they had to make, considering that I was from a large family.

I started living in digs at the age of sixteen which meant it was impossible to run home whenever I needed help. It was difficult at times, but I enjoyed my new independence. It certainly meant that I grew up sooner.

Every couple of months, I would travel the 130 mile journey from Hull to Liverpool, although I never used the train or coach. I hitch hiked every time, since public transport seemed a luxury to me. I enjoyed hitch-hiking and it did not cost me a penny. Often, the driver would stop at a transport cafe and insist on buying me a plate of sausages and chips and a mug of tea.

My Liverpool accent, as explained earlier, was a great asset to me at Boothferry High School. However, the situation changed at the Nautical College, where it quickly became my greatest liability. I was training to be a navigation officer in the Merchant Navy, and, according to the lecturers, "Officers and gentlemen do not speak with Liverpool accents." In particular, the English lecturer would often mock me because of it. Thinking he was joking at first, I did not pay him much attention, but he would constantly ask me derisively when was I going to learn to speak properly. He often ridiculed me in front of the other boys in the class, who were all from Yorkshire. I was determined not to let him see that I was upset and would often exaggerate my accent to annoy him. Despite his distasteful remarks he was my favourite lecturer.

Before becoming a student at the College I would often enjoy spending a Saturday morning in the swimming baths. It was therefore a delight to discover that there was a two-hour swimming period each week. However, what had once been one of my favourite pastimes soon became a gruelling ordeal. Most weeks, we would do nothing but swim continuously from the time we entered the water until the time we left. Training for the Bronze Medallion in Life-saving was our first task, and as soon as we had all passed that, training for the Mile Certificate began in earnest. The only break from the strenuous routine was at the end of each term when we would be allowed to play water polo-, a game I did not enjoy.

During the wintry months, we would build twelve foot sailing dinghies in the evenings and, during the warmer months, we used to go sailing on a lake near Brough, using the boats built by cadets from previous years. Friday afternoons were generally spent at the docks doing "Lifeboat Work". At break time, everybody would go for a pie and a cup of coffee or tea in the dockers' canteen. When it was raining, we would play cards in there while we sheltered.

Class of 64/66 - Hull Nautical College
(left/right) Wood, me, John, Parker, Bailey, Ladlow, Dave, and Thornton

In May, 1966, I applied to become a navigating cadet officer indentured to Sir R. Ropner and Company Ltd. I attended an interview

80

and to my delight was accepted. My reason for choosing this firm was that I wanted to serve my Cadetship on board a tramp ship. This is the name given to a ship which has no regular route and is usually on charter to a third party

I enjoyed the two years spent at the Nautical College. It was not always easy living in lodgings, but I found that it helped to develop my character.

My first trip to sea as a Cadet Officer was on board the M.V. Willowpool. The ship had been chartered by the People's Republic of China, and I was away for almost a year.

We took steel plates from Antwerp and army wagons from Algiers to Shanghai via the Suez Canal. After discharging our cargo we spent three months coasting between Shanghai and four other Chinese ports, before we set a course for Port Sudan, Djibouti, Lattakia, Beirut, Marseilles and Genoa. The cargo for these ports ranged from grand pianos to table tennis bats and balls, canned fruit to vacuum flasks, stamp albums to Mao Tse Tung's Bibles... At the time, there seemed to be everything under the sun.

My most memorable occasion of that trip occurred in Antwerp, our first port of call. The evening before sailing to Algiers, a few of the middle-ranking and junior officers took Tony and Ian, the other two cadets, and myself ashore for a night on the town. First-trip Cadets are generally the first to have their legs pulled on such occasions. As Ian, the engineering cadet, and myself were first-trippers, the tradition was upheld. Unfortunately, I became the officers' first victim that night.

We were having a good time moving from bar to bar and listening to all the amazing yarns that each officer spun. It was hard to believe some of them, since they sounded too far-fetched to be true - I thought it was the drink talking. However, I later discovered that the most unbelievable things do actually happen to seafarers.

Eventually, we ended up in "Danny's Bar," in the red light district of Antwerp. We went inside and had a few drinks, while standing at the bar. As time wore on, the steins of Pils seemed to get too heavy to lift, and we eventually went to sit at a table.

A barmaid suddenly appeared at the next table. I had not noticed her earlier, since I had been too busy listening to all the yarns. How my eyes had failed to see her I do not know! She looked gorgeous in her tight mini-dress which, clung to her boyish figure. Her jet-black shoulder-length hair cradled her young and innocent face. Our eyes met and I was in love! Never had I seen such beauty.

I called her over and managed to stutter out my order. The others must have noticed my attraction to her, because as soon as she had gone to the bar to get our order they began laughing their heads off. To make matters worse they urged me to make a date with her. I could feel my face turning bright red in embarrassment. However, when she returned she put the tray on the table and then winked crudely at me. I was taken aback, as this was out of character for the dream-girl I had conjured up in my mind. I decided to pay her and not to take matters further.

"How much is that, please?" I said in an abrupt tone of voice so as to disguise my disappointment.

"It's on the house, love," she said as she fluttered her darkened eyelashes, "wait for me tonight and we'll have a good time!"

The others were splitting their sides with laughter, as I stood there embarrassed and shocked at what I had heard. It was not what she had said that had disgusted me, but how she had said it, since her voice was deep and husky! As I continued to look at her, it suddenly dawned on me that the barmaid was not a "she" but a "he" - a transvestite!

The officers had been in on the joke all along and had gone there on purpose knowing that one of us cadets would be fooled. All I wanted to do was to finish my drink and go back to the "Willowpool," as I felt such an idiot. The officers just laughed and told me that I was not the first to be fooled and would certainly not be the last. This type of trick is often played on first-trippers, so the others soon forgot about it - I don't think, I ever will!

My second and final trip to sea was on board the M.V. Rushpool. I joined her in Rotterdam and then sailed to Hamburg where we completed the unloading of her cargo of scrap metal. From here we sailed light-ship - without a cargo - to Saint Vincent, in the Cape Verde Islands, where we bunkered - refuelled - and then proceeded across the Atlantic to Argentina to load grain for Japan. After sailing halfway around the world, we discharged our cargo in Yokohama and sailed light-ship across the Pacific to Vancouver, once more loading grain for Japan. We unloaded our cargo in Kobe and again crossed the Pacific to load salt at Cedros Island, off the coast of Mexico. Returning to Japan, we discharged half our cargo of salt in Kobe, and the remainder in Sakata. What happened next will probably be my most vivid memory of my life in the navy. During the last night in Sakata, I had a crippling pain on the right side of my stomach I lay awake all night, and it was not until five o'clock in the morning that I called Tony, the other cadet, in the next cabin, to get help. He alerted the Chief Steward, who examined me and then told the Captain. After checking my condition, he immediately telephoned for an ambulance, and I was rushed ashore to a hospital. My appendix was removed that morning, and the ship later sailed for the Panama Canal, leaving me behind in Sakata!

The hospital had been a U.S. Army barracks during the war, but was converted into an infirmary after the Americans moved out. The wards were basically wooden sheds!

When I came to after the anaesthetic, I found myself in my own private room, with a beautiful Japanese nurse holding my hand. Her name was Sachiko and she could only speak two words in English—yes and no! - mind you, I knew only a handful of Japanese words myself!

Later, when the doctor came to see me, I discovered that he was the only person in the hospital who could speak English! Everything had to be interpreted through him. I tried using sign language with the rest of the staff, but we always seemed to end up laughing at each other.

The nurses tried to get me up to walk on the second day, but I thought they were making a mistake, so I refused to get out of bed. When the doctor came to see what the fuss was about, I told him exactly what the nurses had been trying to do. He smiled at me and asked me what was wrong with that. I replied that patients usually stay in bed for four or five days in England before they are allowed to get up. He grinned and told me not to worry. "In Japan, we do things differently to English," he said, smiling broadly. Within half an how, I was walking around without pain, although I had to be careful not to disturb the stitches.

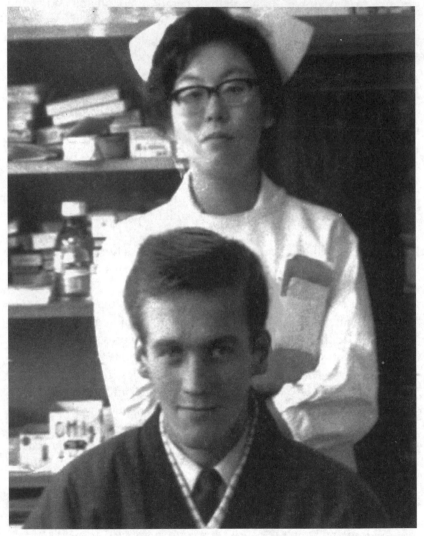

After the appendix operation - Sakata, Japan

On the third day, two students from the local language college came to visit me. Takashi, the boy, and Yoko, the girl, were both my age and were extremely friendly. They spoke English well, although they had difficulty pronouncing some words. They were very good company and taught me to sing "*Suki Yaki*" in Japanese. I knew the tune well, because I had bought the Kenny Ball jazz version of the tune for Gordon the Christmas before. They also took me to the kitchen in the hospital, since the head cook wanted to know how I liked my food prepared. Using the two students as translators, the head cook asked me many questions about Great Britain, and I learned much about their customs.

I remained in the hospital for a further eleven days, and each day the two students would come to visit me. The day before I left, they took me into their College to meet some of their friends before taking me into the town to have a traditional Japanese meal at a restaurant.

The next day, I travelled to Tokyo by train and then flew to Rotterdam via Anchorage, Alaska. I caught a flight from Rotterdam to London and then boarded a train to Liverpool. It had taken me more than thirty six hours to arrive home. My journey had been exhausting.

After being home for six weeks, I attended an eyesight examination at the Board of Trade offices. Unfortunately, I failed the test. I was bitterly disappointed since this meant that my dream of becoming the master of my own vessel had been shattered. I had no other career in mind.

When my paid leave had expired, I went to the Labour Exchange to sign on. After a few weeks, the Ministry of Labour offered me an office job - working at the employment office where I was registered as unemployed! I did not enjoy being a civil servant, but at least it was a stop gap until something better came along. After nine months I left and went to work in the office of a large tobacco company. It was enjoyable working there, but I soon discovered that the conditions for a clerk were much the same everywhere. I therefore decided to change my occupation as well as my job.

I saw that Shell Chemicals were advertising for Trainee Chemical Plant Operators. The training was first-class and the salary was excellent

- even during training! I decided to apply and was accepted after an interview. On completion of a one-week induction course at Shell's Carrington Plant, near Manchester, together with a score of other young men, I began a two-year sandwich course at Stretford Technical College. There was one snag; I had to commute to Manchester every day during the week. Apart from the expense, there was also the travelling time to consider. For the first couple of weeks, I got a lift from another lad from Liverpool, who had started with me, but it meant having to pay him as much as the fare to work. At the end of the second week, I bought a 90 c.c. motorbike and travelled to work on it. It served its purpose well and saved my money.

Chapter 10

Jumping in at the Deep End

Almost eight months had elapsed since the car accident, and it now seemed my life was wasting away at Delph. I was becoming increasingly frustrated at the way my life was being run for me. My mundane existence seemed to be standing still, while I was painfully aware that the world outside the hospital was carrying on without me. My need to take a more active role in deciding my future was of prime importance to me. I was full of enthusiasm and wanted to get on with my life. Something had to be done.

After discussing the situation with my parents, I decided to discharge myself from the hospital. There was some opposition from the doctor, who considered that I was not yet well enough to leave.

He wanted me to stay longer at Delph, but, once I had decided to leave the hospital, there was no way of changing my mind. It was difficult for me to see how I would benefit from remaining at the hospital any longer. I was grateful for what the hospital staff had done for me, but I believed it would now be better for me to live at home. It was essential for me to be re-integrated into society as soon as possible. I realized that it was going to be difficult and that I would have to fend for myself but I was confident society would accept me and help me to lead a normal life again. In spite of my accident, I still intended to make a success of my life. I knew I could do it and knew it had to be done alone.

As I looked back on my recovery, I realized how fortunate I had been. The doctors were unsure whether I would live or die when I was in the coma. They had prepared my parents for the worst, but, fortunately, I had fooled them. They had also assumed that if I did survive, I would almost certainly be a "cabbage" and paralysed down the right side of my body - I had fooled them again. When I did regain consciousness, the doctors had told my parents that I may never walk again - once more, I fooled them. However, they also said I might never speak intelligibly. So far their prediction remained valid, but I was certainly going to try my best to prove them wrong once more.

Physically, I had almost completely recovered - more than anybody had ever imagined possible. My fractured skull and ribs had healed without a hitch. My limb movements were still not co-ordinated properly; I was still unsteady on my feet and walked with a limp, but it would merely be a matter of time before I was able to walk correctly. Although my double-vision was still frustrating me greatly, and my right wrist was continuing to cause much pain and discomfort for me, the most important thing was that I was alive and could think properly. I felt proud of what I, with the help of the medical profession, had achieved.

The greatest problem was my speech, which had not improved significantly. I decided that it would be best to try to ignore the cruel remarks that some people would make about the way I spoke. I realized that it would be easier said than done, because my nature would always ensure that I defended myself. It would be difficult to keep my temper when a stranger insulted or rebuffed me. I tried to comfort myself with the knowledge that my critics might not have been able to recover as well as I had done, if they were involved in a similar car accident. Naively, I fooled myself into believing that if I showed people that my speech did not worry me, it should not worry them. After all, it was my problem and not theirs.

My mental health had certainly improved over recent months, largely because my memory had returned. At least, I was able to recall most of the events that my family asked me about. I could vividly remember details of some past events that the rest of the family had forgotten. However, there was a four-month gap in my memory from about the October before the crash until the day in February when I had regained consciousness in the Infirmary. I could clearly look back to the day when I started work as a Trainee Chemical Plant Operator for Shell Chemicals, early in September 1969. I also remembered playing football at Stretford Technical College with my friends from Shell, but I had no recollection of my twenty-first birthday party in November nor the accident in early January - something I certainly did not want to recall.

I discovered that on the day of the accident I was doing a period of industrial training at the Carrington plant. It surprised me to discover I was travelling to work in a car - not on my motorbike; I had left home on it but had decided to get a lift in a workmate's car. It had been snowing heavily the day before and the roads were treacherous. I had naturally thought it would be safer to travel by car. My workmate also gave a lift to another lad, who fortunately escaped the crash uninjured. The driver had received two broken ribs. I was the unlucky one and received the following injuries: a fractured skull, two broken ribs and a broken wrist, that was still troubling me. I had a deep incision on my right forehead, which was very tender - this injury had led to my being unconscious for twenty-one days, and, as a result, I had to have an emergency tracheotomy. The lack of co-ordination in my limbs, double-vision and greatly impaired speech were other indirect results of my head injuries.

We were travelling through Lymm, Cheshire, at the time of the crash. While taking a bend we hit an icy patch on the road, skidded and had to overtake a wagon to avoid colliding into the rear of it. As we were overtaking, we saw a petrol tanker coming towards us, so my driver tried to avoid it by turning. Our car went into a spin, and the rear end of it careered into the front of the oncoming petrol tanker. I was in the back seat and had therefore received the worst injuries.

The first thing I did on leaving Delph was to visit Tommy and Mr. and Mrs. Forbes at Winwick. They were pleased to see me but surprised to hear I was leaving. Once I explained my reasons they fully understood. I thanked them for everything they had done for me. They were sorry to see me go, as they had got to know me well and hoped I would continue to recover. I told them that it would not have been possible for me to achieve anything had it not been for their help.

I believed that living at home would give me the confidence needed to make greater strides forward in my recovery. At the time, my dearest wish was to practise speaking with my family and to learn how to live in the community again. I was also very much looking forward to visiting my friends at Shell Chemicals, even though it would mean having to travel to Carrington. I wanted to see their faces when they saw how well I was recovering.

I will always be grateful to the Welfare Department at Shell Chemicals. As well as sending my wages and a basket of fruit to me each week, one of their welfare officers had often visited me in hospital to see if they could help in any way. My Statutory Sickness Benefit had not been deducted from my wages, and since I had not spent much money while in hospital, I had quite a little nest egg in the bank.

When I arrived home, we had a family reunion - I enjoyed it, probably because I was the main topic of conversation. Everybody remarked on how well I looked, and my ability to remember certain details of past events in my life. Talking was strenuous for me, so I soon began yawning and decided to go to bed.

I could not have had more considerate and supportive parents - they were wonderful to me. My father, who had recently retired, would do his best to help me - nothing seemed too much for him to do. My mother was so caring and would always bring me my breakfast in bed, even though I had asked her to treat me as she had before the accident. However, although I appreciated their kindness, it got to the point when they would insist on doing almost everything for me. Eventually, it occurred to me that they were unwittingly stifling any progress I was making. I needed more independence in order to make a complete recovery - something I had vowed to do.

After staying at home for two days, I soon became bored and decided it was time to go to Liverpool city centre. My parents wanted to escort me, saying that the pace of city life would be too fast for me, but I insisted on going alone. "Look, I know you have the best intentions for me, but it's no good if you're going to wrap me up in cotton wool for the rest of my life," I said to them, careful not to hurt their feelings. "The sooner I find out what life is going to be like for me the better." In the end, they fully understood.

Although the two women in the coffee bar in Warrington had rebuffed me, I was confident that Liverpool people would not behave in a similar fashion. After all, they were renowned for being amongst the friendliest people in Great Britain.

My spirits were high as I went alone to the city centre. I could not have been happier. I was about to begin my lone crusade - to learn to speak properly again.

I spent the afternoon going from coffee bar to coffee bar, in the hope of finding somebody who would have a conversation with me. Amazingly, nobody would sit and listen to me. No matter to whom I spoke, strangers always ended up insulting or rebuffing me. Some would not even bother to reply when I tried to speak to them, while a few would just look and smile derisively at me before gulping their coffee and walking away. The others would accuse me of being drunk or insane. It was too embarrassing for me to look around in case other customers had seen what had happened.

When I boarded the bus to go home the conductor automatically assumed I was drunk or simple-minded. The passengers merely looked at me in disgust. It was awful - so unlike the reception I was expecting.

On arriving home, I did not tell any of my family about the trouble I had met with. I went straight up to my room to lie on my bed to feel sorry for myself. Full of frustration, I tried to force myself to cry to relieve the anguish within me but the tears would not come. I asked myself why it was that people were so cruel? Did I have bad manners or was it because I looked repulsive? I knew the reason but it was difficult for my pride to accept - people thought I was drunk or a numskull. It was heart shattering for me, especially when I looked back over the many difficulties I had overcome.

Nevertheless, I continued going to town to sit in coffee bars in an attempt to speak to people. By the end of the first week, I realized that the treatment I was receiving from strangers was making me apprehensive, which made my slow babble sound even stranger. I often felt like screaming.

To make matters worse, I was still finding it difficult to swallow liquids and would often make a spectacle of myself. Sometimes, while drinking coffee, I would suddenly cough - anybody in front of me would be showered with coffee. People nearby would look at me in disgust. I would try to apologize and ask somebody to pat me on the back, but they would turn the other way as if to pretend I did not exist. I would despair and, on arriving home, would often vow never to go to the city centre until my speech had improved. However, my need to be accepted by society was so strong that I still went to town everyday, nonetheless.

After being home for a month, I was beginning to feel depressed. The task of learning to speak properly again was more difficult than I had imagined. I needed a change - a respite from the cruel remarks that strangers would hurl at me. Since Mr. Regan, my boss at Shell, and some of his staff had been kind enough to come to see me in hospital, I decided to go to visit him to let him see how well I was recovering. He had not seen me for a few months, and, although he was aware that I had signed myself out of Delph, I knew it would surprise him to see me walking into his office.

I was filled with pride and excitement when I set off to visit my friends at Shell. Sitting on the bus to the city centre, I no longer felt depressed but supremely confident. When I arrived at Lime Street Station, I went to buy my ticket but was very embarrassed after having an argument with the clerk in the ticket office, who assumed I was drunk. It was annoying but I managed to keep my temper.

I bought a newspaper, even though my double-vision meant that it was almost impossible for me to read, and boarded the mid-morning train to Urmston. It was empty so I went to sit near the window. An attractive young woman, carrying a suitcase, was grateful when I took hold of her luggage and put it on the rack above me - fortunately, it was light enough to lift with just my left hand. She thanked me and sat on the seat opposite. I could not believe my luck.

She was about twenty and wore a smart black business-suit. She wore little make-up, which only seemed to emphasize her vibrant youthfulness. I imagined that she was a secretary.

I did not speak but picked up the paper and pretended to read it, while trying to work out how to start a conversation with her.

Suddenly, the train began to move out of the station, which gave me the excuse to glance at her. I looked at her and smiled, but, to my amazement, she was already looking at me and smiling back. Not knowing what to do, I became flustered. I dearly wanted to speak to her, but knew I would make a fool of myself. At that moment, I would have given anything to be able to speak properly, but life is not like that.

My nervousness increased even though I continued to tell myself to calm down. I could feel my face reddening, so I decided to hide behind my newspaper once more to avoid any danger of our eyes meeting. Although afraid to speak to her, I was even more petrified that she would speak to me first. I knew the sound of my speech would ensure that she never smiled at me again.

I would glance at her when I was turning over the page, and, to my surprise, she would always smile back. Twenty minutes later, the embarrassing silence became too much to bear, so I decided to count to ten and then say something to her. I began counting many times but I always seemed to lose my nerve on reaching nine. After what seemed a lifetime, I did build up enough courage to get some words out. I took a deep breath and babbled "Are you going to Manchester?" Unfortunately, a train travelling in the opposite direction drowned my words as it sped by. She looked at me and smiled before asking me to repeat my question. I immediately became nervous again, knowing that my speech would sound awful. I took a deep breath and blurted out a mouthful of babble. Since my nervousness was rapidly getting worse, I was afraid she would think I was drunk. I became flustered again and could not control my nerves so I just continued babbling, forgetting that she would not be able to understand a word of what I said.

Suddenly, the train slowed down and then stopped at a station. A young man got in and sat opposite her, next to me. By the time the train pulled out of the station, my nervousness increased at the idea that he was able to overhear our conversation, but my nerves ensured I continued babbling to her. Out of the corner of my eye, I suddenly saw the young man at my side making fun of me for the girl's benefit. I turned my head to look at him and caught him red-handed. Glancing back at the girl, I saw that she was also doing the same. Feeling very embarrassed and stupid, I tried to explain to her, but she looked at me in horror, turned, and immediately began speaking to the man at my side, leaving me babbling in mid-sentence. Shortly afterwards, they moved away and sat on the other side of the carriage.

I wanted to die of shame. "What's the matter with you ignorant people - have I got leprosy?" I wanted to shout. I could hear the blood pulsating in my ears, and felt thoroughly demoralized. I knew I would make the situation worse if I were to say anything further, so I merely sat there, red-faced and fuming while praying for the ground to open up and swallow me.

I gave a sigh when I discovered that Urmston would be the next station. However, the train appeared to travel at a much slower rate, so my agony seemed to be prolonged. When the train finally arrived at my destination, I stepped off feeling hurt and rejected.

As I walked along the deserted lane leading to Shell's massive chemical plants, I tried desperately to dismiss my most recent rejection from my mind. It was difficult but it was no good getting upset over the matter. If I allowed such events to unnerve me I would probably end up with an ulcer at best. I told myself that I should be ashamed for allowing such a paltry thing to linger in my mind. My thoughts went back to the deranged patients in Winwick and the ridicule that they too would suffer. In the end, I came to the conclusion that there was nothing about which to feel sorry and that I should be grateful for being alive. A confident and positive attitude soon replaced the vengeance and the negative thoughts that I was harbouring.

By the time I walked into Shell's Training Centre my confidence was so high that I decided to ask Mr. Regan if I would soon be able to return to work . I had convinced myself that I would be able to lead a normal life again.

He was astonished to see me walk into his office and congratulated me on how well I was recovering. Despite my new feeling of confidence, it was difficult to make myself understood, and, at times, I had to revert to using a pen and paper to communicate. He was astonished to learn of my intention to return to work and tried to discourage me, stressing that I should convalesce for a further year. I told him that the sooner I began mixing with people again the sooner my speech would improve. He tried again to dissuade me from the idea, saying that it would mean having to live in Manchester during the week. I replied that it was exactly what I wanted, since I would then have to stand on my own two feet. He left me and went into another office to discuss my request with my supervisor. On his return, Mr. Regan told me that he would allow me to begin the two-year sandwich course again at Stretford Technical College, in the following January, providing my doctor agreed.

Upon arriving home, I told my parents of my decision to go back to College after the Christmas holidays. They were amazed and did not like the idea, saying, like my employers, that I should have more time to convalesce. At first they saw it as a bad reflection of the way they had been looking after me. I explained that they were treating me excellently, while very diplomatically pointing out my need to have more independence and to learn to stand on my own two feet again. They tried to get me to change my mind by stressing that the world would be a cruel place for somebody in my condition, but I would not listen to them. They saw my point of view in the end.

I spent most of my spare time articulating words during the two months before the course was due to begin. I would talk to myself in the mirror and even bought a portable tape-recorder to try to improve my speech. I was horrified to hear myself talk. My speech resembled that of a deaf man, except that it was much slower and very slurred. I felt like crying. In the end, I gave the recorder to Colin and made a vow never to listen to my speech again - it was too upsetting for me.

It was very difficult coming to terms with my defective speech. I had always been the type of person who was never afraid to speak up in a crowd, even though my sense of humour was not always appreciated. It was apparent that I would have to be more careful in the future.

I continued going to the city centre. In the mornings, I would go to the library to revise but found the work boring. I would locate the right book and then sit down at a table to try to read it. My double-vision was still very troublesome. The words on each page appeared to jump about, which made it difficult to get halfway along the first line before losing my place. It was frustrating. I usually ended up sitting in the library coffee bar, looking at the pictures in an encyclopaedia.

In the afternoon, I would go around the large stores and coffee bars to practise speaking to people. I was very lonely and would constantly be on the lookout for someone with whom to have a conversation, but I always met with rejection. To make matters worse, the manageress of one cafe refused to serve me. She banned me, and when I tried to explain she frog-marched me out of the shop, assuming I was drunk - it was so humiliating.

Chapter 11

A Moment Can Never Be Relived

In January 1971, twelve months after the accident occurred, I began the two-year sandwich course in Chemical Plant Technology again at Stretford Technical College. I was sure that I would be able to do the coursework, since I had already successfully completed the first three months of the training at the College the previous year. I had found it interesting.

Although I assumed that I would find the coursework terribly boring this time around, I did not mind having to go through it a second time. The previous year, I had got on very well with the lecturers and was looking forward to seeing them again. What was more important, I would be mixing with fellow Shell trainees - people with whom I had a common identity and with whom I would be able to relax. I could barely wait to see my friends who started working for Shell at the same time as myself.

Upon my arrival at the College, I had to report to the head of the science department, since he wanted to hear first-hand how I was recovering. He spoke to me in his study for half an hour, during which time he paid me many compliments about my constitution.

When I arrived at my class, the lecturer, whom I knew well, was extremely pleased to see me again and introduced me to the other students in the class. Since the departmental head had already boosted my confidence, I was feeling very self-assured. I even stood in front of the whole class and explained about the car accident and told them not to worry about my speech. It gave me great pleasure, especially as all the students appeared to understand what I was saying. However, it later became known that the lecturer had previously told them about my predicament, so they would not be too alarmed when hearing my babble. I became nervous and embarrassed halfway through my explanation and attempted to hide it by trying to be a comedian. I started laughing at my own jokes and then could not control my laughter, so it was not long before everybody, including the lecturer, was laughing too. Due to the previous year's lack of exercise, my stomach muscles were not taut enough to control my fits of mirth.

Although the course was terribly boring for me, it was also extremely difficult to comprehend. No matter how I tried to understand each lesson, I just could not concentrate. I often found myself talking to the lecturer and making the other students laugh. It soon became apparent that organic chemistry or any other academic subject no longer interested me. I only wanted to learn to speak properly again.

The students who had started with me at Shell the year before were now completing their second and final year of the course. We had all been very keen on playing five-a-side football in the gym, the previous year, but times had now changed for me. I dearly missed not being able to play with them. However, when they were having their sports period, I sometimes missed my lesson to join them in the gym. I used to get changed into my old strip, but they would never allow me to play. I still felt unsteady on my feet and my lack of co-ordination ensured that I was unable to run - not to mention the trouble I had with my right wrist and my double-vision. To make up for this, at the end of each period, they would allow me to take penalties. With the ball on the penalty spot, I would skip up to it - I could not run - and try to kick the ball as hard as I could into the net. I would usually miss the ball when trying to kick it and fall back on my backside. On the rare occasions that I did hit the ball, it would usually go sideways instead of towards the goal. I would always be the first to see the comical side of my antics, and, as soon as I started to laugh, everybody else would join in. The problem was that once I started laughing it was difficult to stop. On many occasions, the tears would stream down my face, as I lay on the gym floor holding my stomach, trying desperately to stop laughing.

I got on exceptionally well with these students and would often go to their lesson, knowing that their lecturer would not object. Although embarrassed about my speech, I would try to show them that it did not worry me by acting the clown. I would say something and then watch the other students trying to work out the meaning of my babble. The expressions on their faces would inevitably make me laugh, and then everybody else would join in. These times made me happy, for my old classmates made me feel as if I was human again - as if I belonged with them. The fact that they would sometimes laugh at me and not with me, did not worry me. I believed that by showing people I was still alive and kicking, after all I had been through, they would admire my resilience. So, whenever the opportunity arose to crack a joke I would do so - even though few people could understand my wit, never mind my speech, we would all end up laughing.

After completing the three-months course at the College, I began my industrial training at Shell's plant at Carrington. I did my training on the ethylene plant, where I was supposed to learn how to oversee the production process. The Plant Manager knew of my circumstances and had been told to look after me. He lived near Lymm, the scene of the accident and had seen the mangled state of the car I had been in. He said that I was lucky to be alive, let alone ready for work again, especially so soon after the crash. All he insisted I do was to turn up for work with a chemistry book, which I never read due to my double-vision and lack of interest. All I did at work was to sit in the Control Room, drinking coffee. It was boring, sitting in front of the control panels all day. Time seemed to drag, especially since there would rarely be anybody with whom to speak.

Even though I turned up for "work" five days a week, I only "worked" two of them. The company doctor had arranged for me to go to Salford Royal Infirmary three mornings a week. Shell would always provide a chauffeur-driven limousine, usually reserved for executive use, to take me to the Infirmary. After each session at the hospital, I would have the rest of the day off.

On Mondays, I would have Speech Therapy, on Wednesdays I would attend the Physiotherapy Department to have co-ordination exercises on my legs, and on Fridays, I would go to the Orthopaedic Department to see about my right wrist.

I would always enjoy myself when attending Speech Therapy. The Therapist was a dear old lady, who was approaching retirement age. She always wore a tweed suit and a pair of heavy brogues upon her feet. Her pale facial make-up contrasted against the rouge on her cheeks and the bright red of her lipstick. Her straw coloured hair was shoulder length and seemed to stick out at a tangent to the contour of her head.

Despite my babble, we had some very fine conversations. She would always tell me to take my time when speaking and not to worry about the delay in getting the words out. She always seemed to understand what I was trying to say, which would boost my confidence no end. I had to do many facial exercises, as well as extending my tongue in different positions. It was tiring and much more difficult than it sounds. I also had to memorize a tongue twister. It went like this:

> Betty Button bought some butter,
> But she said this batter's bitter.
> If I buy some better butter,
> It won't make my batter bitter,
> So she bought some better butter,
> Better than the bitter butter,
> And when mixing with the batter,
> Did not make her batter bitter.

I used to babble the rhyme so often that it would be difficult to ever forget the words - that is, of course, as long as I do not lose my memory again. I would be exhausted at the end of each session and even though it was hard work, I would thoroughly enjoy every minute of it.

At the Physiotherapy Department, I joined a class of patients who were all recovering from broken legs. It was not difficult for me to do the exercises, and it only dawned on me after doing them for a few weeks that the therapy did little to improve my co-ordination. I told the Physiotherapist so she treated me individually, since the lack of co-ordination is not a common complaint.

The Orthopaedic Department was always packed with patients

whenever I attended, and I would have to hang about for most of the morning before seeing the doctor. I used to enjoy it, as it provided me with an opportunity of speaking to strangers. I met the Consultant at my first attendance but rarely saw him after that. Instead, one of his junior doctors would attend to me. I do not think I ever saw the same one twice. My case history had a special fascination for the doctors and they would often ask me to describe in detail my loss of memory and my hypnotherapy sessions. Hearing about my recovery never failed to impress them and they would always tell me how fortunate I was to be alive. By the time a doctor had got around to examining my wrist, my poor tongue and jaw would be aching with use. I did not mind as it was good practice for my speech, and their admiration for my achievement gave me the incentive to continue to recover. I would always leave the hospital feeling ten feet tall.

I saw the Consultant again after a couple of months. He informed me that my wrist had never mended properly. Apparently, it had broken in a very awkward part and could not be set normally. He told me that I would have to undergo an arthrodesis operation and explained that my wrist would be "stiffened" by the insertion of a metal plate, through which my hand would be screwed to my arm. This meant I would not be able to flex my wrist, since I would no longer have a joint to bend. In addition, I would have to wear a plaster for a year.

I had the operation the following month. After coming around from the anaesthetic I got a shock when I caught sight of my fingers protruding from the plaster on my right arm. I will never forget their colour or their size - each finger was black and blue with bruising and as big as a banana due to the swelling.

Even though I had to stay in hospital for six weeks, my parents travelled from Liverpool to Salford to visit me every day. Each week, Shell would send my wages and a basket of fruit.

After being discharged, I returned home to Liverpool and spent my time going around the shops and coffee bars during the weekdays. Nothing seemed to have changed, since I rarely met with any friendliness or courtesy from the people with whom I spoke. No matter where

I went, strangers always seemed to ridicule me. Upon arriving home in the evenings, I would lie on my bed and forcefully beat my left fist into the mattress simply in an attempt to relieve the dire frustration that was burning within me.

A few weeks of this treatment was all I could bear. I decided to go back to work, even though I was still wearing the plaster on my arm. I was feeling guilty for staying away from work and remember even apologising to my boss at Shell. He told me not to worry about it and insisted I take a further year's sickness leave.

I returned home to Liverpool and continued to spend all day in coffee bars, talking to people - or at least trying to talk to people. Although the vast majority of folk rejected me out of hand, I did have one success. I used to meet and speak to a married couple who worked in the city centre. They had rejected me at first, but my persistence had made them realize that I was not a drunk nor a drug addict. They would sit and listen to my babble, and, after a few weeks, were able to understand some of what I was trying to say. It was my first great breakthrough. I had met two strangers and had managed to explain my predicament to them. Unfortunately, a few months later, they moved to London to work, and I never saw them again.

In August 1971, I went on a fortnight's holiday to Lloret de Mar, Spain. I refused to allow the heavy plaster on my wrist discourage me. Since I did not have any friends in Liverpool - they were in Manchester and most of them were married or engaged - I went alone. I also considered that the challenge would be greater if I could meet and talk to strangers by myself.

On my arrival in Lloret de Mar, I discovered that most of the guests at the hotel were British. I was glad and thought it would be easier to mix with my own countrymen. However, during the first week, the tourist with whom I tried to strike up a conversation rejected me. Although some people spoke to me first, they would usually be making a wise crack about the plaster on my arm. Despite the cruel remark, I would always feel elated that people were at least communicating with me.

Attempting to explain my predicament to people was a painstakingly slow and difficult process, especially since I would have to take a breath for every word I tried to say. The listener would usually assume I was drunk and walk away before I had time to explain my situation. It was frustrating. Whenever I approached somebody sitting by themselves, I would begin babbling to them, and would receive a variety of responses - depending on their sex, they would either run away, start laughing at me and tell me to get lost, or do any number of embarrassing things. As I had no desire to insult or harm anyone, I would usually approach people who were sitting in small groups. They would listen but just when it seemed they had understood what I was trying to say, one of them would usually accuse me of drinking too much tequila. I would feel awful and walk away to hide my embarrassment.

Sometimes, my worries would constantly prey on my mind, and I would feel too insecure to emerge from my room. I would often miss the evening meal, because another guest had earlier humiliated me. On many occasions, I would sit on my bed and practise speaking to myself in the mirror. Fits of self-pity would often get the better of me and I would often end up cursing myself for not being able to speak properly. I would wonder how long people would torment me like this. My dearest wish was to be able to speak properly again and make friends with people, but few people had time for me. The only ones that did would end up mocking me. "Why are you doing this to me, God - why, oh why?" I would ask aloud, as I lay face down on the bed and thumped my fists into the mattress. "What on earth have I done to deserve such pain and anguish?" I would ask myself. I felt like crying to relieve the anger and frustration within me, but, although this would have eased my anger, I was raised to believe it was wrong for a man to cry.

In the evenings, while most of the other holiday-makers would be out having a good time, I would sit at the hotel's bar with a lemonade, feeling lonely and embarrassed. I would be green with envy as I sat and watched people going out of the hotel to enjoy themselves.

I often played table-tennis with a young boy, who had been allowed to stay up late. I knew who he was, because his parents had accused me of being drunk at breakfast on the second day of my holiday.

They had not accepted me, but their ten year old son had.

I used to go to bed early, hoping that the next day would hurry up and arrive, so I could be near people again. Even if the majority rejected me, there was always the chance that I would find someone who would treat me humanely. However, my mind would be too active to allow me to lie down and sleep. I would try anything if it meant that I was in the presence of people with whom I could talk. It would not be long, therefore, before I would get up again, have a wash, and put on something smart before going down to the ground floor. I would sit alone at the bar, always hoping to meet and converse with somebody. At around midnight, the other guests would begin returning from their night out. They would be much more approachable with a few drinks down them - the only trouble was that this time it was often difficult for me to understand the speech of some of them. Nonetheless, they were accepted but I was not.

During the second week, Monica and Maureen Lowden, two lovely-looking sisters arrived at the hotel. They were from Newcastle and had charming personalities. Maureen was seventeen while Monica was twenty and due to be engaged in a month's time. They were very patient as they listened to me and we would talk for hours at a time, even though it would be very strenuous for me. I spent the rest of the holiday with them and thoroughly enjoyed it. During the day, we would go sightseeing or sunbathing and in the evening would go out to a club or to another hotel.

They still had another week of their holiday due when the time came for me to leave. We promised to keep in touch - I remember thinking back to the many times I had made that promise but had never kept it.

I returned home to Liverpool and continued going to coffee bars in the long quest to improve my speech. Having met two girls without any help from anybody was a great boost to my confidence. I went to the city centre with renewed enthusiasm but little had changed - strangers merely continued to insult me whenever I tried to speak to them. I knew that people would not criticize my speech if they knew about my situation. The problem was that it took too long to explain and people always seemed to be in too much of a hurry to stop and listen to me.

One morning I unexpectedly received a letter from Monica inviting me to her engagement party in Newcastle. I was delighted to accept her invitation.

Three weeks later, I went to Newcastle for the party. Monica and Maureen were pleased to see me and introduced me to their parents, who were very friendly and did their best to make me feel at home. The following day, they took me to the station to see me off. I was very grateful to Monica and Maureen, since they treated me as a human being and gave me more encouragement to continue speaking to people.

(Left/right) Me, Maureen and Monica Lowden

I had to attend appointments once a month at Salford Royal Infirmary to have my wrist examined. I used to enjoy going to the hospital. The doctors and nurses would be stunned when they first read my file and discovered what I had been through. They were very understanding and would treat me as a hero, since they realized how difficult it must be for me.

After twelve long months, the plaster was removed from my wrist. It had been a burden and not simply because of its weight. It was awkward for me to have a bath as well as to do many other everyday jobs.

For the next three months I had to attend appointments at the hospital fortnightly. Fortunately, the operation was deemed a success and I was discharged.

I returned to work at Shell, but was officially classified as "disabled" by the company doctor. This meant that I was unable to continue my career as a Chemical Plant Operator. It did not come as a surprise or as a disappointment. I had long realized that it would be impossible for me to remain in that position. The accident had made my actions far too clumsy and my heart was no longer in the job. I was grateful to Shell for giving me the chance to try to pick up from where I had left off. Now, circumstances had changed and I could no longer do many tasks. Although difficult for me to accept at first, I eventually came to terms with it for the sake of my own peace of mind.

Shell offered me a position in the Personnel Department. I was more than happy to accept the position, even though I knew my mind would not be on my work. When I began working at my new post, it soon became obvious to me that it would be difficult to achieve the level of concentration that the job demanded. My mind was far too active for me to sit behind a desk all day. At the end of the first day, I felt as if I were a wild animal locked in a cage and by the end of the first week, I had already made excuses to have time off. I ended up spending more time haunting coffee bars in Manchester than at work. The only thing that mattered to me at the time was to be free to spend every available moment talking to people.

Shell had always treated me excellently, and I soon began to feel guilty at the way I was taking advantage of their kindness. I was ashamed of my continued deception and realized that things could not go on as they were.

After holding down the new position for a month, I decided to leave Shell. It was not an easy decision to make, but I knew that it would be better for all concerned. My boss tried to dissuade me from leaving, but my mind was already made up. My most pressing concern at that moment was to learn to speak coherently again. By this time, my crusade had taken on the nature of an obsession, since I knew society would not accept me until I could talk intelligibly again.

Shell had employed me for only four months before the accident, so they were under no legal obligation to continue employing me. Soon after the accident, they could have forgotten me, but they did not. They had continued to pay me an excellent wage and look after my welfare for more than two years and a half years after the crash. They certainly knew how to look after their employees. I will always be indebted to them for the excellent manner in which they treated me.

I'm not Drunk, Honest!

Chapter 12

Escape From Reality

Although sorry to leave Shell, it felt good to be home again. My family were overjoyed to hear that I was back home permanently. I could certainly tell by the look in my mother's eyes that she was ecstatic. My father was not as expressive but I knew he felt the same.

Linda had passed her A levels and was attending a teacher's training college in Liverpool, while Colin and Janet were still at school. They were happy to have me back at home too. I remember Colin pointing at my two sisters and saying, "Now I won't have to play cards with those two babies any more!" That was typical of him, especially as he immediately declared afterwards: "Hey, now the four of us can play monopoly together!"

Although my speech had not significantly improved, I still went to the city centre on shopping days. It was all the more frustrating to receive an insult, since it was difficult to explain my situation. I would try to justify my slur, but the majority of people would still ignore me and say something distasteful under their breath. I would always feel degraded - as if I had no right to breathe the same air as they. In my frustration, I would attempt to tell them about my speech, but they would turn and walk away. I would raise my voice, so they would hear my explanation, but this only made matters worse, since my voice had a wide range of pitch. It would start off sounding very deep and powerful, but would then taper off to a high-pitched squeak. This alone would make bystanders turn and look at me in disgust - without my slurred speech into the bargain. It was embarrassing but if I wanted to speak properly again, I would have to forget my pride and carry on regardless. I knew there was a mighty task ahead of me and that it was not going to be easy. I tried not to lose heart.

I used to detest Friday and Saturday evenings, since I was well aware that other young people of my age would be going out to enjoy themselves. I would just sit at home and watch television, even though I would secretly be longing to go out to a pub or a club. The trouble was that I was terrified of speaking to a girl of my own age. I used to ask myself what kind of girl would want to date a guy who spoke as I did. I often read the advertisements for computer dates but never had the nerve to complete the form and send it away. I needed a girlfriend but how could I meet one?

To make matters worse, I did not have a job - not that I was in any fit state to work. I felt as if I had no identity and was not pulling my weight in society. Although appearing perfectly "normal" I was officially classed as disabled. The fact that my handicaps separated me from other people made me feel even more of an outcast.

Sundays and Bank Holidays were equally frustrating for me. Since most of the shops and cafes were closed, there would be little to do except sit at home watching television.

As my co-ordination improved, I took up running, but there were still many problems to overcome. At first, I could not run properly and felt as if everybody was looking at me. The nearest I could get to running was to move forward skipping. My breathing was terrible and I would often have to gasp desperately for air or have a fit of coughing. It was always embarrassing.

I was awarded £27,500 compensation for my injuries in May 1972. I did not know what to do with the money at first, so I sought advice from my bank manager. He advised me to put most of it in a range of stocks and shares, deposit some in a building society and leave the rest in a deposit account. I followed his advice and a portfolio of investments was compiled for me. He assured me that they were "safe bets to provide me with a steady income."

I bought myself a new wardrobe of clothes and some luxuries. Having been rejected by society because of my speech, I naively fooled myself into believing that you can always judge a man by his clothes. I also bought some new furniture for the house, although my parents were adamant that I was not to spend any of the compensation on them. They went to great lengths to convince me. "That money is for you, so don't be foolish with it," my mother used to say.

At the time, although the amount of compensation sounded substantial, I would have gladly given it back and have gone through the trauma of being in a mental hospital merely to be able to speak properly again - but life is not like that.

I realized that the most fundamental difference between man and beast is man's ability to communicate through reason and not just by instinct. For the first few months after regaining consciousness, I had not been able to reason or communicate effectively. My mind had been very confused but I eventually improved insofar as my ability to think logically and rationally. Speech is the gift given to man to communicate with others. I had tried repeatedly but could not articulate words well enough to communicate effectively. I was constantly embarrassed and afraid of what people might think and say about me. I was becoming a nervous wreck, which made my speech sound even worse. It was hard for me to come to terms with my impediment, and at times my spirits would be so low that I could not imagine my speech ever improving. However, for the sake of my own sanity I had to rid my mind of such negative thoughts.

Apart from the occasional twinge in my wrist, my speech was the only thing preventing me from making a complete recovery. It was important that I remedy this as soon as possible. I was tired of being treated as a social outcast and wanted people to give me the respect that all human beings should receive - no more, no less.

Although my speech had improved, it was not enough for it to be noticeable. The only people who reassured me that I was speaking more coherently were acquaintances that had not seen me for many months. I did not know if they were being honest with me, but I badly needed to believe they were.

I asked my doctor if anything could be done to improve my speech, so he arranged for me to see a speech therapist the following week. I was looking forward to going, since I was desperately in need of help. While I was waiting for the day to arrive the time seemed to drag.

I turned up for my appointment expecting to meet a speech therapist of a similar age to the one in Salford Infirmary. However, I was in for a surprise, since my new therapist was a young woman of about twenty-one years of age, who was soon to be married. Much to my dismay, it was difficult for me to relax in her presence, since she was far more interested in telling me about her fiance than in listening to me talk. At times, it seemed she was comparing me with her fiance. My ego was thoroughly deflated. The first three appointments had disillusioned me, so I did not go again. I made up my mind to teach myself to speak properly by continuing with my visits to shops and cafes in the city centre.

While I was unconscious, the doctors told my parents that it might help if Gordon came over to England from Canada to speak to me; since we had always been close the doctor hoped that my sleeping brain would react to his voice. Gordon flew to England the day of the accident, even though Frances, his wife, had given birth to Helen, their first child, some months earlier. I learned that he had rarely left my bedside, while he spoke to me in a desperate attempt to awake me from unconsciousness. He often stayed all night at the hospital and only left my side to go to our house for a wash and a change of clothing. Unfortunately, his huge effort bore no fruit as I was in too deep a coma to respond.

Since I was usually up to some kind of mischief when we were growing up together, Gordon would often try to chastise me. "You never listen to me, do you?" he would always say to me. After his unsuccessful attempt to awake me from unconsciousness, it seemed the situation had still not changed.

In July 1972, I telephoned Gordon and Frances in Canada. They invited me to stay with them in Arvida for a month. I readily accepted.

A week later, I arrived in Montreal and caught a domestic flight to Bagotville, northern Quebec. Gordon and Frances, along with baby Helen, were at the airport to meet me. I remember that they remarked on how well I was looking - apparently, they had been expecting to see me looking as though I had just returned from a war zone.

We drove the short distance from the airport to their home in Arvida, a small town where a large number of people either worked or had relatives working for Alcan - the Aluminium Company of Canada.

That evening, a few of Gordon's friends came around for a barbecue and fondue party. Most were young couples who had recently arrived in Canada, hoping to make a new life for themselves. I do not recall ever seeing so many nationalities in the one room before: there were Norwegians, Danish, Swedish, Dutch, Germans, South Africans and of course British - it was like the League of Nations. Everybody was very friendly and tried to make me feel at home. Gordon had informed them about my accident, so he told me not to worry about anything and to merely be myself.

I was nervous at first. Whenever I spoke to anyone, I would babble incessantly, and, as a way of hiding my embarrassment, I would begin to joke. If the other guests had been able to understand me, they would probably have thought I was an idiot. Later, I began to relax a little and my joking stopped.

That night when I was lying in bed, it occurred to me that I could not be myself. In fact, a major psychological effect of my trauma was that I did not know who "myself" was any longer. It was as if I had lost my identity. Since the accident, people had often told me to relax, but it was easier said than done. My identity had been lost among my worries, fears and embarrassments arising from the need to cope with my impediment. I was too preoccupied with trying to conform to the behaviour of others and was worried about how people would react to my speech. I dearly wanted people to like me and would always try to please those I met. It had been so long since I had been able to fully relax that I had forgotten what my true character was.

I got up the next day after Gordon had gone to work and found Frances busy doing the washing. I rushed eating my breakfast, since I was eager to see Arvida and to meet the French-Canadians. I had heard that few of the residents spoke, or were willing to speak, English, and realized that I would probably have both a language and speech problem. I decided, therefore, to take along my English and French pocket dictionary.

Arvida was not a very big town, and it did not take me long to discover that there was only one coffee bar to my liking - *"La Claire de Lune."* I spent all morning listening to the jukebox in there, playing six records by the Beatles - I gave the French-Canadian songs a miss. The waitress did not appear too friendly, so I did not try to have a conversation with her. She understood me when I asked for a Coke, since it is a word used all over the world.

I returned to Gordon's for lunch and then went back to the coffee bar in the afternoon. To my surprise, the waitress seemed a lot friendlier and we had a good discussion. It was not easy but we managed to communicate by inventing our own French and English sign-language. I only used the pocket dictionary as a last resort.

Gordon could not take the time off work to entertain me properly, so he asked me if I would like to stay in an apartment in Montreal for a fortnight. Frances's brother owned the flat, but he was working away for a few months and had given his permission for me to use it. I jumped at the offer.

The first thing I did after arriving in Montreal was to buy a good camera. Gordon had recommended a photographic shop in Saint Catherine Street, so I went and bought a Minolta SRT 101. I was delighted with it and was like a kid with a new toy.

Montreal was fascinating and had many places of interest to visit. During the first week, I went around many of the tourist attractions: the Botanical Gardens, a number of museums and art galleries, and the "Man and His World" exhibition, formerly the 1967 "Expo World Fair." I also went to the Flea Market, near *Place Jacques-Cartier,* which was an amazing place and reminded me much of France.

During the second week, I spent most of my time sitting in the open air cafes on *Rue St. Denis,* in the Latin Quarter. I found that many University students, writers, and artists frequented this district. Most of the students I met could speak English, but at first it was too embarrassing for me to have a lengthy conversation with them.

However, the day before leaving Montreal, I decided to try to forget my impediment and to have a conversation with a student that sat at my table. His name was Jean-Paul and he was a very interesting character. He had travelled extensively and had lived in Kobe, Japan for two years, when his father took a job there. We spent some time talking about our experiences in Japan, before I became aware of my speech. He noticed the operation scar on my neck and asked how I had got it. Making a joke of it, I told him I had cut myself shaving. He had recognized the scar at once, of course, as he was a medical student. I told him about the injuries I had received in the accident and he seemed fascinated. We spent the rest of the afternoon talking about the problems of the world, or at least he did - I was ignorant of such things, for I had been too busy trying to recover from the accident to consider problems of the world around me. When we were parting he invited me to a party the next evening at his apartment. Unfortunately, I could not go since I was due to return to Arvida the next morning.

Gordon began his holidays the day after my return to Arvida. During the next fortnight, he took Frances, Helen and me touring around Quebec and Ontario.

When he returned to work after the holiday, I spent most of my time frequenting *"La Claire de Lune."* I would sit for hours drinking coffee and talking to people who could speak English.

When the time came to return home, Gordon and Frances took me by car to Montreal Airport. As I sat in the Departure Lounge, waiting to board the plane, I reflected on my month-long holiday in Canada. I had got on well with the people and they had never insulted me or accused me of being drunk. It had been a very enjoyable vacation, especially since people had made me feel human again.

However, I was soon brought back to reality with a jolt, when, on the flight back to the U.K., a business man from Birmingham sat next to me. We began chatting and I told him all about my holiday.

"I had a great time - went to plenty of parties," I said, forgetting my babbled speech.

He looked at me and laughed. "I suppose you drank them dry

- how many have you had today?"

I immediately ignored him and began flicking through a magazine, since it was too embarrassing to look him in the eye. His words echoed in my ears, and it felt as if he had kicked me in the stomach. It suddenly occurred to me that nothing had changed. A month had passed since a stranger had mentioned my speech, so it was perhaps understandable that I forgot to make the effort to speak slowly and to pronounce my words correctly,

Nothing was said until the stewardess came with our in-flight meal. When she asked me for my order I was unable to even babble, let alone speak - it was as if my Adam's apple was choking me. I needed to drink something, before I was able to order my meal.

The businessman realized that he had been mistaken about my speech and sincerely apologized. After that we got on well, and I found it much easier to converse although I still sounded very slurred.

Whenever people remarked that I was drunk, my speech would always sound worse and I would sometimes be too embarrassed to answer. It was only after I had spoken slowly and explained, if I was permitted, and received an apology that I would be in the right frame of mind to continue a conversation.

Chapter 13

Snap Happy

I returned home from Canada in early September 1972. During the weekdays, I continued to go around the shops and coffee bars in the city centre trying to improve my speech. I was feeling much better and less nervous about approaching strangers, even though the majority of the folk I came across would still insult me. My pride would take a heavy battering, but I refused to let people see that their cruel remarks were affecting me. To some extent I was learning to cope with their insults by keeping my true feelings bottled up inside me, until I returned home in the evening. I would lie on my bed, cursing myself for not being able to speak clearly. The abuse that people gave me was badly affecting me. I would feel so inadequate at times that I would blame myself for not being able to speak correctly.

Although most people rejected me, I found that it was usually easier for me to speak to middle-aged or older women than to younger women or men - this may have been due to a maternal instinct that seemed to make them more approachable. Nevertheless, regardless to whom I spoke, their initial reaction to my speech would usually be one of horror. If strangers allowed me to explain about the car accident, I would point to the trachcotomy operation scar on my neck. As soon as I had pointed to it, a few of them would become concerned and show great interest in what I was trying to say. It soon dawned on me that those people who did not insult me and allowed me to explain would feel sorry for me and drown me in sympathy - and sympathy was not what I wanted. I was in a dilemma. I knew that people would feel sorry for me, once they allowed me to tell them about my accident, but, at the same time, I wanted to be treated as a normal person and not to be pitied.

I was very lonely and needed a girlfriend - somebody with whom I could be myself, somebody whose problems I could share, somebody whose life I could be part of. I never had any trouble finding a girlfriend before the accident but times had changed. What type of girl would want somebody that always sounded drunk? I fooled myself into believing that this question would not be answered until I went out to a pub or club. I did not have any friends with whom to go out socially in the evening, so there was little option but to go by myself.

One Friday night, I went to the city centre in the hope of meeting the girl of my dreams. I selected a pub that caught my eye. My nerves were getting the better of me and I remember having to pace up and down outside many times, before I was able to build up enough courage to walk into the pub.

The bar was crowded with young people enjoying themselves. The confidence that I had worked up earlier soon deserted me. It felt so strange for me to stand in a room full of people who were enjoying themselves, while I was feeling very alone and inadequate. It was as if I was on a different planet. My initial response was to walk straight out but I realized it was merely a negative reaction.

Taking a deep breath, I went up to the bar and ordered a drink from the barmaid. She could not understand me at first, so I had to repeat my order. Finally understanding me, she laughed at me and went to get my drink. My face reddened as I looked about embarrassed. Most of the other customers were busy chatting to their friends and had not been paying any attention to the barmaid's remarks. The others were looking at me in disgust.

"Make this your last," she said, as she laughed and looked at me contemptuously. "You've had enough!"

Totally humiliated, I could not bring myself to take the drink or the change from a five-pound note I had given her. I simply walked straight out of the pub despondently and headed for the nearest bus stop to go home.

While waiting for my bus to arrive my anger began to mount. I was cursing myself for speaking as I did. I worked myself into a thoroughly bad temper and wanted to seek revenge for the way society was treating me. I wanted to scream at the top of my voice to relieve the tension that was pent up inside me.

For some reason my mood suddenly altered. I weighed up my situation again and realized vindictiveness would certainly not improve my predicament. I remembered there were many people far worse off than me: some were severely paralysed and unable to perform the simplest of tasks for themselves; some were blind; some were crippled; some were homeless - the list was endless. I began to feel ashamed for allowing myself to become unnerved by the barmaid. "Was I going to be a loser for the rest of my life?" I asked myself. I knew the answer as soon as the question entered my mind.

Shortly afterwards, I walked back into the same pub and went up to the bar. The barmaid saw me, gave me the change I had left behind earlier and poured me another drink, even though her perception of me had not changed. My nerves were still rickety, but I stayed until "last orders" had been called despite merely drinking a glass of beer. It was obvious that the more I drank, the more my tongue and jaw would tire and the worse I would sound - if that was possible.

Feeling daring after having the courage to go inside a pub and order a drink, I decided to go to a night-club. The bouncers would not let me in the first club, assuming I was drunk. It was frustrating - the more clubs I went to, the more downhearted I became.

My confidence had all but gone when I knocked on the door of "The Pyramid Club." As the door was opening, I took a deep breath and was about to ask the bouncer if I could come in when he nodded for me to enter. Amazed, I walked up to the reception desk but I became so unsure of myself that I suddenly turned to the doorman and blurted out my story. After the initial shock of hearing my speech, he became interested in what I was trying to say. I was surprised he could understand some of my babble - probably because he was accustomed to dealing with drunkards. I showed him my tracheotomy scar, and, judging by his facial expression, it was obvious I had met a friend.

The bouncer's name was Joe Philips. He told me I would always be welcomed at the club, which helped me to relax and feel more confident. I offered to buy him a drink, but he refused saying he did not drink while working. He insisted I did not pay the admission charge and later introduced me to the owner, Roy Adams, who owned a number of clubs on Merseyside, the most famous of which was the "Cavern," where the Beatles had made their name. I felt my luck was changing.

There was a dance floor in the basement and another upstairs. I went downstairs. It was dark, crowded and the music was deafening. Cigarette smoke floated upwards in the light thrown out from the disco.

Standing by the bar, while looking at the other people in the club, I realized that I had no idea how to start a conversation with a girl. Should I go up to her and ask her the time or say something like: "Do you come here often?" or "Haven't I seen you somewhere before?" or "What's a nice girl like you doing in a place like this?" These clichés had seen their day, so I decided at first not to use them, but changed my mind since I had no idea what else to say.

Upon seeing a girl that took my fancy, I would first decide how to approach her and what to say to her. I would desperately try to think of something witty to say but could only come up with an old cliché. At this point my confidence would begin to waver, so I would decide to count to ten first. Unfortunately, I would always lose my nerve by the time I had reached nine. Whenever I was bold enough to walk up to a girl, the situation would overwhelm me, and I would be reduced to simply standing there, staring at her dumbly. I would be terrified to say anything to her, assuming she would think I was drunk or stupid.

Wanting to find out how to chat up a girl, I decided to eavesdrop on some of the other people's conversations and got quite a surprise. I have never seen so many junior doctors, lawyers, sales executives and brain surgeons in one room before. Although eventually seeing through this charade, I was still too afraid to be myself, to be natural, and most of all to speak - society had made me feel ashamed of the way I spoke.

I was making good use of my recently acquired camera, since it was a good way of getting to know people or at least of introducing myself. I carried it around almost everywhere I went and took dozens of photographs daily. My interest in photography grew so I bought an enlarger and other dark-room equipment to teach myself how to develop black and white prints. I was pleased with the camera, since it produced some excellent negatives. However, it took much longer than I anticipated to produce any good quality prints. Developing and printing required much patience, which, at the time, was another of the qualities I was lacking. I would always be in too much of a hurry to see the finished product. After a few weeks, however, I was able to produce prints of a satisfactory standard.

Since I was a very keen amateur photographer, I decided to make photography my profession. My dream at the time was to become a wildlife photographer and to travel the world making films of animals for television. I enquired at the local education offices and discovered that Blackpool College of Art offered a three-year course set by the Institute of Professional Photographers. A place on the course was available and I was interviewed at the College the following day. The Principal listened carefully to my babble, and, after looking at the examples of my work that I had taken along, he told me that I could start immediately since the course had already begun the week before. I could barely believe my luck.

When I returned home and told my parents the news, they were delighted and did not mind that I would be leaving home again. They knew I was able to fend for myself.

I was particularly pleased to be accepted onto the course, because it would give me the opportunity to show my capabilities. In addition, it was important to acquire an identity again and to feel as though I belonged somewhere. If I could successfully get through the course at the College, I would have a career in photography. It was important for my self-esteem that people should not be able to say I had only been successful because of the money I had received as compensation from the crash, besides, photography interested me greatly and was something I thoroughly enjoyed doing. I was looking forward to the new challenge and determined to be successful.

I arrived at the College at nine o'clock in the morning. I was a nervous wreck at first, since I was afraid of how the other students might react to my speech. The Senior Lecturer was a very affable man, and I knew immediately I would get on well with him. Our conversation lasted almost an hour and centred mainly on my accident and rehabilitation. He told me that he was very impressed and that he was delighted to have me as a student - I began to relax.

After settling into my digs, I returned to the College where I met the other lads doing the same course. The lecturer had informed the other students about the car accident and about the way I spoke, so I was not too nervous. They appeared to accept me at first, so I soon settled down, even though they had great difficulty understanding my speech.

However, as soon as I had gained enough confidence, I began to answer questions and put my views forward during the tutorial periods - much to the displeasure of a few students. Because of this, I became unpopular with a small clique within the class. Ultimately, I began to make enemies. Apparently, some students felt that it was not acceptable for me to compete with them. They did their best to make my life a misery by ridiculing the way I spoke - alas, I was an easy target.

I was in a dilemma. Should I allow people to say what they liked about me without arguing back, or should I stand up for myself and become unpopular? It was a difficult question - either way, I was the loser. I decided to stand up for myself, of course.

The small clique in the class almost made my life unbearable for nearly a month. Fortunately, an event took place that changed their attitude towards me. Three of my friends and I were returning to our digs one night after a visit to the cinema, when we saw three lads beating two of the students who had made my life a misery. I forgot our feud for the moment, and my three friends and I chased the three bullies away. The two students were grateful and put an end to the hostility towards me.

Shortly before the beginning of the Christmas vacation, two of my friends and I were walking back to College after having our lunch. A man stopped us in the street to ask if we had change of a pound. As I went to get my money out, my right thumb got caught in the opening of my trouser pocket, and I felt an excruciating pain in my wrist. I yelled out in agony. When the pain had subsided I was left with that old familiar aching sensation in my wrist and remembered it had been troublesome before on many occasions. It began to throb and, in trying to explain, my voice sounded as if I was whining. I ended up saying nothing further and returned to College, hoping that the pain would at least ease but it did not. Although it was possible to hold my hand in a position where the pain in my wrist was not too severe, the least movement of it would produce an unbearable ache. I sat in the classroom grasping my upper forearm in an attempt to divert the pain from my wrist - it was constant agony.

After finishing my lectures that day, I went to hospital for treatment. My wrist was x-rayed but the doctor could do little to help me due to the complexities involved in the operation carried out at Salford Royal Infirmary. He needed to compare the current x-ray with one taken when the operation had first been performed, before he would be able to give me any treatment. All he could do was to give me painkillers and to advise me to see the doctor that had performed the operation - I left the hospital a worried man.

The next morning, after staying awake most of the previous night nursing my wrist and pondering over my future, I sought the advice of the Senior Lecturer. Realising it would be a lengthy business to have my wrist mended, we both agreed it would be best for me to terminate the course at the College and to return home. I certainly did not take the decision lightly, since I was only too aware that I would again become merely a statistic on the "sick list." It was so frustrating especially since it meant losing my new identity.

I remember how miserable I felt as the train pulled out of Blackpool Station. I reflected on the way things had turned out and the opportunity that I had to relinquish.

Returning home, I attended the Orthopaedic Clinic at the Liverpool Royal Infirmary the next day. Although my wrist was x-rayed again, it was still necessary to send to Salford Royal Infirmary for details of the operation. As a temporary measure, my wrist was encased in plaster, and I was given more painkillers. Before leaving the hospital, an appointment was made for me to attend the following week.

As arranged, I attended the Infirmary and met a number of doctors who said they were amazed at the recovery I was making; naturally I felt proud. I was always cheerful and never let them see that I was becoming despondent.

I began to regularly attend the Orthopaedic Department and rarely saw the same doctor twice. Most of these were junior doctors, which may explain why I lost count of the number of plasters I wore during that period. Occasionally, I would see Professor Bentley, the Consultant, who would always be surrounded by a throng of student doctors. Since he continued to emphasize how well I was recovering to his students, it made me feel as if I could overcome any pain. When he got around to asking me how my wrist was, I would make light of it. My pride would not let me complain about my discomfort.

Realizing I was lucky to be alive and generally in good health. I might easily have died or remained a cabbage - I might have needed to stay in Winwick. I certainly had nothing to feel sorry about. Nevertheless, my fits of depression were occurring more frequently. It was becoming increasingly difficult to force myself to think how lucky I had been to have survived the accident. When alone, however, I would begin to feel apathetic. There was nobody else to blame for my misfortune, so I blamed myself - it eventually dawned on me that my mood was largely the result of my negative thinking.

It became clear that if I wanted people to be cheerful to me, I would first have to be cheerful to them. Although I did not think I had appeared hostile or miserable when speaking to strangers, I made up my mind to try to be as cheerful and as positive as possible. It was not always easy to accomplish this, but, in my new frame of mind, I did begin to view my life differently. At times, I was able to laugh at my own bad luck.

Sometimes I would take my new approach to life too far. During the shopping days, I would go to town early and would say "Good Morning" to everybody who passed me in the street. In response, some people would look at me as though I was stupid. In the end, I decided just to greet the people I knew.

Although the majority of strangers continued to be hostile towards me, my new approach to life meant that I met with fewer rejections when I striking up a conversation with a customer in a store or cafe. Some people would also stay and listen to me longer. My new approach to life was just what I had needed. I felt content and believed that anything was possible, as long as I believed in myself.

I continued going to the city centre to improve my speech. I would catch the bus at the same time when returning home, trying to give commuters the impression that I was leading a "normal" life. It was important for my self-esteem and did not want people to know I did nothing all day but walk around the city centre. If a stranger was willing to listen to me, I would always tell them about my battle to speak properly again.

Every evening, I would watch the news on television to keep up to date with what was happening in the City. I had bought stocks and shares expecting to make money from my investments, so that I would have financial security for the rest of my life. However, things do not always turn out as expected. Most businesses at the time were performing badly on the Stock Market due to the state of the economy. Some of the companies in which I invested went bankrupt and the rest of my shares were depreciating rapidly. When I first received the compensation I thought my worries were over. My assumption was wrong and I was beginning to worry incessantly.

I lost a substantial part of my compensation, so my confidence in my bank manager was severely dented, to say the least. I would often complain to him, but he kept telling me that I should hold on to the stocks and shares in the hope that they would recover. In the end, I did not know if I should trust him or not. It was a nightmare.

Eventually, the bank manager grew tired of my pestering and told me that all I could do was either to hold on to the shares or to sell them at a loss. I was beginning to feel apathetic and decided to sell some shares and have a damn good holiday. I liked going abroad because non-English speaking people seemed to accept me more readily than my own countrymen and women, and I would meet with fewer rejections.

Since I was a very keen photographer and interested in wildlife, I decided to go to South Africa for three weeks. I flew from Heathrow and landed at the Jan Smutts airport in Johannesburg the following day.

The flight had been very tiring, so, after booking into my hotel, I went straight to bed. The next day, I went on safari and spent six days travelling throughout Kruger Park, a large game reserve. I saw many animals in their natural habitat. It was a wonderful experience, I had often dreamt of. I was amazed at the beauty of the impala, an antelope, but they were so numerous that it was not long before they became boring to watch. I saw a pride of lions, herds of elephants, wildebeest and zebras. There were also giraffes, hippopotamuses, baboons and vivette monkeys - not to mention the many species of birds I saw.

On Safari - Kruger Park
(I am the one wearing the hat!)

After the safari, I returned to Johannesburg. I remember the many skyscrapers, but that was all I care to recall about the city. I spent a full day in the town but found it difficult to relax. I tried talking to a few White people, but they immediately shunned me. It was much easier to talk to two Black men, even though they found it difficult to understand what I was trying to say. They were very friendly and seemed afraid to speak to me at first. As soon as the conversation was over two policemen approached and cautioned me, saying it was forbidden to mix with the Blacks. I was amazed at the injustice. However, they were dubious about my speech and I had to convince them I was not drunk - a lengthy and embarrassing process.

The following day, I flew south to Cape Town. The country we flew over was contrastingly beautiful - from the rust-coloured rugged earth of the Kimberley Mine to the breathtaking mountainous views of Francheshook.

I booked into my hotel. At dinner on the first night, I had an interesting conversation with the Asian waitress who was serving my meal. When she disappeared into the kitchen, the Hotel Manager came up to my table and abruptly told me that I was only allowed to fraternize with "Whites." That was my second confrontation with the apartheid system - a system I found utterly repulsive.

As expected, South Africa did not bear much resemblance to Great Britain - except that the buses in Cape Town were double-deckers. Although I had visited many countries, this was the first time I had seen such a mode of transport outside of the U.K. I vividly recall this particular feature of South African life because I was disgusted at what took place when I boarded one. I immediately went on the top deck to get a better view of the town. However, no sooner had I sat down when the conductor came running upstairs shouting for all he was worth. I turned and looked at him - his face was red with anger and his language was foul. "Whites downstairs, Blacks upstairs," he yelled or words to that effect. That was my third confrontation with apartheid.

The countryside around Cape Town must be amongst the most spectacular in the world. I went on several tours, and on each one I often held my breath in wonder at such an abundance of natural beauty. I saw one of the seven wonders of the world - Table Mountain - and went to the southernmost tip of Cape Province, where the Atlantic meets the Indian Ocean.

I arrived in Durban for the final week of my holiday. On the second day, I went to Hluhluwe Game Reserve, and saw many rhinoceroses. However, the highlight of my stay in Durban was watching the surfing. From a pier stretching out into the sea, it was possible to see the surfers artfully balancing on the crest of a wave. It was spectacular.

As I flew home, I reflected on the previous three weeks. I was truly fascinated by the natural beauty of South Africa and had made great use of my camera. However, I felt subdued when in the company of strangers, and my feelings about the place were mixed. Despite its beauty, I could never abide with its system of apartheid. In spite of my gregarious nature, I did not meet any White South Africans with whom I wanted to speak. My conversation with the guide who took me around Kruger Park was brief, because he was not the kind of person with whom I could have an in-depth conversation. His attitude towards Non-White human beings was totally repugnant to me, since he looked upon them as less than human. When I questioned him about the apartheid system, he became inflamed and told me that Blacks especially were ignorant and had no education. I was about to ask him about the educational opportunities available for the Non-White population but thought better of it. Fortunately, I realized that it was not the individuals I detested but the system of apartheid.

The holiday did give me a much needed respite from the barrage of insults to which I had received in England. What was more important, after witnessing the injustice of the South African apartheid system, it was clear to me that I was able to empathize with the Non-Whites. Like me, they had to live for twenty-four hours a day with their struggle. But they had never been accustomed to receiving respect from the Whites, while before my accident I had.

Chapter 14

A New Venture

Although I had rarely sunbathed while in South Africa, my suntan was a deep bronze. It made me feel good and helped to give me the confidence to continue speaking to strangers. I often found that when sitting in a cafe, a fellow customer would start a conversation with me by asking where had I been to acquire such a tan. This was a great help to me, although my speech would still be unintelligible, especially if I did not take a deep breath before answering.

I would travel to the city centre every working day and would try to spend as many hours as possible, sitting in the coffee bars and large stores drinking coffee. I had become well-known by some of the staff and by many of the regular customers. In particular, I used to have a coffee at the horseshoe bars on the fifth floor of one store. Esther was the waitress there and a lovely person. She was popular with the customers and always seemed to have some famous personality sitting at her bar.

Although one of my dreams was to meet a girl who would accept me, I would never willingly speak to young women of my age group, since I was nervous of meeting them. It was not because I was shy, but simply that I did not want to give them the opportunity to accuse me of being drunk or of making fun of me. Every day, I would walk past scores of attractive young women of my age group and deliberately ignore them. I certainly did not enjoy doing this, but feared I would only make a fool of myself if I stopped and spoke to them - it was difficult.

My life was becoming boring again since there was nothing to do but to go to hospital appointments, sit in the library or go around drinking coffee. I would set out from home in the morning feeling happy and confident, expecting something good to happen that would change my life completely - but nothing did.

Due to the constant rejections, my ego had been deflated to such an extent that I had a very low opinion of myself. I did not have a job and my speech was pathetic, despite a slight improvement. My loneliness haunted me and I was terribly inhibited. I was still finding it difficult to relax and be natural in the company of others. Whenever I went somewhere unfamiliar, I would be terrified to speak and generally very apprehensive. I still felt ostracized and alienated, as if life was proceeding at its busy pace, while I was standing still.

I would always apologize to people when something did not go according to plan, even though I would be blameless. I remember, in particular, a time when I was going up an elevator in a large store in the city centre. A young woman, carrying an armful of shopping, almost knocked me over as she hurried past me. The carrier bag in her arms could no longer take the weight of its contents and burst open showering me with groceries. A bottle of sauce hit the side of the elevator and smashed open, spraying the contents over my new trousers. I simply looked at her and apologized sincerely.

However, I did not want to remain in this pathetic state for the rest of my life, so I plodded on regardless of the insults or the way strangers treated me. I firmly believed that one day with constant practice I would speak properly again. I still had many dreams, but my most cherished wish was for the people I met to accept my speech.

Although most strangers still continued to insult me when I spoke to them, I would occasionally meet somebody who was more understanding and willing to talk to me. It would usually be somebody who had experienced a certain amount of trauma themselves. They would listen attentively to me and would sometimes tell me their troubles. At the end of the conversation they would usually say that it was a pleasure to have met me. To receive such a compliment would greatly surprise me at first, because most strangers would greatly underestimate me. Such moments were rare but they would spur me on to continue my quest to improve my speech.

I was still going to the "Pyramid Club" on Friday and Saturday evenings. Before leaving home to go to the club, I would always have to build up my confidence and convince myself that I was going to meet the girl of my dreams that night.

However, once inside the club the environment would at first be far too intimidating for me even to try to have a conversation with a girl. My slurred speech meant that I was self-conscious and would be all too aware of how a girl would probably react if I spoke to her. My imagination rarely ceased to tell me how lonely I looked standing by myself. Most of the time, I would be convinced that all the girls thought I was weird. Everybody else in the club seemed relaxed and with their friends, having a good time. I would desperately wish that I too could be like them.

Eventually, I would realize that I was being a wimp and would decide to break the ice. I would always attempt to count to ten to build up my flagging confidence, but, before reaching nine, I would usually conjure up an excuse for discontinuing the count. It would not be until shortly before the club was due to close that I would be able to pluck up enough courage to ask a girl to dance.

I often went up to a girl but would suddenly feel so embarrassed that I would start babbling to her. She would immediately give me a nasty look and walk away hurriedly, mumbling something about my state of inebriation. It seemed ironic when I remembered how long it had taken me to build up my confidence only to be immediately rejected.

One night, I stood and watched to see why other lads never seemed to have any trouble finding a partner. It did not take me long to realize how they never failed. They would simply go up to a girl, grab hold of her hand and then nod towards the dance floor, without saying a word or even looking at the girl - the girl would always follow.

"Brilliant," I thought, "I can easily do that without having to worry about my speech." However, having been isolated and unaware of the social behaviour of young people for so long, it occurred to me that such behaviour was indeed ill-mannered. Although I did not like the idea, the girls did not seem to object, so I eventually decided to try it. "If they can do it, then I can as well!" I told myself.

I looked around the dance floor. There were so many attractive girls that I was spoilt for choice. Some had an air of sophistication and intelligence, some appeared to be auditioning for a chewing gum advertisement, while others looked sweet and innocent. In the end, I would realize that I was only going to dance with the girl I chose - not marry her.

Eventually, I selected a "sweet and innocent-looking" girl. As usual, I found myself attempting to count to ten but always losing my nerve before reaching nine. I tried to invent excuses for not dancing, but, after exhausting these, I finally admitted to myself that I was thinking negatively. After taking a deep breath, I walked towards the girl of my choice. She was facing away from me, so I walked up to her, took hold of her arm, turned and went to walk towards the dance floor. However, as I turned, I suddenly heard her friend scream out. I looked around in surprise to see that I had knocked the glass of fruit juice her friend was holding out of her hand; it spilt over the front of her dress. I attempted to apologize, but only managed to babble, which made matters worse, especially since the girl accused me of being both drunk and stupid. I decided that I would not try to copy others in future.

One night, I left the night-club and had difficulty getting a taxi. Nevertheless, I enjoyed that time of the day and the exercise was good for my limp, which had improved greatly and was not very noticeable. I was walking through the city centre when a policeman stopped me. He was much bigger than I was and about thirty.

"Well, Laddie, how much have you had to drink?" he asked facetiously.

I was petrified and began trembling as his beady eyes looked down to examine me. I tried to speak but the words got stuck in my throat.

"Lost your tongue, have you?"

I began to babble, trying to explain about my speech impediment, but it was obvious he could not understand my speech and assumed that I was drunk. He looked at me and began laughing.

I had to do something fast, so I put my hand into my inside pocket and brought out a newspaper clipping about my accident, while he watched my every move. My nerves were already rattling, and I found myself reciting one of the few things people could understand - "Betty Button bought some butter, but she said this batter's bitter ..."

The policeman suddenly stopped laughing as he began to read the article. Realizing I was not drunk, he apologized sincerely and even flagged down a passing taxi for me.

Afterwards I had a good laugh at what had happened. I thought it would be good to make a film about some of the amusing events that had happened to me since my accident.

One afternoon, I was sitting at Esther's horseshoe bar, when two young women sat down next to me. I had often seen them at the bar but had never spoken to them. One of the women, whose name was Toni, was obviously well-known to the other customers. She was a jovial type of person and appeared very confident.

As I sat drinking coffee, I overheard Toni telling Esther that she had been involved in a collision when driving into Liverpool that morning. Although nobody had been physically injured, the shock had badly affected Toni. At that moment, Esther went to serve another customer, so I realized that this was my opportunity to join in the conversation. The trouble was that I did not know how to start talking to the two young women, nor how they would react to hearing my speech. I was flustered at first but eventually decided to count to ten, take a deep breath and see what happened.

"Excuse me," I said, before taking another deep breath, "but may I speak to you?"

The two young women looked at me and then smiled at each other, as I suddenly realized how naive my question must have sounded. I quickly pointed to my tracheotomy scar and tried to explain that I knew what it was like to suffer from shock. They became very understanding once they realized I had been injured in a car accident. With growing confidence, I was able to illustrate how shock had affected my speech and was therefore able to empathize with Toni. We had a good conversation and I discovered that Toni owned a leather fashion business.

The prices of my stocks and shares were continuing to fall, so I seriously considered buying a small business. The more I thought about the idea, the more attractive it seemed. Apart from anything else, it would give me something to do during the day. It soon became obvious to me that there was much to learn and that I had to choose the kind of business to buy. I was in a dilemma, since I had the money but did not know how to use it effectively. I finally decided to open as a newsagent in the city centre.

However, shortly before I was due to sign the contract, I was having a coffee at Esther's bar when I met Phil, a teacher in his late twenties. I had met him in the "Pyramid Club," although we had never spoken at length. We started talking about being in business and he remarked that he would like to open a night-club in Gloucester, where his parents ran a pub on the outskirts of the city. Apparently, there was only one decent club in Gloucester, despite the growing demand for another. The idea excited me, but I remained calm and asked him how much he thought it would cost. He told me that his father would be willing to lend him £6,000 and that he would prefer to have a partner to help him run it. I immediately showed my interest. Phil seemed relieved and invited me to stay at his parents for a week, so that we could hunt around for adequate premises. I felt that this was the opportunity I had been waiting for.

The next day, I was supposed to see the estate agent to sign the contract to set up as a newsagent, but I cancelled the deal. The following Friday, Phil drove me to Gloucester.

He told me he had many things to sort out while he was in his home town, so I would have to look for premises alone. I was surprised and disappointed because he had always been so keen on the idea, whenever we had discussed it. My suspicions were aroused at first, although I finally put his sudden change of plan down to the fact that he had not been home for a few months.

I spent most of my time during the day inspecting various sites for the club that the estate agent had offered me. It was a tiring business, especially as I did not drive. At the end of each day, my feet were sore due to all the walking I had to do. After inspecting the sites during the day, I would select the best locations, and, in the evening, Phil and I would examine them together. By the middle of the week, I felt as though I had tramped around every empty building in Gloucester.

We eventually chose an old hotel that had not been used for a couple of years. It was outside Gloucester and had adequate parking facilities. It resembled an alpine cabin and would make an ideal country club. We decided to call it "The Lawns" and to decorate it inside with items relating to various sports. We were both delighted with it, and I clearly remember imagining the club packed with young people enjoying themselves. The only snag was that the property was for sale and not for rent. I decided to seek the advice of a solicitor the next day.

There was a strange atmosphere around the house when I came down for breakfast the next morning. I sensed there had been a family row. Phil suddenly informed me that he would not be able to get the £6,000 from his father. I was stunned and dismayed by this revelation, having set my heart on part-owning a night club. After Phil had left the house, his father told me his son had never intended to open a club and had merely used me as an excuse to visit Gloucester. I was surprised and wondered what he meant by that. According to him, Phil needed to come to Gloucester to see his girlfriend, who was expecting his baby. This news came as a great surprise to me, since he had never mentioned anything about his girlfriend, nor that she was pregnant. It was difficult for me to believe what I had learned at first and thought it odd that Phil should need an excuse to visit his parents. In the end, I decided it would be best to confront Phil later to explain - that was before his father told me the full story. Phil needed a reason to visit his parents, because his wife in Liverpool suspected he was having an affair with a girl in Gloucester. I was amazed. He had never even told me he was married, so I had naturally assumed he was single. I did not listen to any more - I caught the next train home.

I was still attending hospital appointments in the hope of finally having my wrist fixed. Whenever I enquired about it, the doctors would merely tell me that the difficulty was due to a small bone in my wrist that had broken in an awkward position.

Eventually, I was measured for a surgical wristband, which I received a month later. It fitted over my hand and had holes for my fingers and thumb to fit through. It was much lighter and more comfortable than wearing a plaster. I was able to take it off whenever I needed, which meant that I could have a bath without constantly having to keep my right arm out of the water. Nevertheless, it was still necessary for me to attend the hospital every week to have my wrist embalmed in warm wax. This was supposed to have a therapeutic effect, but after the wax had been removed the soothing effect would quickly be replaced by the same old aching sensation. It was disappointing but I realized that the doctors were trying their best. I can remember often walking down the ramp outside the Casualty Department and saying to myself, "Well, that's life."

Chapter 15

Save Petrol and Lose Money!

I was having a coffee at Esther's bar one afternoon when I began talking to another regular customer called Peter. He told me that his friend's father was the inventor of the petrol-saving device that had recently been featured on "Tomorrow's World," a television programme devoted to new inventions. I had seen the very programme and was impressed by the comments made about the device. Peter told me that he had bought some shares in the company that was to market the new invention. He went on to add that the inventor was looking for financial backing. My ears immediately pricked up. I told him that I would like to find out more about the project and asked to meet the inventor.

Being brief, I met the inventor and he explained how his device functioned. I was able to understand how it operated and was very impressed. Its effectiveness was confirmed by equally impressive results from tests that the Motor Industry Research Association had carried out. In addition, the device would shortly be featured on a Granada TV news programme.

I thought that it had to be the invention of the decade, especially since the industrialized world was in the grip of an oil crisis at the time. The invention seemed an ideal solution to the problem. However, although convinced of its effectiveness, I decided to ask my bank manager to run a check on the company.

A week later, the bank came back to me, saying that investment in the device was not advisable and suggested that the inventor might find it easier to interest a large car manufacturer. Apparently, the company had insufficient capital to produce and market such a product. This was the last thing I wanted to hear, since my heart had been set on the idea. I had wanted to be told that it would be a lucrative way of making money - not simply because it might earn me a fortune, but for the inventor's sake as well. He had spent a great deal of time and money on the device, and it seemed a shame that he could not get enough people interested to back him financially. I knew that, in theory at least, the device was technically sound and worth a try.

Later that day, I met Peter and informed him what the bank had suggested. In reply, Peter told me that the company did not want to involve a large manufacturer, since it would demand control over every facet of the business and try to increase profits by cutting costs. To avoid this, the inventor had formed a limited company, which would provide the finance for the device to be cast, for the special rubber tubing to be made and for the necessary gaskets to fit the device onto the engine. When fitting the unit, different attachments were required for each model of car. Thus, the plan was to have the device first fitted to one model, and the profit received from the sales would provide the finances for the fitting of another model. It was expected that once the device was on the market sales would flourish and the company would rapidly expand. Peter described the company in glowing terms.

I went home and thought seriously about the whole proposition. After discussing it with my parents, they advised me not to invest in such a risky business.

It was a difficult decision to make. I thought about what the inventor and his small company were trying to do; he certainly had my admiration for being so bold as to take on the large manufacturers. Then I thought about the state of my stocks and shares that the bank had advised me to buy. I was in a dilemma. Should I stand by powerless to prevent my shares tumbling, or should I take a risk by investing in this new invention? It would mean having to sell a substantial amount of my shares, but, at least, I would not have to worry incessantly when watching the evening news every night to hear about the latest company bankruptcies. Since my most important ambition was to learn to speak coherently again, I decided in the end to invest in the petrol device, on the condition that I became a paid employee of the company.

The next day, I saw the bank manager and informed him of my decision to invest. He simply looked over his spectacles perched on the end of his nose and told me he thought it unwise. I reacted by asking him how the Stock Market was doing, but he did not answer me.

Naturally, the inventor was delighted when I informed him of my decision to back his company and offered me the position of Despatch Manager. I felt at last as though I was beginning to lead a normal life again and was serving a useful purpose.

The device still had to be cast and would not be ready to market for another three weeks, because of a small number of teething problems in the manufacturing process. I was becoming restless so Peter suggested I go and enjoy myself abroad for a couple of weeks. His friends in the travel business acquired a cheap package holiday in Tenerife for me. Since I did not have any friends, I went by myself. I did not object to going alone, especially since it would be a challenge for me and an opportunity to speak to more strangers.

While sitting in the Departure Lounge at Manchester Airport, waiting for my flight to be called, I felt my familiar nerves mounting as I sized up the other passengers. They seemed to be very friendly but I did not speak to any of them in case I was accused of being drunk. In the past, I had often landed myself in trouble for merely arguing to the contrary; the more I protested to people, the more convinced they would become. Since I did not want to ruin the holiday before it began, I decided not to get into a conversation with anyone.

On the plane I was given a seat next to the window. Sitting next to me was a middle-aged woman and her daughter aged about twenty. My heart began to race faster with the sudden realization that I would have to speak to them. Although I smiled cordially at them, I was secretly praying they did not ask me a question.

My speech would always sound very slurred if I were asked an unexpected question, since it would mean having to consciously take a deep breath and think at the same time. This may be the natural thing to do, but I was all too aware of my impediment and would often try too hard to articulate my words. The result was that they would sound over-pronounced and disjointed. Also, by this time, my expectation of receiving an insult increased my apprehension and made my slur sound worse. My jaw and tongue would often become tired, and it would be very laborious for me to speak. At such times, I would often resort to using the least amount of words as possible to get my message across

However, the woman and her daughter did make the first move. They had not flown before and asked me if they could sit by the window - a question easily answered with a nod and a smile from me. I was only too pleased to change places, since I felt as though I was doing them a favour - it was a good start to our relationship and helped to put me at ease. We had an interesting conversation which lasted all the way to Tenerife. As usual, the accident was the main topic of discussion. Although they told me my speech was lucid, I knew they were merely trying to give me confidence. In fact, they treated me as a V.I.P. The mother was a social worker for an organisation that worked alongside the mentally handicapped. She told me that the manner in which society generally treated both the mentally and physically disabled often meant that the mental health of some of her clients would deteriorate. Unfortunately, I knew exactly what she meant. They were staying at a different resort to me so we parted shortly after arriving in Tenerife.

"Los Aiguilos," the hotel where I was staying, stood on a hill a few miles from the resort of Puerto de la Cruz. It provided the necessary amenities, so there was little need to venture outside of the hotel.

After unpacking my case, I lay down on my bed to weigh up my situation. I remembered the first time I had been on a package holiday to Lloret de Mar. Many unwanted memories of the first week I had spent there were all too vivid in my mind. I remembered how lonely it had been, as well as the numerous insults and rejections that had plagued me during that first week. I was determined not to go through a similar experience this time.

My decision to avoid socializing with other guests and to spend most of my time in Puerto de la Cruz seemed a good idea at the time. Since I was ashamed of my life, ashamed of my speech, ashamed of having to accept pity from people and afraid of what people might think of me, I decided not to give other guests the chance to reject me.

I also made up my mind not to tell anyone about my big invest-ment. I did not want to give people the impression that I had an excessively good opinion of myself. If it was necessary to give some account of my livelihood, I would say I was a stock-control clerk. It was important for my self-esteem that other holiday-makers saw me as having an identity similar to their own. Fortunately, I had a table to myself at meal times, so it was not necessary to make conversation with anyone.

It soon became apparent that I was the only person to have come on the holiday alone and I felt embarrassed about it. To overcome this, I decided to say that my girlfriend had recently changed jobs and could not get the time off work to accompany me. Consequently, she had insisted that I come by myself.

For the first couple of days, I spent most of my time walking around the town, drinking coffee at various hotels and bars. Whenever I saw two lovers holding hands I would feel very inadequate and lonely. I had not had a girlfriend since before my crash and felt odd because of it. Although it was true that the state of my health had often preoccupied my mind since the accident, and that no girl had ever looked at me twice after hearing my speech, I realized that these were merely excuses to disguise my inability to have a girlfriend. I had become terrified of mixing with young women, since the vast majority of them had treated me scornfully or had simply rejected me as being unworthy. I found it difficult therefore to relax in their presence. I felt as though it was beyond my capabilities to have a girlfriend and would always be terrified of a girl rejecting me. It was not that I had not thought about women - after all, I was only human.

After a few days, it became obvious that some of my fears were unfounded, since the other guests at the hotel were very friendly. I realized that I was being anti-social by not mixing with any of them. Since my arrival, I had only spoken a few words to the guests I had met in the lift or had passed in the hotel. I had often greeted them cordially since I dearly wanted to be friendly but I had never engaged in a conversation with any of them. I was terrified of being rejected or insulted by another guest, but even more so of being accused of acting offensively to one of them when simply trying to justify the reason for my slurred speech.

Eventually, I became embarrassed about my self-enforced isolation and was afraid my fellow guests would imagine that I thought myself superior; if there was one thing I detested it was snobbishness, so I decided to change my habits. It occurred to me that if I wished people to treat me as "normal" I would have to act as the people around me, so I made up my mind to socialize. It was not going to be easy but, at least, I had to try.

I decided to sunbathe by the hotel's swimming pool instead of travelling into the town every day. I made my way to the far side of the terrace where it was not too crowded and lay on one of the beds provided. It was not long before a man and his wife came to lie on the vacant beds next to me. They were in their forties and, after hearing them speaking to the waiter earlier, I realized they were German.

I smiled at them, took a deep breath, and said *Guten tag*. They replied similarly but we were interrupted by the appearance of their daughter and her friend, who were both in their early twenties.

We all introduced ourselves. Since they were very friendly, I was soon able to relax. Fortunately, they could all speak some English. Having spoken to many foreigners when I was in the Merchant Navy, I realized it was only polite to speak slowly - not that I had any choice. I hoped that my speech impediment would not be immediately apparent to them. We began a conversation, and I was pleased that they appeared happy speaking to a foreigner, which boosted my confidence.

Later, at a time when I did not have anything to say, I became nervous again and pretended to be drunk. I began joking and did not seem able to stop. However, I eventually told them about the accident and my impediment. I knew it would only have been a matter of time before they realized my speech was abnormal.

Despite a few problems with language, I got on very well with my new friends. The father, George Leidl, was an architect and could not speak English very well; his wife knew even less. His daughter, Anna-Maria, also knew only a few words but was forever trying to make herself understood. Her friend, Helga, could speak English well. She had arranged to meet her boyfriend, Jan, a Dutchman, who had travelled from Holland to meet her. He joined us later and, like many of his countrymen, was fluent in English as well as a couple of other languages.

The six of us would sunbathe all day together by the pool, and, in the evening, we would go into Puerto de la Cruz for a meal. They left at the end of my first week, unfortunately, and I was sorry to see them leave. We had got on very well together and exchanged addresses, even though, at the time, I did not think I would meet any of them again. They were foreigners who had accepted me for what I was - another human being. I will always remember them.

I stood in the driveway to the hotel and waved good-bye to my foreign friends, while their coach set off to take them to the airport. As the coach disappeared from view, I felt isolated again. I walked slowly back into the hotel and went straight up to my room to lie on my bed. Foremost in my mind were the happy times I had spent with the Leidls during the previous week.

Shortly after lying down, I was suddenly distracted by an uproar coming from the sunbathing terraces outside. I jumped up, rushed out onto the veranda and peered down to see a crowd of people gathering around the swimming pool. As far as I could make out from the balcony, an elderly man had developed cramp while swimming and had lost consciousness in the water. A man had dived into the pool and had brought him out. A young man then began trying to give him artificial respiration, but it was apparent that he did not have much idea about how to do it correctly.

I rushed down and onto the terraces. Fortunately, everybody was too busy watching the rescue to notice that I had to skip since I was still unable to run normally. I elbowed my way through the crowd and looked down at the unconscious man rapidly losing his colour. Somebody asked the young man trying to revive the man if he knew what he was doing. He looked up, shrugging his shoulders and said he hoped so.

Since I held the Bronze Medallion in Life-Saving, I immediately indicated to the young man that he was doing it wrong and that I knew how to do it correctly. Looking relieved, he quickly stood up and let me take over.

I extended the man's tongue out of his mouth, and, with the help of others, I rolled him onto his stomach and lifted him by the waist to empty his lungs of water. Laying him on his back, I correctly positioned his head and proceeded to give him the kiss of life.

Shortly afterwards, an ambulance arrived and the unconscious man was immediately given oxygen before he was rushed to hospital. His much distressed wife was in tears, while the rest of her relatives comforted her. The Spanish waiter brought her a glass of whisky, but I told him angrily to take it back and bring some warm tea instead.

After learning that their father was making a good recovery, the rest of the family showed their appreciation for what I had tried to do by buying me drinks all afternoon - not that I drank much. They appeared to be typical farmers and, judging from their accents, were from Lancashire. We sat talking in the bar, and I discovered that they did not live far from Liverpool. I suddenly had a feeling that I had known them from somewhere. On questioning them further, I learned that they did not live too far from Bill Tyrer, the farmer, for whom I had worked when I was a boy - talk about coincidence.

The elderly man spent three days in hospital, before he was flown home. It is debatable whether I saved his life, but, nevertheless, everybody at the hotel treated me as a hero. Those who had witnessed the event wanted to shake me by the hand, and I soon became popular with the other guests.

I was feeling elated by this unexpected turn of events. All of a sudden, I felt as if I was no longer in my alien and lonely world. All the frustration and anger that was pent up inside me seemed to evaporate. The insults and rejections were soon forgotten - I could only think of my present popularity.

At first, I did not mention my accident, because everyone at the hotel accepted me and treated me with respect. The nervousness about my speech was not so evident, and I was much less self-conscious of the way I spoke. Later that day, I was surprised that nobody had mentioned my impediment. I was thrilled and decided not to tell people about my crash.

The next day, I was still on cloud nine and enjoying the attention from everyone - that is, until one of the teenagers looked at me in admiration. "'Your bill at the bar must be sky-high; how much do you drink each day?'" he asked.

At first, I felt as if my world was collapsing around me and my confidence quickly began to ebb. My mouth and tongue seemed to freeze and I could no longer speak.

Suddenly, I had an idea - since everybody seemed to assume that I was a drunkard, I decided to act as though I was drunk. I had always felt very ashamed when falsely accused in the past, but then I decided to change my tack. If everyone thought I was inebriated, I might as well do away with my embarrassment altogether and enjoy myself.

I saw the comical side of the situation and burst out laughing. I found it so absurd that it was difficult for me to control my laughter. Eventually, a crowd of guests gathered around, wondering what was the cause of the commotion. I pretended to act as a drunk and began cracking jokes and generally acting merry. Everybody was laughing, and, this time, I did not seem to mind when the other guests accused me of being a sot. I was enjoying the deception, especially since my fellow guests apparently accepted me, in spite of it.

For a couple of days, I acted as inebriated and continued to enjoy the ruse. I even had my own party-piece - whenever there was a lull in the activity around the pool, I would suddenly shout "Happy Holidays," to which everybody in my vicinity would shout the same back to me. I felt on top of the world.

Although I had spoken to many of the guests, I had never had a lengthy conversation with any of them . However, a few days before the end of the holiday, Val, a young woman, was talking to me on the terrace. As usual, I was trying to be both a sot and a comedian to justify my slurred speech and to hide my embarrassment at speaking to a young woman. The mood of the conversation changed when she asked out of the blue if she might ask me a question.

"Sure," I said, "but don't ask how much I drink!"

"No, it's nothing like that."

"Go on, then."

"Well, me and my friends were wondering where about in Germany do you live."

"Germany - I'm not German!" I said, looking puzzled.

"I knew it," she quickly replied, obviously pleased with herself. "I knew I was right! The others said you were German, but I knew you were Austrian."

Flabbergasted, I told her I was British but she merely laughed, assuming my wit was at work again.

It was at this point I suddenly realized why nobody had remarked on my speech. Val and the other guests had assumed that I was Austrian or German because I had mixed with the Leidls, my German friends. The fact that I spoke "funny" and often omitted adjectives and adverbs from my speech only added weight to their assumption. Val would not believe that I was British, until I had shown her my passport.

When I had convinced her and explained about my speech, she burst into tears and ran into the hotel.

I soon began to hate my pretence and felt as if I had betrayed myself. The respect I had earned from trying to save the elderly man's life had begun to diminish. Some guests seemed to dislike the idea of my always being "drunk." I realized it would be best to tell them the truth.

However, it was easier said than done. It was difficult to convince some of the guests that I was not drunk and never had been. They refused to believe me at first and thought I was merely jesting again. In the end, I had no option but to tell them about the car crash and my resultant speech impediment. They all apologized guiltily and admitted that they had thought I was a drunken German.

Surprisingly, my image changed again; although I had regained people's respect, there no longer seemed to be any more laughter when I was amongst them. The guilt people felt about their mistaken view of me made them serious whenever I was in their presence.

I had been thoroughly enjoying my popularity, until the other guests learned about my accident. The enjoyment soon dissipated and was replaced by a mood of solemnity. I began to feel as if the whole situation was my fault. I had to do something, so I simply acted as a drunk again. The laughter soon returned and remained through to the end of the holiday.

Some of the guests arranged a farewell party for me on my last night. This time they really did get me drunk. I had not enjoyed myself so much for a very long time. The party must have gone on until the following morning, because I did not remember going to bed.

Most of the guests turned out to see me leaving on the coach to the airport. The driver left the door of the bus open, so I could stand on the steps to wave to my friends and shout "Happy Holidays," as we pulled out of the hotel driveway.

Whenever I look back at this episode in my life, I have to laugh to myself because of so many mistaken assumptions about my identity. At first, the Leidls told me they had assumed I was French, because they had heard me saying *"Bonjour"* to a French family and the French family had assumed I was Canadian, because they had heard me say "Quebec" when trying to tell them my brother lived there. Even the British had initially believed that I was German or Austrian, because I had first mixed with the Leidls and because I "spoke funny."

On arriving home from Tenerife, I was feeling confident. At last, Lady Luck seemed to be on my side, and I had begun to believe in myself again. I began to hold a picture in my mind of future success for myself, hoping that it would turn my dreams into a reality. I also found that I had begun to like myself again; it had been such a long time since I had any real self-esteem.

My right wrist was still causing concern, although my speech was still my major problem, but I was alive and that was what mattered most. I looked back on my life and thanked God for letting me come through such a traumatic experience. I knew only too well that many people have died in much less serious accidents. I thought that I had been through the worst now, so my situation was bound to improve. This new frame of mind must have been triggered off by the happy times I had in Tenerife.

I was expecting a letter from the inventor of the petrol-saving device to inform me that the casting was completed and that the advertising and marketing could begin. I was excited at the thought of starting work again. Unfortunately, there was another hitch in the casting of the unit, so another teething problem remained unresolved.

Before my holiday to Tenerife, I had written to Gordon about the device and asked for his opinion. A letter had arrived from him while I was away, informing me that he was interested in investing in the company. I was delighted and realized that, with his knowledge and experience, if he thought that it was a proposition worth backing, then my instincts must have been right. If I could trust anybody to tell me that the device was sound in theory, Gordon would be that person. I met up with the inventor the following day to tell him the news about my brother's investment. He was delighted.

As usual, I still continued to go to hospital appointments. It was still my hope that the doctors could find some way of relieving the aching in my wrist, but they did not seem to have any solution. Nevertheless, I used to enjoy attending, since it was a break in my monotonous routine.

Whenever I was in a hospital environment, I would feel particularly confident about my speech. While waiting in the queue I would usually have a conversation with the other patients. I rarely mentioned my accident to them, since they had their own problems. I did not mind listening to their worries, because it would remind me that many other people had troubles.

Since the time of my accident, I had experienced so many difficult situations that I felt able to cope with most of the stressful events in life. I realized also that whenever anybody is in a situation that is causing them concern, there is a great tendency to assume that their problem is worse than everyone else's.

Whenever I had a problem, my initial response would be to worry and begin to let the situation get out of hand. However, I would realize eventually that constantly worrying is harmful to the mind. It was difficult but I would always try to remember the wording on the plaque on our bathroom wall: "Worry is like a rocking chair, keeps you busy, but gets you nowhere!"

After three long and frustrating months, the teething problems concerning the device were solved. The Company had rented an office in the heart of Liverpool's business district, so I went down to meet Martin, the office manager and accountant. He told me that the following week, the first batch of two hundred devices were to be delivered to an engineering works not far from the office.

I spent the next day going around to various garages. I had to buy the gaskets and other accessories that were needed to fit the unit between the carburettor and the inlet manifold of the engine.

When the devices arrived, I examined one of them and was surprised at its size and weight. It was big and cumbersome and not at all like a device that was supposed to have a dramatic effect on the internal combustion engine.

However, things do not always work in practice as set out on paper. There were many more minor teething problems to sort out, before we could begin to market the device. The major problem was that each car had to be re-tuned for the unit to work effectively. After the inventor had worked out a way of getting around this, the biggest problem was convincing the public that the device did save petrol. Few people believed us, and the company was eventually declared bankrupt.

There was a meeting in Manchester to officially liquidate the company. The inventor did not turn up, which I thought was disgusting. Afterwards, I remember thinking that my dreams of being successful had once again not materialized. I also realized that I had spent a substantial amount of the compensation and had little to show for it. However, it was not such a blow to me as it might have been, for my main concern was to speak properly again and not to make money. I remember saying to myself "Well, that's life!"

Chapter 16

Survival

I returned home from the meeting to liquidate the company to find my parents waiting eagerly to discover what had taken place. I told them briefly that the company no longer existed and then went upstairs to my room to lie on my bed. My bedroom was my sanctuary - the only place I could be myself. So often I had lain there thinking about my problems and my dreams of success.

I reviewed the past five years since the accident and realized that, although there had been a significant improvement in the state of my health, the money from my compensation had greatly diminished. My dream of being successful with the petrol device had become a nightmare. "What went wrong?" I asked myself. I tried to blame other people for my mistakes, but I had to admit that they were mainly my own doing. I should have taken the advice of my parents and my bank manager and have looked after my money more sensibly. My carelessness with my finances had largely stemmed from my overriding obsession to speak properly again.

I came to terms with my financial losses, although the advice my parents had given me was still audible in my ears. "There are too many people out to rob you soft - you've got to be careful when you have money - people won't want to know you when you've none." They were right, of course, but whenever they had given me this good advice, I had ignored it. I had honestly believed I knew better and that as long as I lived my life without causing harm to anyone my success would be assured. In the end, I realized that life was not so simple.

Since I always believed that it is no good crying over spilt milk, I decided to look upon my past mistakes as a lesson, albeit an expensive one. Fortunately, there was still a few thousand pounds stashed away in my building society account, so I was not exactly down on my uppers. However, I did realize that in future there was a need to be more prudent in the way I spent my finances.

I began to notice that fewer people would insult me when I approached them in the coffee bars, probably because I was now beginning to feel more confident. However, I would sometimes forget to take a deep breath before speaking and would sound more slurred than usual. My speech had continued to improve, although my impediment was still obvious. I often suffered badly from having a heavy cold or a sore throat and as a result the clarity of my speech would suffer.

As usual, I continued to attend the hospital to have my right wrist examined and to have it embalmed in wax. The pain was becoming worse, and the back of my hand was beginning to swell. On examining it, I could feel something sharp beneath the surface of my skin.

I eventually reported it to one of the student doctors at the Infirmary. After examining me, he admitted to have never seen a wrist like mine before - one that contained a metal pin and screws. He went to seek the senior doctor's advice.

After what seemed like hours, he returned with the senior doctor, who did not look at all pleased to see me. He had examined my wrist on previous occasions and had often been abrupt with me. In a manner so uncharacteristic of his profession, he took hold of my wrist brusquely and proceeded to twist and bend it. I eventually cried out in pain and pulled back my arm. I looked up at him in amazement, but he quickly looked away.

He sent me to have my wrist x-rayed when I continued to complain. Later, after returning from the x-ray department, I sat and waited in a cubicle for his arrival.

The senior doctor came at last, and, after scanning the x-ray, he sat on a small stool in front of me. "Look Mr. Lever," he said, crossing his legs and staring at me, "I've examined your x-ray, and there does not seem to be anything out of place." He suddenly looked down at the tiled floor before running the fingers of his right hand through his dark brown curly hair. He slowly shook his head. "How long have you been coming to this clinic?" he asked, abruptly.

"About three years now, Doctor," I replied, instinctively aware he was about to say something distasteful to me.

He waited a moment before replying. "After that amount of time, you know, it's easy for your mind to play tricks on you."

I immediately felt indignant and found it difficult to remain silent. It was hard to believe what I had heard, since I had always thought of myself as being a model patient.

"Come back in a month's time and we'll have another look at it," he said, patronisingly.

My throat suddenly seemed to dry up and I knew that my speech would sound awfully slurred if I tried to reply, so I simply stared back at him, in response. His attitude was difficult for me to understand. It was ironic since I had always shown the greatest respect for every member of the medical profession. I decided that in future he would be the one exception.

As the weeks passed, the pain in the back of my hand became more intense and the lump grew in size. The back of my hand had become so inflamed, that the leather support would chafe against the swelling. In the end, I had to give up wearing it, since it was too painful to wear and increasingly difficult to fasten.

At my next appointment, I reported the inflammation to another student doctor. Fortunately, he could see that the back of my hand was swollen, so, after a short examination, he sent me to have it x-rayed. Later, after scanning it, he told me to wait to see the Consultant, Professor Bentley, who would shortly be coming to the clinic.

On his arrival, he was smiling broadly as usual. I don't remember ever seeing him without a cheerful look on his face. One pace behind the Professor was the senior doctor who had indirectly accused me of faking the pain. An entourage of junior and student doctors was following in his wake.

The student doctor, who was attending to me, reported my condition to the Professor, who immediately came to see me.

"Well, Mr. Lever, how are you this morning?" he asked, before looking at my records and smiled.

"Very well, thank you, Professor Bentley," I said as cheerfully as I could. I was trying not to let him see the expression on my face, since it clearly betrayed the statement I had just made.

"It's a long time since I last saw you," he said, looking down at his diary. "Let's see, it was almost three months ago."

I smiled at him and then looked at the senior doctor, who was looking at me. He smiled but quickly looked away.

The Professor turned to his students and proceeded to tell them about my injuries and how I was coping with my recovery. His words embarrassed me, but I could not have been more proud.

"How is your wrist feeling now?"

"Well, I'm sorry to complain but it's very painful at the moment - it's like a stinging sensation which doesn't go away," I babbled. "And there's a swelling on the back of my hand, which is smarting."

"Yes, I can see it's swollen," he said, as he gently examined my hand and raised his eyebrows in alarm. "How long has it been like this?"

"About a month," I replied.

"Well, why didn't you tell anybody?"

I looked directly at the senior doctor. His face was red and the smirk, which always seemed to be fixed on his face, had been replaced by a look of guilt. I was satisfied to see him in this state and did not to want to prolong his embarrassment. "Well, you see, Professor Bentley," I said as clearly as I could, "I've been coming here so long I was afraid some of your staff might think I was imagining it."

"No, I'm sure none of the staff in this hospital would think such a thing! They only have to look at your case history to see that you are not that type of person."

I looked at the senior doctor again, who immediately looked at the floor.

The Professor turned to scan the x-ray and stood deep in thought as he folded his arms. Turning back to me, he took hold of my wrist and gently felt the lump on the back of my hand, which made me whimper aloud.

"Sorry," he said, "but do you know what is causing the problem?"

"Is it my bone - has it moved out of its position?" I asked.

"No, it's a screw!"

"Really!"

"Yes, one of the screws that was put in to hold the steel plate in your wrist is protruding beneath your skin."

"I knew there was something there!" I said, feeling my complaints had been justified.

"The screw has done its job, and, since the bone has grown around the plate, it is no longer needed. We'll be operating next week. It's only a minor operation so you'll only be in for a day."

The following week, I had the operation and had to wear yet another plaster for a further six weeks.

I realized that it was time to stop going to the "Pyramid Club." I had become so self-conscious by this time of always being alone. It was embarrassing merely to imagine how the other club-regulars perceived me. I was also aware that some of them had begun to watch to see how long it would take before I succeeded in dancing with a girl.

I decided to go to another club. As usual, I was very nervous and had to build up my confidence by telling myself that I was as good as the next person. I stood at the bar and did not speak to anybody apart from the occasional barmaid or waitress. The other people would be enjoying themselves, while I simply watched and wished that I could be happy like them.

After a few months of this, I managed to strike up a conversation with John, who was the same age as me and another regular at the club.

He was a representative for a large food manufacturer on Merseyside and, as might be expected, was a good conversationalist. The first night I met him, we became friends and he gave me a lift home afterwards. Every Friday night, he would call for me, and we would go to the club together. Afterwards, he would drop me off home.

I got on well with John. I used to admire him, because of the stories he told me about some of the things that had happened to him when he was "on the road." In particular, I respected him because he had so much confidence - he certainly had the gift of the gab. He would tell me of his many conquests with girls. I would be green with envy.

Eventually, he would persuade me to get up with him to have a dance with two girls. The music would often be too loud to hold a conversation, which suited me fine. In time, I began to feel guilty because my presence made it difficult for him to take a girl home. He told me that he did not mind, because he was helping me, and that he saw plenty of girlfriends during the week. I thought he was a good friend.

I had known him for about a year, when, one Friday, he phoned to say that he could not come with me. I was disappointed but decided nevertheless to go to the club by myself.

It was almost a year since I had been there on my own and I was feeling more nervous than usual. The plaster on my forearm meant that I was even more self-conscious than normally.

When I arrived at the club, it occurred to me how much easier it was for a person to feel confident when in the presence of a friend. I asked myself if the other men around me were really as bold as they seemed, or were they just pretending. I convinced myself that much of it was false confidence they were portraying. I began to feel better and promised myself not to be nervous.

As usual, I broke my promise. Although I stood by the bar, looking confident, in reality, I was feeling terribly nervous and lonely inside. At that moment, I would have given anything for a girl to come up and be nice to me - as they do in the movies.

There was another regular who had come by himself. We had never spoken, but he nodded and came to stand next to me at the bar when he saw I was standing alone. He was friendly and we soon got into conversation. Feeling self-conscious as usual, I explained about the car accident and how it had affected my speech. He was understanding and I began to relax.

Much to my surprise, he had heard about my accident from his brother-in-law, who had also worked for Shell at their Carrington plant at the time of the crash.

I felt as if he was a friend - somebody who knew what I had been through and what it was like for me at that moment. My usual feelings of inferiority lifted, so when he suggested we should have a dance with two girls. I agreed.

However, my nervousness soon mounted again. At the beginning of each record, I would try to delay going onto the dance floor, usually by saying "Oh, I don't like this one, wait for the next."

Eventually, he twigged on to my delaying tactic. "They won't bite your head off," he told me.

In the end, I counted to ten, took a deep breath and then nodded. "All right, you choose," I said.

We went onto the dance floor and the girl he chose for me was attractive, even though she wore little make-up.

When we began dancing, I was nervous and afraid to glance in my partner's direction in case she was looking directly at me. If our eyes had met, I knew my first reaction would have been to panic and say something to her. To make matters worse most of the other couples were deep in conversation. Our eyes did eventually meet and she smiled at me. This was unexpected and gave my confidence a welcomed boost.

I was about to speak to her, but, fortunately, the record came to an end. Still feeling confident, I took hold of her hand and guided her towards the lounge-bar at the back of the club. I do not know where I found the pluck from - I did it without thinking. It felt marvellous to hold a girl by the hand. It had been such a long time since I had done anything so natural. The longer I held onto her hand, the more confident I became. Once inside the lounge, I took her over to a table and let go of her. My confidence soon began to ebb when it struck me what I had just done. However, the girl smiled at me and my confidence perked up again.

I smiled back and took a deep breath. "Would you like a drink?" I asked, sounding as clear and as confident as I could manage.

"'Babycham', please,'" she said, as she sat down.

I was thankful to walk away to the bar, since it gave me the opportunity to compose myself. I could barely believe that I was doing what I had desperately been trying to do for years. "But what happens now?" I thought desperately. I did not want to disappoint her by telling her I was disabled and could not speak properly. I imagined that she would react by drinking up and going back to her friend as fast as she could. She must have noticed the plaster on my arm, so I made up my mind to tell her that I worked in an office but had broken my wrist playing football and was off work sick. I was determined not to mention the accident.

Carefully carrying the two drinks on a tray, I walked back to where she was sitting. "What's your name," I asked, remembering to take a deep breath and praying at the same time she did not jump to the conclusion that I was drunk.

"Jane, what's yours?"

"Hal," I said, suddenly losing my confidence and wondering what to say next.

"It's the first time I've been here - nice inside, isn't it?" she said, looking around the lounge.

"Yes, I come here every week."

"You don't, do you?" she asked in surprise.

I was not expecting that particular reaction and became flustered. My confidence soon began to desert me, and I suddenly found myself telling her all about my accident. Fortunately, the lounge bar was quiet, which gave me the opportunity to explain properly to her. To my great surprise, she was genuinely interested and wanted to know more. My confidence began to grow and I felt marvellous.

That night, I took her home and she invited me in for a coffee. We spent most of the night talking about me. I could not help it, since she was so interested in the things I had done. I tried not to mention the accident, but we always seemed to end up discussing it, no matter what we started talking about. I apologized for always relating everything to the car crash, but she merely replied that it was understandable and that she did not mind. We arranged to meet the next evening and, by the time I kissed her good night, it was early morning.

She lived in my neighbourhood, and I felt so jubilant that I skipped all the way home. I had met a girl, had a dance, bought her a drink, told her about myself, taken her home and arranged to meet her the following night. "Miracles do happen" I thought.

The following day, I telephoned John and told him what had happened. After thanking him for his help I told him he would not have to look after me any longer, assuming he would probably be glad, because he would now be free to enjoy himself. I asked him if he wanted to go for a drink during the week, but he said he was busy. He did not sound very pleased for me.

I was supposed to meet Jane at eight o'clock that evening and arrived at our rendezvous ten minutes early. She arrived five minutes late, after what seemed like the longest period I had ever waited. She apologized for having been delayed at home. I remember fibbing by telling her that I had only just arrived.

We went to the "Pyramid Club." I had particularly wanted to go there to show the regulars that I did have a girl - an attractive one at that. Being honest, I was posing.

Jane told me to relax and be myself, so I decided to try to be as natural as possible. I must have been relaxed, because I did not worry about my speech. It was a tremendous relief not having to remember to take a deep breath or to worry about what people thought of me. I felt perfectly happy and as if my troubles were now behind me. I could not remember being happier than I was at that moment.

We left the club at one o'clock. As we walked towards the taxi rank, we had our first quarrel. To my surprise, Jane accused me of getting drunk and making a fool of her.

I felt awful and realized that maybe I should have at least remembered to try to speak properly. I certainly did not want her to think I was the sort of person who would take a girl out and get drunk - especially on the first date. Taking a deep breath and speaking as clearly as I could, I explained that I had merely done as she had suggested: simply to relax and not to worry about my speech. She suddenly burst out crying, realizing that she had been mistaken.

We saw a lot of each other in the ensuing weeks, although we never went to a club again. Since Jane had a car, we would usually go to a country pub.

As we became more intimate, I began to worry as I had not been near a woman since before the accident. I had almost given up hope of anything like this happening to me, because of the way people had treated me in the past. I had a very low opinion of myself and never imagined a woman would look twice at me, let alone desire me in a sexual manner. I was scared that my mental turmoil and my long period without sex would render me impotent. However, as things worked out, the only problem was not impotency - I simply ran out of breath. It was too exhausting for me. At first, I thought it was because I was not physically fit but eventually realized that it was due to my breathing. I tried to ignore it but to no avail.

Jane was a secretary for the personnel officer at a large manufacturing company in Liverpool. One evening, she told me that the company for which she worked was recruiting storekeepers, and that she had arranged for me to be interviewed for the position.

I was speechless at first and found it difficult to believe what she had told me. When I had taken it in, I realized that getting the job would take me another step towards leading a "normal" life. I remember hugging her tightly, as she gave me the good news. "My troubles will soon be over," I said to myself. If I had a job, I would be able to talk continuously with my workmates and my speech would soon improve.

My hopes were shattered when I came through the interview successfully but failed the medical due the lack of co-ordination in my hands. I was bitterly disappointed.

Jane and I went out together for the following six weeks. One day she told me that her former fiance wanted to begin their relationship again. We parted as friends.

I was grateful to Jane for what she had done to for me. She had helped me considerably on the road to recovery and had made me feel human again as well as giving me the idea that it was possible get both a job and a girlfriend. I decided to have a go at achieving both of these aims. However, I knew in future I would not get too intimate with a girl. My breathing would make it impossible to have an intimate relationship.

The next Friday, I went to the club and found John there. He was not his usual confident self that evening. From his conversation, it dawned on me that all he had told me about his numerous girlfriends had been a fabrication to disguise his own inferiority complex. He had only been building up his confidence at my expense. I also discovered that, when we had taken two girls onto the dance floor, he would tell his partner that he felt sorry for me because I had no confidence, and that he would take me out dancing merely to help me. My image of him was instantly shattered.

I stopped going to night-clubs after that. I had never felt relaxed in them, and I realized that they were not my scene.

A few weeks later, I was lying on my bed thinking about my plans for the future, when I suddenly realized that I could not breathe properly. Often it had happened when I was doing something strenuous, but, at that moment, I was merely lying on my bed. I was inhaling normally but was still short of breath. Although my chest was fully expanding not enough air was entering my lungs. I tried taking deep breaths, but it did not seem to make any difference. I attempted to clear my throat but found it difficult to do so. I was mystified and began to worry. As the condition tended to come and go, I would try my utmost to put it to the back of my mind, but it was not easy to do.

The following month, I asked my doctor to examine my chest. He did so but could find nothing wrong with me. It was a great relief for me to hear this, since I had begun to imagine I had cancer or some other terminal illness. He told me that after having been involved in such a terrible car accident, I was lucky to be as well as I was. He also added that my condition was probably psychosomatic. Feeling relieved, I agreed that it must have been my imagination. After what I had been through, nothing else could go wrong - or could it?

Chapter 17

Getting a Job

Early in 1976, I tried my utmost to get a job, even though I was still officially classed as "Sick" and "Disabled." Ideally, I was looking for a clerical position, since the work would not be physically demanding. Simply because my life was so boring, I would have willingly taken on any job available. I seemed to be wasting away on the sidelines and not performing any useful function in society. If I found work, I would not bother going to my weekly hospital appointments, since there was nothing they could do to mend my wrist.

Each day, I would visit the Employment Exchange in the hope of finding suitable work. On rare occasions, I would be fortunate enough to be given an interview and would make a special effort to look presentable. While travelling to the rendezvous, I would be full of confidence and attempt to convince myself that it was going to be my lucky day. I was aware of the sort of questions the personnel officer would ask me and would always prepare my answers in advance. Upon arriving at the office where the interview was to take place, my nervousness would mount and my speech would inevitably sound very slurred. To a certain degree, the personnel officer would have genuine sympathy for my predicament. However, once he discovered that I had not worked for six years, he would usually tell me that he was looking for somebody with recent experience, or disqualify me on similar grounds.

It was ironic as I would have been very conscientious and an asset to any company if only to show my appreciation for their giving me a job. It was soul-destroying to realize that it was only my speech that was preventing me from being accepted. I tried for what seemed a lifetime, but I still remained unemployed. It always felt as if I was waiting on a railway platform for the next train to arrive but never allowed to board.

My speech had much improved since the time of the accident, although my words still sounded slurred, especially when tired, or when something happened unexpectedly. Speaking was not as tiring for my jaws or mouth as it had been, although it was still an effort for me. In recent years, I had at times been short of breath, which was beginning to affect my already impaired speech.

I had often tried to analyse the way I spoke. Doctors had said that the shock of the collision had caused the paralysis, but I realized that the barrage of insults people had hurled at me, undoubtedly aggravated the problem. It was only natural that such continual rejection would adversely affect me. At one stage, I seriously began to wonder if I had developed an inferiority complex.

The possibility of having such a complex appalled me. The very term was distasteful to me, since it was often used to discredit a person's character. The idea of being labelled as having an inferiority complex was so repugnant to me that I would rather have received my usual insults than be written off in such a way. I was determined, in future, not to give people the opportunity to talk like that about me!

I had often wanted to be able to attract the full attention and admiration of people in a crowded room by simply opening my mouth and speaking. It was one of my most cherished dreams. I decided to prove once and for all that I did not have any kind of complex by showing a crowd of people that I was not afraid to speak in front of them. I was looking forward to the challenge.

One Wednesday evening, I went to a night school in my area to enrol for a course in Public Speaking. It had taken great courage for me to make such a daring decision. I walked up and down outside the school trying to build up enough confidence to go inside. When I eventually joined the class, I discovered my apprehension was unfounded, since the lecturer and other students, most of whom were women, were very friendly indeed. Nevertheless, I found the situation far too intimidating for me to relax or to speak to any of them at first.

Our first assignment was to present a five-minutes speech on a topic of our choice. The lecturer allowed us fifteen minutes to prepare the talk. I chose to speak on "A Safari in South Africa," since I could not think of anything else except my accident - I was sure nobody wanted to hear about that! When the fifteen minutes were up, the teacher asked for a volunteer to speak first - guess who put his hand up!

I was extremely nervous and knew my speech would sound all the more slurred as a result. To lessen my embarrassment, I realized it would be best to explain first about my speech impediment. During my explanation, my captive audience were amazed that I had the courage to volunteer first. However, nobody was aware that I had done little else but talk about my crash for the previous six years so I knew exactly what to say. The very favourable response from the class encouraged me greatly and gave me sufficient impetus to continue.

I spoke for more than ten minutes about my accident and was about to carry on with the speech I had prepared about South Africa. To my great surprise, the class suddenly erupted into applause. Alas, I never did get to give my prepared speech, since the teacher asked for the next speaker to begin. When we stopped for a break, I was the main topic of conversation and was amazed to be so popular with the others in the class. On my way home later, I could barely wait for the next session.

The following day, I went out early in the morning feeling very confident. I went to the Job Centre in Speke, on the other side of Liverpool. On my arrival, I asked to see the Disablement Rehabilitation Officer, but, after taking my name, the receptionist told me he was busy and asked me to wait in the queue.

I sat alongside three other men. Every few minutes, a man would come out of an office and say "next," to the men sitting beside me. Eventually, my turn came so I took a deep breath and went in.

There was a man sitting behind a desk, who looked up at me and smiled. "Good Morning," he said, standing up and offering me his hand.

"Good Morning," I replied, cheerfully.

"Right, I haven't got much time, so I would like you to answer the following questions. What's your name?"

"Hal Lever, Sir." I said.

He looked down a list of names but could not find mine. "Did you give your name in at the reception?"

"Yes, Sir!"

"Tut, secretaries!" he said, raising his eyebrows, as he wrote down my name.

"Where did you last work?"

"Shell Chemicals."

"Have you worked in a car factory before?"

"No, Sir."

"Have you done this type of work before?" he asked, not bothering to look up, as he continued to take down my particulars.

"Erm, yes, Sir." I said hesitantly, while wondering if he had a position for me in the Civil Service. I was about to tell him that I had worked in the Labour Exchange but was not given the chance. He continued to fire a series of questions at me. These merely required "yes" or "no" answers, which suited me fine.

Suddenly it dawned on me what was going on. I had blundered into the wrong room and was actually being interviewed for a job as an operative for British Leyland Motor Company. I was amazed and could barely believe what was happening.

"The medical is at 10.00 o'clock tomorrow morning - don't be late," he said, not bothering to look up. "Ask the security man on the gate where the Medical Centre is - he'll show you. Take your P.45 and your birth certificate along with you - without them you won't be able to start, so don't forget to take them. I've filled in the application form already - you only need to sign it. If you pass the medical, we want you to start on Monday, is that all right with you?"

"Certainly, and thank you very much." I blurted delightedly.

Suddenly, the man looked at me baffled - a look I had often seen before. I realized that I had not taken a deep breath before speaking.

I had to act quickly. I pretended to wince and held my jaw. "Sorry, but I've just been to the dentist and my mouth is rather numb," I said, quickly signing the form.

"All right, send the next man in when you go out."

"Phew," I said to myself, walking out of the office in a daze. It was just as well the next man in the queue knew it was his turn, because I would not have been capable of telling him. I was ecstatic.

However, I came down to earth with a bump, when I remembered that there was the medical to pass. I began to worry.

The following morning, I attended the medical examination. The doctor did not ask many questions, and most of those he did merely required "yes" or "no" answers. It was surprising that he failed to notice both the twelve inch scar, stretching from the back of my right hand to my elbow, nor the tracheotomy scar on my neck. It amazed me how easy it was. However, he asked what was wrong with my speech. I replied that a bus had almost knocked me down when I was six and the shock had affected the way I spoke. He did not press me on the subject but began to write notes before telling me to wait outside. A little later, an elderly nurse came out and told me to report for work on the Monday morning.

I was euphoric. "At last, my luck is beginning to change," I said to myself. As I walked out of the Medical Centre I was laughing at the ease at which I had secured a job. It was strange to think about all the office jobs for which I had unsuccessfully applied and for which I was better suited. By pure accident I had passed an interview for a job - one for which I would never have thought of applying - and I had even sailed through a medical examination. However, the real test would come when I actually started work.

Understandably, I was nervous when reporting to the factory on the Monday morning along with twenty other new employees. Apart from my speech my greatest worry was that my right wrist would be a hindrance. In addition, I had not worked for many years and was not sure whether my fellow workers would accept me.

The workers starting along with me were a mixed bunch, aged between twenty and forty. Some were loud-mouthed and uncouth, while others were more reserved by nature. Despite this, I got on well enough with all of them, although I did not talk much. I was aware that some of the other recruits had been surprised to hear my speech.

We had to attend an induction course on the first day. After completing it we were each given a position on the production line.

Another young man and I were allocated to the same station on the track. Between the two of us we had to fit the front and back wheels, complete with their tyres, onto the right-hand side of each car. We then put on the nuts with the help of a pneumatic spanner. Considering the combined weight of a wheel with its tyre that had to be lifted to shoulder-height and positioned onto the axle, it soon became apparent that it was only a matter of time before I would be dismissed.

When the track began to move, it was difficult to keep up with the cars passing my station. I soon had to catch up on a backlog of vehicles I had been unable to do. I managed to stick it out for a quarter of an hour, but only because it was possible to stop the track by pressing an emergency button.

Eventually, Harry, the Foreman, came up to me with another lad to replace me. "You can't half tell you've never worked in a factory before," he said, with a friendly grin on his face.

I apologized and smiled back.

"Come on, I've got just the job for you!" he said, shaking his head and smiling to himself.

My new job was not as strenuous, but was equally difficult. I was supposed to bolt the water bottles for the windscreen wipers onto the body of the car. It was a job that most people could do without any trouble, but I still made a hash of it. My lack of co-ordination ensured that I kept dropping the nuts and bolts or the spanner - ultimately, I had to stop the track.

When Harry approached me again, I was expecting him to sack me. I did not give him time to complain.

"All right, Harry, you've been patient with me," I blurted out. "I should not have started here. I should have explained at the interview. I'm sorry," I said.

"Why, what do you mean?"

"Well, six years ago I had a very bad car accident, and I haven't worked since."

"I realized you had some difficulties in your movement - is that why you speak the way you do?"

I simply nodded, surprised he was taking such an interest in me.

"How bad was the accident?"

I explained what had happened but did not mention that I had been in a psychiatric hospital. I was receiving more than enough cruel insults about my speech and certainly did not want to hear any about my sanity.

Harry looked at me in admiration. "Look, I'll find you an easy job - don't worry, you'll be all right."

He gave me a job ripping off the masking tape from each car, after it had passed through the paint-spraying booth. It was easy for me to do, but, like most other jobs on an assembly line, it was terribly boring. I did not mind because after many years of frustration I had finally found a job. It felt as if I was no longer at the railway station, waiting for the train to arrive but was sitting in a carriage, watching the station grow smaller in the distance.

After I had been doing my new job for almost three weeks, Harry came up to me on a Friday morning.

"Hello, Hal, how are you getting on?"

"Great, thanks, Harry. By the way, I know I've told you before, but I'm really thankful to you for not reporting me. And for giving me this easy job."

"Oh, forget it - there are times when we all need a helping hand! Talking about jobs, there's a vacancy on the notice board that I think would interest you. I'm not saying it's easy, but it's a damn sight more interesting than what you're doing at the moment."

"What's it for?" I enquired.

"They're looking for a storeman."

"That would be great!"

"Well, if you pass the interview, you'll never look back."

"Thanks a lot, Harry, you're a friend!"

"You haven't got the job yet."

"I know, but I would never have known about it if you hadn't told me" I said gratefully.

"Well, you can go for your break early. You'll find a pen and paper in my office - go and write a letter to the Store's Senior Foreman. Do it now and I'll take it around to his office - he may see you today," he said, as he turned to walk away. "I'll go and tell the relief man to come and give you a break."

I went to his office and thought about what I would write. I finished the letter after much contemplation and was pleased with the finished result. Later, I attended an interview and was given the job.

On the Monday morning I reported to the Stores and met Frank, my new Foreman. Harry had told him about my accident, so he gave me a job that did not involve lifting heavy materials. If the job did entail lifting anything heavy, I would always be able to wear my wrist band. Frank, like Harry, was amazed to hear about my recovery. This surprised me greatly because, since leaving Winwick, I had developed a very low opinion of myself. So many people had treated me as a third-class citizen during the previous six years that I had come to accept their assumption as true. Although many people had congratulated me before, I had believed that they were merely being polite. Thanks to Harry and Frank, my self-opinion began to change. I realized that I had achieved something significant and began to like myself again.

In the excitement of being employed, I forgot to attend the course in public speaking. However, it had greatly boosted my confidence and helped to ensure I would never be afraid to talk.

I was enjoying my work at British Leyland and found myself accepted by the other workers. A few men had tried to ridicule me at first, but their attitude changed once they heard about my car accident. They soon treated me as an equal.

I also discovered that I could make people laugh, especially the operatives at work. At first, it was difficult to relax in their presence, but as they got to know about my accident I became less tense. However, I was still embarrassed about my speech and, in attempting to disguise it, I would often joke. Much to my surprise, it soon became apparent that my work mates found my wit hilarious. It may well have been the way I was speaking and not so much my sense of humour. On many occasions, I must have become too confident because it almost got to the point when I merely had to open my mouth, and the others would laugh at anything I said.

I eventually shared a job with another storeman, called Jimmy. He had been brought up in a poor part of Liverpool and had a heart of gold. He was not a well-educated person, but was, nonetheless, very intelligent. At times, he would have difficulty understanding my speech, but he was always patient with me and would often tell me to take my time. When we were not busy we would have some interesting conversations. He had a thirst for knowledge and when he learned that I had been a Navigating Cadet in the Merchant Navy, he wanted to know about navigation and astronomy. I often ended up giving him trigonometry lessons during the meal-breaks.

After working for a couple of months, I began to feel secure in my job and decided it was time for me to leave home and get a flat. I wanted to be considered as a grown man of twenty-eight who was leading a "normal" life, so it was no good living at home with my family. I needed my independence. When my parents learned of my intention to leave home they fully understood.

A friend at work knew a landlord who was looking for a tenant for a vacant flat. I went along to see him and agreed to move into the flat the following week. My father, Colin and I redecorated it throughout in two days. I was delighted with how the flat looked on completion. The only problem was that I had no friends to invite.

My double-vision was still troubling me, although it had much improved. I was beginning to take a greater interest in reading, even though it was a very slow process. The problem was that at the end of each line, it was difficult to continue reading onto the line below. It was a painstakingly slow and tedious ordeal, so it would not be long before I became bored.

While I was trying to read one evening, the room was suddenly plunged into darkness. After finding a spare bulb, I stood on the 'stepladder and stretched up to fit it into the socket. Suddenly, I realized my breathing had become erratic. My life had been so busy during the previous few months that I had not had time to worry about my chest.

I took a deep breath, but my lungs still felt empty. My mind suddenly went blank and the next thing I remembered was falling to the floor and injuring my right wrist. The pain was so severe that I went to hospital. As expected, I later left the Casualty Department wearing a plaster on my wrist and was told to take six weeks off work. It was so frustrating and annoying to end up on the "sick list" again at a time when I was beginning to enjoy my new lifestyle.

Still worried about my breathing, I went to see my doctor about it. He examined my chest again but was confident it was fine. Despite his reassurance, I was convinced something was wrong with my chest but greatly feared he would accuse me of hypochondria if I continued to complain. I tried to forget my erratic breathing, but the problem kept niggling at my mind. It was a strange situation. "Surely," I said to myself, "the doctor must know what he was talking about?" I decided, in the end, to try to put it down to an overactive imagination but it was far from easy.

I took advantage of my time off work by frequenting the coffee bars and stores in the city centre, talking to old acquaintances. I was expecting the people that knew me to tell me my speech had improved. However, it was disappointing to discover that they were finding it more difficult than usual to understand what I was trying to say. I was very dismayed. It felt as if I was fighting a losing battle.

On returning to work I began working a shift system. I did not mind doing the night-shift, because it meant that I was able to spend two or three hours in the city centre speaking to people during the afternoon.

The factory closed down for a fortnight during the summer, so I decided to spend the time off in Ibiza. I made up my mind to enjoy this holiday and was not going to worry about what people thought of my speech.

For the first few days of the holiday, I spent most of my time drinking coffee and having an occasional beer at the many bars in the town. For some reason I was not as confident about speaking to people as usual, probably because I knew I would start talking about the crash.

I did not believe that many other people would want to hear about it, certainly not when they were on holiday. I would watch the other holiday-makers sitting in the sunshine, relaxed and happy, while I was a bag of nerves in comparison.

Eventually, I began sunbathing by the pool at the hotel and got talking to Ian, a young man, who was also from Liverpool. He was quiet and reserved and I enjoyed his company greatly. His parents joined us later. They were very sociable and we spent most days sunbathing together.

In the evening, I met two married couples from Holland. They all spoke excellent English. Dan and Ria lived in Zutland and had a business in Rotterdam, supplying industrial washing machines to the armed forces throughout Western Europe. Their friends, Koosh and Yoke, lived near Rotterdam. Yoke was a secretary, while Koosh worked for Shell as a research engineer. I was surprised when he told me his job involved improving the performance of the internal combustion engine. He was interested in hearing about my failed attempt to break into business in that field, so we had plenty to talk about.

However, as soon as the introductory conversation was over, I became tongue-tied. It was difficult to think of anything else to talk about except my crash. I suddenly became nervous at the thought that, like many others, they too would assume I was drunk. I had promised myself not to mention the accident, but my nerves got the better of me, and I found myself telling them about my speech. I would occasionally crack a joke in the process, which went down well. They seemed to enjoy my sense of humour, and I soon found myself the centre of attention again.

We became good friends, and Dan told me that there would always be a job for me if ever I wanted to work in Holland. I told him that one day I might take him up on his offer. I spent most evenings at the bar with them, though I never drank much. I preferred to act as a drunk than to let people see that I was conscious of my speech.

As usual, everybody exchanged addresses when we were leaving, and we all promised to keep in touch. I decided that I would certainly visit my friends if I ever went to Holland.

When I was sitting on the plane home, it struck me that the holiday had not been as enjoyable as my earlier trip to Tenerife. I wondered if I had finally had enough of strangers insulting me and as a result had not gone out of my way to meet people.

Two months after returning from my holiday, I decided to buy a house. I could afford to do this, since there was still enough money left from my compensation, and I was earning a good wage at British Leyland. When working on the night-shift, I would get up at mid-day and spend most of the afternoon looking around houses for sale.

I eventually bought a modern three-bedroomed house in Gateacre, a residential area of Liverpool. I managed to get a ninety per cent mortgage, which left me with enough money to furnish and decorate my new home, with some left in reserve for an emergency.

A fortnight after moving into my new house, I slipped and fell halfway down the stairs, badly injuring my wrist again. As a result, I had to wear yet another plaster on my arm and was obliged to stay off work for six weeks. I was dismayed, especially since the company did not pay operatives any sick pay.

To add to my troubles, the work-force went on strike for thirteen weeks shortly after my return to work. When the strike was over, all the production of British Leyland cars in Liverpool was transferred to their factory in Coventry. In June 1978, British Leyland closed their two factories in Liverpool, making me redundant.

It was a great disappointment for me, since I had settled very well at British Leyland. Realistically, I knew that it would be difficult for me to find another job in the future, especially during the recession.

Chapter 18

Going Dutch

After finishing work in May 1978, I realized how lucky I had been to be employed by British Leyland. It was an exceptional stroke of good fortune that I had got the job in the first place, and if it had not been for Harry, the foreman, I would probably not have lasted beyond the first day.

I had been paid until late June, so there were still six weeks to find employment before becoming eligible to register for "Unemployment Benefit." Since my health had greatly suffered as a result of attempting to lead a "normal life," I decided to enquire at my local Social Security Office about claiming all of the benefits, to which I, as a severely disabled person, was entitled. However, when I applied the clerk assumed I was drunk. The other claimants overheard my arguing and, assuming I was intoxicated, began to heckle me. It was so humiliating, especially because, since the car accident, I had refused to admit to myself that I was disabled. Degraded, I walked out of the office, promising myself never to return. I claimed Unemployment Benefit instead!

During the week, I would go to the Job Centre every day in search of work but was never even offered an interview, let alone another job. My frustration grew when I discovered that most of the other men working with me at British Leyland had little difficulty finding employment. I felt like screaming but I told myself that my situation would change if I remained patient and continued to go to the Job Centre.

My wrist was still giving me trouble. The stinging sensation was becoming more acute, so I began attending the hospital appointments again. However, the situation had not changed - there was nothing they could do for me. I saw a whole string of doctors who had not previously attended to me. As usual, I would have to explain my case to them all over again. Despite their initial interest in my medical history, I was beginning to get the impression that nobody took my problem seriously any more. It felt as if they were merely going through the motions of giving me my next appointment.

At the beginning of August, I received a postcard from Dan, Koosh, Ria and Yoke, the four Dutch people I had met on holiday in Ibiza. They had just returned from their vacation in Italy and were wondering how I was getting on. My Dutch friends had often been in my thoughts, although I had never got around to writing to them. Many a time, I had thought of writing to Dan to ask him for the job he had promised me, but I did not want to impose on him. My greatest fear was that if Dan gave me a job, I might get injured, or be the cause of another employee being hurt.

However, the more I thought about working for him, the more attractive the idea became. I had been to Holland twice before, when in the Merchant Navy, and had always found that the folk there were fond of the British. In my opinion, the Dutch were amongst the friendliest people in the world.

I wrote to Dan to tell him I was fine and casually mentioned my unemployment. A fortnight later, I received a letter in reply inviting me over to Holland for a holiday. Dan mentioned in his letter that Koosh and Yoke had also invited me to spend a week in their home.

Feeling that I had at long last found some true friends, I was more than pleased to accept the invitation. However, it occurred to me that people do not always behave the same way on holiday as they do when at home. I was in a dilemma - I did not know whether to act as though I was drunk, as I had in Ibiza, or whether to be sober and try not to let my speech get me down. I finally decided to try the latter.

I caught the overnight ferry from Hull and arrived in Rotterdam the following morning. Dan and Ria were waiting to greet me warmly as I walked into the reception lounge. We went to a nearby restaurant, where we had a fine breakfast. Later, we travelled to a hamlet, outside Rotterdam, where they lived in an ultra-modern luxury bungalow.

Built to Dan's specifications, the bungalow included a right-angled corner window - the glass pane was right-angled and did not have any brick corner-support. I had never seen anything like it. At the back of the bungalow was a large compound, where Dan kept a horse there while Ria kept three pet goats.

At first, I was nervous, but Dan and Ria did all they could to make me feel at home. I soon began to relax. Dan told me he would give me a job as a storeman and, as if that was not enough, told me he would help me to find a flat and settle in Rotterdam. The salary he was offering me was excellent I could barely believe it, when he told me. It was decided that it would be best to spend a week's holiday with Dan and Ria, followed by a week with Koosh and Yoke, before returning to England to obtain a work permit and to lease my house.

As Dan had various dealings in towns around Holland, I travelled with him on his ventures and managed to see much of the country. One day, he took me to Volendam. We travelled along a motorway that ran along the top of a dyke. There was a fresh water lake on one side of the road and the North Sea on the other. When we were in Volendam I tasted my first eel, which was about six inches long. It had to be cut into three pieces, before I could eat it. With my mouth open, I had to tilt my head back and allow a piece to slide down the back of my throat. I only managed to swallow one piece and nearly choked myself in the process.

On one occasion, I caught the train to Amsterdam. Since I had to change some traveller's cheques, I went to the nearest bank. Upon entering, a cold shiver ran down my back with the sudden realization that I had forgotten to bring my traveller's cheques. I did not know what to do, since I only had four guilders in my pocket. The Gods must have been smiling down on me that day, because I put my hand in my shirt pocket and found a crumpled five-pound note. Even though it had been through the washing machine and had lost some of its colouring, it was still recognisable. I took a deep breath and went to the nearest teller.

"Excuse me, I would like to change this five-pound note sterling into guilders, please," I said, remembering to speak as clearly as I could to the very smart young woman behind the counter.

"Certainly, Sir," she said, smiling and taking the five-pound from me. Suddenly, the smile vanished from her face, as she carefully examined the faded five-pound note. She looked back at me and excused herself before going to speak to her supervisor, sitting behind a large desk at the back of the bank.

Her superior looked at me over his gold-rimmed spectacles, and said something to the young woman, who then went into the manager's office. She later returned and asked me to take a seat.

Shortly after sitting down, two burly-looking men dressed in rain coats walked into the bank. They were acting suspiciously and apparently looking around for someone. I was half expecting each of them to pull out a gun and rob the bank. My assumption was wrong, for I saw the young lady teller pointing in my direction and then the two men rushing over to me.

"Excuse me, Sir, we are police officers, would you mind accompanying us to our headquarters? It's in connection with our enquiries into counterfeit money coming into this country."

My poor heart was racing as I tried to think of what to say. I attempted to reply but was unable to speak. I could do nothing but allow them to lead me out of the bank and bundle me into their car.

There was silence as we drove through the city. We pulled off the main road and into a car park, next to which was a huge circular building - the Police Headquarters.

We went inside and took the lift up to an office where I was interrogated. One of the policemen began examining the five-pound note, using a magnifying glass, while his colleague asked me many questions about the money I had and how many five-pound notes I had exchanged on the ferry.

After summing up the situation that I had inadvertently got myself into, I showed the two policemen the tracheotomy scar on my neck and babbled that I needed a glass of water. Afterwards, I was able to speak a little better, although they were still unable to understand me. In the end, I asked them for a pen and paper and explained that the five-pound note had been left in my breast pocket when my shirt was washed. I also wrote about my car accident.

As soon as they had read the note they walked to the other side of the room to discuss what I had written. It did not take them long to realize their error. They quickly returned and apologized sincerely for the mistake and for having inconvenienced me. They took me back to the bank where both the manager and the teller apologized profusely. I realized that they had only been doing their job and saw the funny side of the affair. The manager was relieved I had not made a big issue out of the event.

After spending a week with Dan and Ria, I went to stay with Koosh and Yoke. They made me very welcome and Koosh had a few days off work to take me sightseeing. I told him about Jan the Dutchman, in Tenerife some years previously. Koosh said I should try to get in touch with Jan, but we left the subject there.

The next evening, we had a fondue party with Dan and Ria. The five of us were having a good time, talking about our experiences abroad when the telephone rang. Koosh answered it, speaking in his native Dutch tongue. After finishing his conversation, he spoke to the other three, who laughed heartily at what he said. I asked him what they were laughing at, and, after first apologizing for speaking in Dutch, he told me that one of his neighbours wanted to join the party. Apparently, Koosh detested the man because of his arrogance and because he was such a bore. Without warning, my five Dutch friends excused themselves and walked into the kitchen.

Suddenly, there was a knock on the door. Since I was the only one who was not busy, Koosh asked me to answer it. Opening the door, expecting to see the boring neighbour, I was stunned and amazed to see Jan standing before me. I turned around and saw my other Dutch friends, each of them grinning broadly. Apparently, I left my address book lying around the house, so Koosh found his telephone number and invited Jan to the party.

Jan did not live far live from Koosh, and I went to stay at his home later that evening. He owned a fruit and vegetable business that exported to several European countries. He offered me a job in the market, but my wrist would not have been strong enough to take the heavy labour.

He dropped me off the next day in Vlaardingen where I was picked up by Dan and Ria. As I was opening the car door, the fingers of my right hand got caught in the handle and I injured my wrist again. I was in agony, and eventually told Dan what had happened. He wanted to take me to hospital to have it examined, but I knew there was nothing they could do for me. Fortunately, I was able to relieve the ache temporarily by taking the painkillers I always carried with me. I decided not to accept his offer of employment, since it would not have been fair on him if I were to cause an accident and possibly injure other workers.

My injury ruined the trip to Holland for me. The atmosphere seemed to change although it was probably only my frame of mind. I thanked my Dutch friends for their warm hospitality and decided to return to Liverpool.

I caught the ferry home two days later. I was cursing the opportunity that I had missed because of my wrist.

Life was terribly boring for me when I arrived home. My breathing was continuing to trouble me, and all I could do was to put it down to my lack of fitness. Since I had plenty of time on my hands I decided to take up running. I was only able to run for a mile each day at first but was eventually able to get up to two or three miles. I was determined to get fit and rid myself of my breathing difficulty.

However, although my leg muscles were getting plenty of exercise, my breathing was not improving, indeed if anything, it seemed to be worsening. I often suffered spasms of breathlessness when I was running - it was a mystery to me. On many occasions, I was close to the point of collapsing and would have to stop to gasp desperately for breath. It was embarrassing since it often happened when other people were around. It worried me but what more could I do, since my doctor had often told me my lungs were fine. In desperation, I began to imagine it was a symptom of cancer or some other terminal disease. This only made matters worse, since my worrying became almost constant. I ended up trying to dismiss it from my mind altogether but it was far from easy.

Every day, I would go to the Job Centre but still could not get a job. I would often become depressed since I felt as if my life was in a vacuum. Eventually it became clear that my situation would not change unless I actively changed it myself. The possibility of my finding a job was almost non-existent, so I had to find an activity that would interest me and keep my mind off my worries.

I decided to teach myself French, especially since I had often recalled how envious I had been in Canada, after hearing Gordon speaking it fluently. I had intended to learn to speak French but had never got around to doing it. Remembering how the doctors at Warrington Infirmary had said that I would probably never speak again gave me an additional incentive. I decided to prove them wrong conclusively by not only speaking in my own tongue but also speaking in another language.

I often heard about people beginning a correspondence course but becoming bored and giving it up after a few months. I was determined it was not going to happen to me. In August 1977, I bought a complete course in French: tapes, a manual and exercise books. I put all my efforts into learning this language, when I was not looking for work.

Every morning during the week, I would arrive in the city centre at 9.30 and look at the vacancies in the Job Centre before going to the Central Library. I would study French until early in the afternoon. It was tedious especially since my reading was still badly affected by double-vision. I remember asking university language students about various aspects of the grammatical points that I had not fully grasped. After I had first explained about my speech, the students were usually happy to oblige and would often go out of their way to give me their help. I would spend the rest of the afternoon in the city centre trying to speak English properly. In the evenings, I would listen to the French tapes. Sometimes I would go to night school to compare my progress with other students.

At first, I found the French language difficult to understand, and often thought of throwing it in the bin. My past attempts to be successful had always ended in failure for reasons beyond my control, but this time I only had myself to rely on. My poor health was not a factor - that is, apart from my breathing. Fortunately, I recalled the saying "When the going gets tough, the tough get going" I decided to get "tough."

I soon fell in love with the French language and would often buy *"Le Monde,"* from the newsagent during the week. I would enjoy attempting to translate some of the articles into English. It was not easy and I would spend many hours trying to comprehend the full meaning of one article. This effort did lead to improvement eventually and my interest in French became a great distraction from my worries.

I decided to enter for the General Certificate of Education at O level in French. Apart from the written papers, consisting of translations from French to English and from English to French, there was also a comprehension as well as an oral examination, which entailed speaking in French for five minutes to an examiner. I was worried about passing this part of the examination for obvious reasons. I made a special effort to prepare myself for the exam and would often practice speaking to university students I met in the library. My efforts were rewarded when I successfully sat the examination in June 1978.

The day after the examination I went to see my family. Colin was going to visit Gordon and Frances in Canada the next day. As usual, my mother was her old smiling self, but my father was ill. I sat at his bedside, and he seemed to brighten up when he saw me. Later, I left when Colin offered to drive me home.

A few days later, my mother phoned me in the early hours of the morning. "Your father has just died," she said, sobbing.

"I'll be there in ten minutes, Mum," I said, desperately trying to think of what to say - but what could I say at a time like that?

I called a taxi, which was quick in coming, and, on the way, my thoughts were of my mother. I tried again to think of the right words with which to comfort her, but in vain. I had often met and spoken to people who had recently lost a loved one, and I liked to think my words were comforting to them. Now the tragedy had happened to me, and to a greater extent my mother, I felt helpless.

I arrived ten minutes later to find my mother in the living room, still sobbing. I tried to comfort her but all I could do was to let her cry on my shoulder.

Shortly afterwards I went up to see my father. He had both feet on the carpet and was sitting on the side of his bed. His sky-blue eyes, often so expressive, were now so inanimate. I felt the top of his head. It was stone cold.

My stomach was in a knot as I looked down at his corpse and realized how fragile and precious the gift of life is. I wished I could have brought him back to life for my mother's sake.

I telephoned Gordon to tell him the bad news. He said that he and Colin would fly to England that day.

Chapter 19

Success at Last!

My spirits were very low when I returned home after my father's funeral. The feeling uppermost in my mind was guilt. In some vague way, I felt that he had been disappointed with me for not spending the money I had received as compensation more wisely. He had gone to great lengths to stress the importance of using the money carefully, but I had reassured him that I knew what I was doing.

Although wanting to be successful in business, my real ambition was always to learn to speak properly again. I had always been looking for ways to make money but it was difficult, not least because of the way people perceived me. Most people assumed that my inability to speak properly meant that I was not fully in control of the rest of my faculties. Consequently, people often underestimated my potential.

I recalled some of the main events since my crash almost ten years earlier: life in the Infirmary; recovering in Winwick; my holiday in Lloret de Mar; leaving Shell; injuring my arm when studying at Blackpool College of Art; the disappointment of Phil and the club in Gloucester; my holiday in South Africa; the disappointment of the petrol-saving device; my redundancy at British Leyland; my trip to Holland when I injured my wrist and the many hospital appointments I had attended, not to mention the seemingly endless volley of insults I had received from people during this period. It would have been pointless to bury myself in self-pity, since there was nobody else to blame for the mistakes I had made. *"C'est la vie,"* I said to myself.

I wondered why my attempts to be successful had always ended in failure and tried to make excuses - I could find many but that was all they were. My obsession to speak properly again had taken precedence over everything else in my life. As a result, I had not taken enough time and trouble to sort out other areas of my life. It occurred to me that money was not the main importance in life and that there were many ways in which one could be "successful." If success was going to come my way, I knew I was not going to be successful in business, not with so many other preoccupations on my mind. I wondered if I was being honest or merely making excuses for having spent a large part of my compensation. Besides, my most cherished wish was to mix with people without being rebuffed or insulted.

The next day, I went to hospital to have my wrist examined, but the doctors just gave me painkillers. Their responses no longer frustrated me. I merely greeted them with apathy, as I had come to accept that they could not do anything to mend it.

I continued to go to the Job Centre and was willing to apply for every vacancy on the board, but there were rarely any appropriate positions available. Whenever there was a suitable vacancy on the display board, I would always enquire about it, but I would frustratingly hear that the job was no longer vacant.

It was clear that I had too much time on my hands to think about my problems. I needed to be active and to be with people to prevent my worrying excessively.

In September 1979, I enrolled as a part-time mature student at Childwall College of Further Education. On the enrolment form I had to state my choice of prospective career. Initially, I was undecided as to which profession I wanted to enter. My future had rarely been in my thoughts, since it was daunting for me to think about it. I did eventually decide to become a school teacher. Ideally, I would have liked to work with deaf and dumb children. This would mean going into higher education, which required three G.C.E.'s at A level.

I decided to study French, Sociology and Economics A level over a period of two years. Although my double-vision prevented my reading at length, I could persevere with a textbook, since it would generally involve reading only a few pages at a time. Reading was tedious for me, but my vision was slowly improving.

Returning to college at the age of thirty was not an easy decision to make, especially since I had to contend with a speech problem. My words were not as slurred as they used to be, but my breathing had become much more erratic. As a result, I could only speak a few words before having to take a fresh breath.

Most of the students were aged between eighteen and twenty. Having recently left school, many of them had gone to college because they were unable to find work. Much to my surprise, once they had become accustomed to my speech, most of them seemed to accept me as an equal. There remained a minority who did make cruel remarks about my impediment, but I tried not to let them see it bothered me.

Within a matter of months, my breathing worsened and other students would often comment on it. Although my speech had improved since the car accident, it seemed to have reached a point where I ceased to make any further progress. My breathlessness seriously affected my concentration when studying alone. During lessons, I could cope with the coursework but my concentration deteriorated rapidly on leaving the College. On many occasions, I sat at home reading a book, with every intention of doing some revision, but soon after beginning, I would find myself thinking about my breathing. It affected everything I attempted to do or say, and it seemed to be constantly on my mind.

I tried to dismiss such negative ideas from my mind, but it was difficult. When in the presence of other students I would purposely act in a flamboyant and comical way, since I wanted to give the impression that I was content with my life and did not have a care in the world. It was merely an attempt to fool other people, but I could not fool myself.

Whenever I was alone my thoughts would terrify me. I would often be lying in bed when my breathing problem would rear its head again. On occasions, I would stay awake for most of the night, afraid to sleep in case I never woke up.

During the Christmas vacation, a sharp pain in my right wrist suddenly awoke me in the middle of the night. I must have been lying awkwardly and twisted it as I turned in my sleep. "What next!" I said to myself. Although I had experienced the pain many times before, it had never been so bad. It was so acute that I was about to phone for an ambulance but decided against it, since I did not want to make a fuss. I tried to get back to sleep but could not as the pain was too severe. I lay there in agony thinking of my lot.

As soon as dawn broke, I went to the nearest hospital in the hope that a different doctor would be able to help me. After having my wrist x-rayed, the doctor informed me that he could not relieve the pain due to the complexity of the operation carried out on it originally. He merely gave me painkillers and told me to report to the Infirmary.

Fortunately, my regular appointment at the Infirmary was the next day. Rather than inconvenience the hospital staff, I decided to put up with the pain for a day longer.

At the infirmary the following day, a student doctor attended to me. At first, he appeared very concerned about my wrist and immediately sent me to have it x-rayed. On my return, his attitude seemed to have changed. He was abrupt and told me that the senior doctor wanted to see me

I was flabbergasted. What had I done to offend him? Was it my speech or something else? I could not understand it, as I had always made an effort to be polite.

Eventually, the senior doctor arrived. I could tell by the look on his face that he was not pleased to see me.

"What's the matter with you now, Mr. Lever?" he asked, condescendingly raising his eyebrows.

"It's my wrist, Doctor," I babbled nervously, "it's playing up again."

"Look, Mr. Lever, I'm sure your wrist can't be that painful! I'm tired of seeing you come here about such a paltry matter. Do you think we have nothing better to do than to treat you over some minor injury?"

I was stunned. It was hard for me to believe what I had heard him say. I felt degraded and as if I was purposely wasting his time and money. My throat suddenly went dry and I knew that my speech would sound pitiful. I said nothing and merely walked out of the cubicle.

He called me back, probably realizing that he had been wrong, but

I ignored him. I returned home and lay on my bed thinking about what he had said. I wondered if my imagination was playing tricks with me, or if the pain in my wrist was severe enough to justify going to hospital. I knew the answer immediately.

That evening, I thought of writing a letter to Professor Bentley, my consultant, to tell him what had taken place at the Infirmary. However, I decided to think about it for a day, since I did not want to write in anger. I wrote to Professor Bentley the next day and informed him of the developments at the Infirmary. I told him that it was frustrating going to the Infirmary every week and asked if there was any way he could mend my wrist.

The next day, his secretary telephoned to arrange an appointment for me to see him at Broadgreen Hospital.

I attended as arranged and while waiting outside the Professor's office, it struck me that the atmosphere in this hospital seemed more caring than that in the Infirmary.

The Professor apologized for the behaviour of the senior doctor and said that he had good news for me. He explained that he expected to be able to perform a relatively new operation on my wrist in six month's time. It would involve breaking the joint connecting my arm to my hand so as to remove the metal pin and screws from my wrist. A piece of bone taken from my left hip would then be grafted onto the joint. Within a year, the bone-graft should have grown, connecting my arm to my hand - thus "freezing" the joint. Although I would still be unable to bend it, I would no longer be subjected to so much pain and discomfort.

I was ecstatic and felt six months was not too long to wait, especially considering the ten years that I had already endured the problem. My future looked much rosier, although there was still my breathing problem to consider - the only thing to do was to try to put it to the back of my mind.

However, my breathlessness did have me baffled. At my request, my doctor had repeatedly examined my lungs but had always told me that my chest was fine. I made another effort to tackle my doctor. I had to build up my courage to ask him to examine me, since I was sure he would discover I had a terminal illness. However, after he told me that my lungs were "as clean as a whistle," I did not know what to think. Initially, I was relieved and thought my imagination must certainly be playing tricks on me.

That night in bed, I suddenly realized that nothing had changed, when I was attacked by a bout of breathlessness. My breathing was often troublesome when I was lying down and attempting to read a book. There were times when I had to jump up and run to the window to get fresh air, but, as soon as I stood up, I was able to breathe normally again. The only explanation was my imagination, but it was difficult to accept.

Frequently, I suffered from a heavy cold and a sore throat, which only aggravated my speech problems. I was feeling lonely and afraid for my future. Ultimately, my work and attendance at College suffered.

I decided to claim Sickness Benefit during the six months I was waiting for the operation. The N.H.S. granted me permission to attend the College as a part-time student; it was more convenient, since I did not have to report regularly at the Labour Exchange. Even though my claim was accepted, I still remembered the humiliation of my previous encounter, and never applied for any of the other benefits to which I was rightly due.

In May 1980, I was admitted into Broadgreen Hospital to have the operation on my right wrist. I had every confidence in Professor Bentley and was looking forward to the operation. If my wrist was mended, it would dramatically change my life for the better.

I was put into a large ward. Although the other patients seemed very friendly, I decided not to be too familiar with them until they learned about my circumstances through the hospital grape vine. The problem of my speech had become so inhibiting that I was always fearful of speaking. Nevertheless, my gregarious nature always seemed to overcome such worries.

The next morning, I was the first patient to go to the operating theatre. It suited me fine, since I wanted to get it over and done; I detested having to wait for other patients to return from the theatre.

When I awoke from the anaesthetic after the operation, my mind immediately recalled my operation in Salford Royal Infirmary. Again my right arm was in plaster and held up in a sling above my head. Protruding the end of the plaster were my thumb and four fingers - again they resembled bananas and were black and blue in colour. It had been difficult to move about in bed after the first operation on my wrist - this time, it was far worse. I had the added difficulty of being unable to move onto my left side, since the bone graft had come from my left hip and the incision was very tender.

When the Sister came to see me, she was very concerned about my breathing. During the operation, the anaesthetist discovered that I was not receiving enough oxygen. As a result, the operation was halted while the theatre staff tried to discover what was wrong. Although unsuccessful in their search, they completed the operation while prudently monitoring my respiration.

Later, the anaesthetist came to see me in the ward. His concern became apparent by the many questions he asked about the illnesses I had suffered since my birth. Unfortunately, he remained baffled when I was unable to provide information about the matter. Nevertheless, for the following four weeks I received a supply of richly oxygenated air at regular intervals during the day.

At first, I did not connect this to my frequent bouts of breathlessness. I had assumed that the doctors would have noticed if anything was seriously wrong with my breathing and would get to the bottom of what was causing the trouble.

My wrist, hand and fingers were very painful at first. To make matters worse, when the doctor removed the stitches from the incision on my hip it had still not healed. It was very tender and constantly oozed with pus. Each day, a nurse would dress it, but it did not seem to make any difference. Nonetheless, I was feeling much better although confined to my bed for four weeks after the operation.

I enjoyed being in hospital - not simply because of the attention given to me, but because of the opportunity to meet so many different people. The other patients in the ward were in hospital to have surgical operations, so the majority knew what it was like to suffer constant physical pain. Consequently, they were understanding. Nevertheless, it was not until they heard about my speech problem that I would be able to begin to relax in their company.

It was not too difficult for me to act flamboyantly, and the other patients seemed to enjoy my humour. Sometimes they would laugh with me, while on other occasions they would laugh at me. That did not bother me, since I wanted to make people happy.

Although I enjoyed playing the clown, I was merely putting on an act. Little did they know that I was being cheerful only to prevent my lapsing into silence and letting my worries come back to haunt me.

I was finally discharged after spending six weeks in hospital. A district nurse visited me daily for a further ten days to redress the incision on my hip, which seemed to be taking its time to heal. In addition, I had to wear a plaster on my arm for almost a year after that.

It was not until I came out of hospital that I realized why I had enjoyed being hospitalized; I felt secure there. What was more important, the other patients did not reject or insult me because of my speech and it was so much easier to relax.

My mother was living alone for most of the time, as Colin was working abroad on contract to various aircraft companies. She had been very caring and attentive to me after my accident, so I thought I might be able to go some way towards repaying her. I sold my house and moved back to live with her, two months after coming out of hospital.

It was good to be living back home again. Although it meant sacrificing some of my independence, it spared my mother the loneliness. As usual, she treated me well and never seemed to stop doing housework of some kind.

I did not want my family, especially my mother, to know about my respiratory problems. I had caused her enough heartache in the past and certainly did not want to cause her any more.

My breathing was continuing to trouble me, and I could not help being apathetic about my future. It had got to the stage where I did not care what happened to me. Convinced that I did not have long to live, I just wanted to spend what remained of my life doing what I enjoyed - talking to people.

I continued to go into the coffee bars and large stores in the city centre to practise speaking. Although rejected by most strangers, I would have very interesting conversations with some people regardless of their class, age, sex or race. It did not worry me to whom I spoke. In my opinion, we are all human beings, and, since each of us has different experiences, we can all benefit from each other.

Since I was still apprehensive about the possible reaction to my speech, it was often difficult to begin a conversation with a stranger, even if we were sitting at the same table. Eventually, I developed a ploy that rarely failed me; I would catch their attention by dropping something as if by accident, while pretending to curse myself in the process. The stranger would usually smile at my apparent misfortune, which would give me the opportunity to start a conversation.

People would usually begin by asking me about the heavy plaster on my wrist. Wishing to justify myself as usual, I would tell them about my car accident. To my great surprise, I found that once they had learned the details of the accident, they would show genuine concern and even tell me they admired me. Their words of praise often embarrassed me, so I would quickly change the subject. Sometimes they would end up telling me about their own problems in turn. I often found that people would trust me with their most intimate problems and my advice would often be of help to them - or so they told me.

I returned to the College in November to continue the A level course. My favourite subject was French and it became a great distraction from my problems. I even planned to spend some time at a French university once the plaster had been removed.

Early in the New Year, although my breathing had not improved, I was still learning to cope with the inexplicable spasms of breathlessness. I was slowly coming to terms with the idea that I might always have impaired speech, although I was reluctant to accept this notion.

My old problem of rejection by strangers was now occurring with increasing regularity. Again, strangers would accuse me of being drunk and treat me as a third-class citizen. Each time it happened, it would be a stark reminder of the days when I came to expect such cruel remarks. It was the reappearance of the nightmare I had previously dispelled from my mind.

At the time, my speech problem was not so much caused by the paralysis, although this did have some relevance; the principal cause was my breathlessness, which usually depended on the specific activity I was doing at any time. This first became apparent when I was trying to have a conversation with a student as we were walking home from the college. I was gasping for breath and trying to speak at the same time. Consequently, my slurred speech was more evident.

I coped with the spasms of breathlessness the only way I knew how, by making a conscious effort to be cheerful while still trying to push the problem to the back of my mind. There did not seem to be an alternative, since my doctor would tell me it was caused by my imagination. I was terribly confused.

To make matters worse, it became apparent that I was not sleeping as well as when I was living in Gateacre. Sometimes, I would have a sleepless night. The following morning, my blankets would be in a heap at the bottom of the bed, and my three pillows would be on the floor. The lack of sleep would further affect my speech which was remarked upon by the students and lecturers at the College.

There were times when I felt too tired to make the effort to try to speak properly and I would sound very slurred. It was as though I was fighting a losing battle. Whenever depressed, I would try to recall the patients in Winwick Psychiatric Hospital and remember that I was lucky to be alive. That would help me to forget my problems, although it seemed my subconscious would not.

Chapter 20

My Head In The Sand

At the beginning of June 1981, I attended the hospital to have the plaster removed from my wrist. I had longed for this day to arrive, because my wrist had been the cause of so many disappointments during the past eleven and a half years. Fortunately, the operation was deemed a success.

I was overjoyed to finally put this problem behind me. I thanked Professor Bentley sincerely and apologized for having caused him so much trouble over the previous years.

"Don't worry," he told me, "I only wish we had more patients like you."

As I was opening the door to leave, I remember turning back and looking at him. "I really appreciate what you've done for me," I said as clearly as I could. "By the way, please don't be offended, but I hope I never see you in here again!" He looked at me and laughed heartily.

A week after being discharged from the hospital, I telephoned Grenoble University in France to ask if there was a place on their French language course, specially designed for foreign students. Fortunately, there was still a place. Since the course was to start early in July, I decided to leave the following day. I had already prepared my luggage and sorted out my debts. It was only a matter of signing off the Sickness Benefit register, arranging with my bank to send money to me each month and doing some last minute shopping.

With my rucksack on my back, I arrived excitedly at London's Victoria Station late in the evening to catch the overnight boat-train. I arrived in Paris early the next morning.

Although eager to arrive in Grenoble, I decided to spend a night at the youth hostel in Paris. As it was the holiday season, there were many foreign tourists at the hostel so I had plenty of company.

The other guests were all younger than me and were from different parts of the world. Fortunately, none of them were able to speak English fluently, so my speech brought no unwanted comment. The atmosphere was very friendly, and, since a young Swede had his guitar with him, we all had a good sing-song. I mouthed the words as my voice sounded awful. I met a German student who was studying sociology at Munich University. She was travelling around France, comparing the different lifestyles and customs of the Parisian worker with the worker in the provinces. We had an interesting conversation about the Third World. By the end of the evening, we were both convinced that we knew how to change the world.

The next morning, I took the train to Grenoble. I was very impressed by the comfort and service provided by the S.N.C.F., the French railway company. It was far superior to that provided on British trains.

Grenoble was a very modern town. Although many of its buildings appeared new or renovated, occasionally an older building would stand out proudly to boast its cultural heritage.

Not far from the city centre, the space-age bubble car of the *téléphérique* transported many sightseers above part of the town to the old *Bastille*. Situated on the top of a hill, the old fortress looks down and across the surrounding countryside. The view was magnificent especially at dusk.

The University of Grenoble was one of the largest in France and catered for over 32,000 students. The summer courses, *Les Cours d'Étés,* were specifically designed for foreign students wishing to learn or to improve their French.

On arriving at the University the next day, I enrolled as a full-time student, following the Language, Literature and Civilisation Course. I decided to wait until the beginning of October to enrol for the Autumn term. If the University was not to my liking, I would later go somewhere else, probably to Paris.

I would have to take an examination. Usually, the mere thought of sitting an examination would terrify me, since I would relate them to my future - something I dreaded thinking about. However, I did not mind on this occasion, since it was merely to grade the level of my French. I was allocated a class in the fourth grade and was delighted, since the fifth grade was for very advanced speakers of French.

The other students arrived during the following week. They hailed from many countries, including Argentina, Australia, China, Japan, America and the Soviet Union. No sooner had they arrived than the campus suddenly swarmed with Tunisian and Algerian male students. I had not noticed them before, but they seemed to come from nowhere to charm the female students. They made their conquests. I remained in the background while my confidence ebbed away.

The intensive language lessons were from 8 o'clock in the morning until noon. Usually they consisted of grammatical exercises, as well as audio work in the language laboratories. There was no tuition in the early afternoon until half past four when there was a two hour lecture on French literature and culture.

On most afternoons during the week, I spent my free time in the town centre, drinking coffee and speaking to people. I would usually sit outside the cafe on the corner of *Place Victor Hugo,* opposite *Place Grennette.* Many of the local people, who frequented the cafe during their lunch-break, were only too willing to help me with my French. Later, I would sit and chat to tourists. I would spend hours relaxing in the sunshine, while making one cup of coffee last all afternoon.

My breathing was easier when I was sitting in a relaxed environment, although the paralysis in my mouth, tongue and jaw still meant that my speech was slow. Since I was still not completely fluent in French, I would make a special effort to pronounce each word correctly, while trying to give people the impression that I was recalling a certain word, while, in reality, I would be taking a fresh breath. As I was obviously a foreigner, people would willingly make allowances for the slow rate at which I spoke. It was not therefore always evident that I had a speech impediment.

When feeling very confident, I would speak to anyone sitting near me and would be delighted that people could understand me fully. My confidence grew the more people I met, which encouraged me to speak to as many strangers as possible. I soon found myself asking questions, even though I already knew the answers simply to strike up a conversation.

On more than one occasion, I became too confident. This became obvious whenever I tried to tell an English joke in French, since I rarely received the expected response. For once I would have liked to believe it was simply because of my speech, but I fear it may well have been because of my unusual sense of humour.

The University buildings were modern and set in many acres of land. *Berlioz*, the *logement* where I was living, was only one of a number of residences on the campus. The accommodation was basic but cheap and the meals were subsidized by the French authorities. I soon became friendly with the *concierge* - resident caretaker - and his wife, who would often invite me to their home on Sundays to have a meal with their family.

I also met Sylvie, a lovely young French woman, who was single and in her late twenties. She worked in the students' accommodation office at the University. Since we had always conversed in French, it did not occur to me that she spoke any English. However, about a month after we had met, I was explaining something to her in French and could not find the right word. She immediately told me in English the word I was trying to remember - I was flabbergasted. Apparently, she had spent eighteen months in England and could speak perfect English.

In the evenings, most students would sit on the grass outside a selected *logement* and have a good sing-song. The Mexicans would don their *ponchos* and *sombreros* and play their guitars, while the rest of us sang along with them. It was great entertainment and good for strengthening my voice, although not so good for those who could hear me. At first, only a few songs were familiar to me, but I eventually learnt many more, and everybody knew the Beatles' songs regardless of their nationality.

Living in the room to the right of mine was Giorgio, a young major in the Italian army, who was serving with the N.A.T.O. forces. He was very friendly and not only spoke perfect English, but also knew many American, Australian and British colloquialisms. Jokingly, he used to call me "a bloody Limey." I often wondered how it was he spoke English so well, until discovering that his mother taught English in Milan, his home town. He stayed at the University for two months, during which time we had many entertaining evenings in Grenoble. He was a fine companion.

In the room to my left was Richard, a tall bespectacled teacher from Eire. He was a giant of a man and full of fun and laughter. In his true Irish spirit, he had ridden from Calais to Grenoble on an old bike. I found this difficult to believe when he told me, until Sylvie took me in her car one day to watch the competitors in *La Tour de France,* cycling through L'Alp d'Huez, in the Alps. The country lanes were crowded with spectators shouting encouragement to the cyclists as they passed by. On the return journey, who did we see pedalling for all he was worth up a steep gradient and wearing his own "yellow jersey?" - Richard. We stopped to ask him if he wanted to put his bike on the car's roof-rack and have a lift to the campus with us, but he insisted on cycling back.

Richard was taking the fifth-grade course. He greatly impressed me, because he spoke French at such a fast speed and with a very convincing accent. As my knowledge of French improved, I noticed that he often used some words in a different context to what I had been taught to use. On a few occasions, I told him about this, not with the intention of criticizing him, but simply because I wanted to learn more about French. However, he would merely deny it. He must have thought that I was deliberately trying to trip him up, because one day he took me aside and asked me to keep a secret. He told me that he was a teacher - not of French but of Mathematics. His sole qualification in French was the Irish equivalent of an A level, taken ten years earlier. When I asked him about his accent he told me that all he did to impress the other students was to chuck his arms in the air every so often and say, *"Mon Dieux!* or *"Non, alors!"* When I told him it was a wonder nobody else had noticed, he laughed aloud and said he had the luck of the Irish.

Some of the Saudi Arabian and Turkish students thought I had an hilarious sense of humour. For many years, I often used the phrases *C'est la vie* - that's life - and *Tant pis* - so much the worse - to describe many unfortunate events that happened. I used them so frequently that some of these students would place bets amongst themselves to see how long it would be before I used one of these phrases. As soon as I did, they would erupt into laughter.

My room at Grenoble University
(left to right) Ali, Peter, Janet, Julie and me

On most weekends, there were trips to other parts of the Dauphiné and a variety of regions of France. I visited Chartreuse and Annecy. The scenery was breathtaking.

We were given a few days break at the end of each month. On one such occasion, I decided to go by train to Perpignan, a town close to the Spanish border and near to the Mediterranean Sea. When the train stopped at Narbonne a young lady in her early twenties boarded and sat opposite me. She was petite and very attractive with long auburn hair.

I wanted to begin a conversation with her but was rather nervous and did not know what to say at first. I decided that it would be best to break the ice by saying something amusing. I knew a well-known French saying, which is often used when one does not speak French very well, so I decided to use it. *"Excusez moi, Madamoiselle, mais bien que je lise et j'écrive français, je parle français comme un Basque espagnol."* When translated it means: "Excuse me, Miss, but, although I can read and write French, I speak French like a Spanish Basque." She smiled at me but then suddenly looked annoyed and told me that she was a Basque. I felt awful and immediately apologized. She started laughing and told me she too was only joking.

While I was in Perpignan, I stayed two days at the youth hostel. The weather was glorious so I spent most of my time at Canet Plage, a Mediterranean resort. On the final day, I left the hostel early in the morning and made my way to the deserted beach, where I lay down to rest. I fell asleep and awoke an hour later to find that the beach was no longer deserted. I propped myself up on my elbows and looked around me. I was instantly surprised at what I saw - two females on my right and three on my left were topless sunbathers. "Just my luck," I said to myself, cursing my misfortune. I am certainly not a prude and would usually have been more than delighted, but not this time - they were pensioners!

One evening, I was sitting in my room, when a Frenchman knocked on the door to ask if I would do some translating for him. He was a translator by profession and needed a native English speaker to translate a tour guide for the visitors to the local nuclear power station. I readily agreed since I merely had to "translate" his broken English into smooth flowing language - it was more difficult than it sounded. I worked for him for a further six weeks, earning 1,000 francs for each page I corrected.

I got on very well with the other students at the University at first. There was no mention of my speech - or at least I did not hear any comments about it. However, after a few weeks, the lecturers encouraged us to hold debates amongst ourselves. Unfortunately, some of the arguments would become heated. I would forget my troublesome breathing and try to speak as fast as I could and to lengthen my sentences. Inevitably, I would begin to babble and my confidence would suffer.

As October drew nearer, my breathing worsened and the restless nights were affecting my speech to such an extent that some students had begun to make fun of me. I would get annoyed but they would say they were only joking - joking at my expense. My pride was dented and I eventually admitted to myself that I was losing the battle. I did not enrol for the autumn course at the University but decided to return home instead.

Sitting on the ferry, I recalled the many interesting times I had enjoyed in the company of my fellow students and the French people I had met. Despite the common myth that the French are very unfriendly towards the British, none of the many French people I met ever showed any animosity towards me. I found they were very friendly and sociable. I would very much like to spend more time in France one day.

Chapter 21

Apathy

I returned home from Grenoble in October 1981. Although very content with the way my French had progressed, I realized it was time to take stock of my situation again. I felt hypocritical for having advised other people to face facts and to live in the present, since this was something I was now refusing to do myself.

Although dearly wanting to speak French fluently, my true reason for going to France was to get away from my ever growing problems. I was tired of the way strangers would look upon me as somehow less human than themselves. I was sick of being wrongly accused of drunkenness and sick of my breathing problems.

I would often lie awake most of the night, trying to fall asleep. Although exhausted, my breathing problem haunted me when I was in bed. I would ask myself what I had done to be plagued by such illness and bad luck.

Having spent most of the remaining compensation on going to Grenoble University, my situation had not changed for the better. I may well have been foolish with my money, but it did not perturb me too much, since my overriding ambition was to speak properly again. The compensation had been for my future welfare, but since I believed my future would be short-lived, money was the least of my worries. My mind was in such turmoil that no amount of money would have solved my problems. I did not want to think of what lay ahead of me.

It was evident to me that my respiratory problem was related to my lungs and was terminal. I again sought the advice of my doctor. After examining me reluctantly, he told me that my lungs were fine. He went on to comment that it was only natural that I was plagued with illnesses, after having such a serious accident. He also implied that my overactive imagination was probably the real cause of the trouble. I tried to convince myself that my illness was psychosomatic but it proved difficult. I did not have any friends in whom to confide and did not want to tell my troubles to my mother - she was a widowed pensioner, and I did not want to cause her any further distress.

Even though continuing to visit the Job Centres, I rarely had an interview and was never given a job. I would always go in the morning in a cheerful mood, hoping that it was going to be my lucky day - but it never was. I can remember the many occasions when I searched on the vacancy boards. Some of the advertised vacancies were on the boards for months, even though the positions had been filled many weeks earlier. Occasionally, there would be a recently posted vacancy that was suitable for me. I would go to the desk excitedly and give the clerk the reference number. After sitting down, I would prepare the answers to the questions that I expected the clerk to ask me. All too often, however, the clerk would return to tell me the position had already been filled - if not then there always seemed to be some reason to disqualify me.

Still believing my illness was terminal and that I did not have long to live, I was becoming increasingly apathetic. There seemed to be no respite from my worries. It was sickening to remember my many failed attempts to be successful. I no longer cared about my future and felt my life was one long heartache. It had now become far too easy for me to expect and accept failure. Strangers were again rejecting me because of my speech. It was soul-destroying and so frustrating.

I needed something to occupy my time and my thoughts, but what could I do? After spending two months on the dole, I decided to become a part-time student again. Although still registered for Unemployment Benefit, I was allowed to attend a College for twenty hours per week. I enrolled at the North East Liverpool Technical College to study at A level in French, Sociology and Economics again. The other students were friendly, although I could sense they were remarking to one another about my speech, when I first met them.

During the lessons, I would listen to the lecturer and fully understand his meaning. In the Sociology lesson, for instance, we would discuss different aspects of society. Since my experience of life was greater than my fellow students, I would often contribute to the lesson by giving examples of real life situations.

When talking to the other students, I would try to show them that I was not allowing my speech impediment to get the better of me. In an attempt to hide my insecurity I would always act confidently. At times, I disliked myself intensely and would feel miserable, especially since I had lost so much of the confidence I used to have.

My concentration was still letting me down. I would sit at the desk in my room and attempt to do some revision. No matter how I tried, my mind would not be able to focus on one subject for very long, before I would find myself thinking about my breathing. As time went by, it was becoming increasingly difficult to force myself out of my states of depression. Nevertheless, whenever I was in the company of others, I always managed to hide my personal problems.

In March 1983, I decided to apply to Liverpool Polytechnic. I elected to read for a B.A. degree in Social Studies, as I realized that my French was at a high enough level to carry out a fluent conversation on most subjects. My acceptance as a mature student at the Polytechnic was conditional on handing in a 1,500-word essay on the possibility of a social scientist remaining objective while carrying out social research. Later, I attended an interview and was accepted to begin the three year course in the following September.

Although the Polytechnic accepted my application, I still decided to sit the three A level examinations at the College. I was only able to write slowly due to the injuries sustained in the accident, so, after providing the appropriate medical evidence, the examining board allowed me extra time during the examinations. Despite my inability to concentrate, my coursework during the term had always been above average. My lecturers fully expected me to do well in the exams, and I felt sure I would at first, but, as the date of the examination drew nearer, it became obvious that my concentration would let me down. All I could do was hope that once I was in the examination room, my adrenalin would begin working and not allow my mind to stray.

However, at the beginning of each of the three examinations, as soon as I sat down and read the first question my mind would begin to roam. I would sit there in a trance and my confidence would begin to ebb. All I could think of at first was my erratic breathing. From time to time, I would snap out of my stupor but would be too tense to concentrate on answering questions. The purpose of the examination was to contribute towards my future - a future that terrified me. It was as if my mind would refuse to concentrate on anything that was on my horizon. Eventually, I would begin to think of the many failures that had occurred in my life. Towards the end of the examination, I would write desperately about the car accident in the hope that the examiner would take pity on me. Consequently, I did not pass any of the three examinations. Although pretending to be startled by this depressing news, I admitted to myself that I had stood little chance of passing.

At the end of September 1983, I began the three-year degree course in Social Studies at Liverpool Polytechnic. For many years, I had taken a great interest in the social sciences and was looking forward to the course while praying my concentration would not let me down in the examinations. If I had not thought that my future was so bleak, I would have trained to become a social worker.

The Social Studies course run by the Polytechnic was ideal for me. All the students on the course had to study methodology - the science of collecting, collating and interpreting the different forms of social data. In addition, there was a choice of studying four of the following subjects; Economics, Politics, Sociology, Human Geography and History. I decided not to study History.

I found Economics interesting as we discussed Monetarism and Keynesianism as well as the economic implications of Capitalism, Socialism and Communism. In Politics we studied the theories behind the main political systems, while we discussed the major changes in society since the arrival of the Industrial Revolution in Sociology. This included topics such as the Family, Education, Deviance, and Work.

Human Geography focused on urban problems and the Third World, which interested me particularly.

There were other mature students on the course, but I was the only one in my tutorial group. The rest of the students had recently left school. They were friendly when we first met, but as time passed, I found myself excluded from their conversations. It was difficult for me to mix with them, as there seemed to be a barrier between us. I often felt isolated and therefore became nervous when speaking to them, which aggravated my speech problem.

Unfortunately, I was partly to blame for this, since I would always be too conscious of my breathing and ultimately my speech. Embarrassed, I often found myself speaking without thinking about what I was saying. I would often crack jokes, which, because of my slurred speech, nobody understood. Inevitably, I made enemies as well as friends.

The Social Studies Department was in the same building as Modern Languages. Since I could speak French and had attended Grenoble University, I found it much easier to mix with the language students than with those of Social Studies.

In particular, I got to know four girls, who were each aged eighteen. I do not think I could have met four nicer people. They were reading for a degree in French and Spanish and were from Merseyside, apart from Gerry. She was from Northern Ireland and, as most of the Irish people I have met, she had a wonderful personality. Ros was very genuine, despite her "way out" hairstyle that resembled a blob of candy-floss. Katie was always cheerful, despite the often troubled relationship she had with her boyfriend. Fiona, the quietest of the four, always seemed to be deep in thought.

After a few months, I found it increasingly difficult to concentrate on studying because my worries about my breathing distracted me more and more from my work. Despite my fervent attempts to concentrate, I soon found myself falling behind. All that seemed to interest me was talking to the language students. They had accepted me and never seemed to mind the way I sounded.

As time passed, my breathing continued to worsen. I complained again to my doctor. It worried me so much that I even asked him if I had cancer. He examined my chest and declared again that my lungs were as clean as a whistle. It disappointed me because I wanted to hear that there was something wrong with me. I was tired of living in this world of uncertainty and convinced that there was something seriously wrong with me, but nobody seemed to listen to my pleas. They simply believed I was suffering from ailments related to the car crash, fourteen years previously. But what could I do, when I had repeatedly been told by my doctor that my lungs were fine. I could only wonder again if my imagination was the culprit. I dearly wanted to believe his explanation, but my mind would not accept it. It seemed that the doctor had made a mistake, but who was I to question his diagnosis?

I began to feel lazy and often too tired to walk even a short distance. My shirts no longer fitted me, as the collars were too tight - my neck size had increased from 15 to 16 inches in recent years and I had gained two stones in weight to make me fourteen stones. It was hard for me to understand why I was gaining weight, since I had stopped using salt and sugar on my meals, and my mother had always removed the fat from the meat before cooking it. Nor did I eat an excessive amount of starchy or sugary food.

Something had to be done, so I took up running again and would jog two or three miles twice a week. It did not make any difference - apart from nearly killing me in the process due to my breathing. I remember my embarrassment at having to stop to get my breath back while gasping desperately for air. All too often a passer-by would stop and stare at me curiously. Ironically, I had to give up running in the end for health reasons.

I still felt my body needed extra exercise, so I took up gardening. It was not as physically demanding, and I would be able to reap the fruits of my hard work. I disapproved of the chemicals in fertilizers and insecticides used in gardens, since they were potentially harmful to the environment. I borrowed a book from the library and read up on organic gardening, built a compost heap and dug up the back garden.

One day while in the garden, I discovered that I would begin wheezing whenever my head was lowered and my chin was touching my chest. I would start gasping for air and have to stand up straight to breathe properly, otherwise I would have collapsed.

When the time came to take the examinations at the Polytechnic, I was tested orally since my writing speed was slow due to my co-ordination. My tutor had very thoughtfully arranged this concession for me, when I had begun the course. However, my breathing had greatly deteriorated in the meantime and my speech had suffered accordingly. Nevertheless, I did not have the heart to tell him that I preferred a written examination, since he had gone to so much trouble for me.

During the examinations, the lecturers were very patient with me and gave me every chance to answer the questions, without breaking the examination regulations. I tried to concentrate on the question but it was an impossible task. My preoccupation with my breathing problems and my previous failures in life constantly interrupted my train of thought. Despite my attempts to dismiss these worries from my mind and not to be embarrassed about my speech, I failed the examination miserably.

I had not told any of my fellow students or the lecturers about my difficulty in maintaining concentration. I knew they would probably have shrugged their shoulders and have said that everyone had the same problem. Although I was certain their problem was different to mine, I decided not to say anything about it in the end.

The Polytechnic allowed me to resit the examinations three months later in September. During the summer vacation, I tried to revise but was still unable to concentrate. When I sat the examinations again, my concentration let me down badly. It was a terrible ordeal waiting for the results to be posted on the notice board outside the faculty building. While praying that I had somehow passed, I turned cold on discovering I had failed again.

I felt so inadequate, especially when meeting my fellow students and telling them my results. Nevertheless, the Polytechnic allowed me to take the first-year of the course again. My self-esteem, which was already low before receiving my results, now reached rock bottom.

I realized that the odds were stacked high against my passing and was convinced my failure had nothing to do with my ability. It was clear to me that the state of my worried mind was responsible, but how was I to convince the lecturers of my troubles, when my doctor did not believe me? I had revised the course-content well enough, but the problem was my concentration, especially during examinations. It was terribly frustrating for me, especially as I had helped to explain some of the more difficult theories in Sociology to those students who had not studied the subject before. I dreaded having to go through the first year of the course again. Even though I had found the course interesting and enlightening the previous year, I knew it would be terribly boring the second time around.

The new intake of students into the first-year was very friendly. Although surprised when first hearing my speech, they soon got used to it and treated me as a human being at first. Most were strangers to Liverpool, so I helped them to settle down during the first few weeks.

I was determined to pass the examinations the following June. It would be an uphill struggle, since I had tried my best the last time but had still failed nonetheless. I decided to try to put the matter to the back of my mind and hope for the best. That may sound like a very foolish strategy to pass an examination but what else could I do?

One night during the Christmas vacation, I was lying in bed with three pillows under my head. During the early hours of the morning, I was unable to sleep due to my erratic breathing.

My mother overheard my wheezing, coughing and gasping and came into my bedroom to see if she could help. She looked down at me and asked how I was feeling. I will never forget what I said to her in reply. "Mother, I haven't got long to live." I immediately felt awful at my lack of tact and realized she would now constantly worry about me. On previous occasions when she heard my wheezing, she told me I should go to see the doctor, but I always tried to allay her fears by telling her I merely a bad chest cold.

I reflected on the past fifteen years of my life since the accident and realized that I had never stopped trying to be successful but had only failed. However, my perspective on life had generally changed, and the need for "success" no longer obsessed me. All I wanted was to live the rest of my life in peace. My life still seemed to be passing me by, while I was going nowhere. It was lonely for me in my confused state. I believed I was dying.

One day, while reaching up to get some seeds from the top shelf in the garden shed, I suddenly began to gasp for air. In a state of panic, I lost my balance and fortunately fell on some bean-netting. I sat up and immediately my breathing improved. It completely mystified me.

From the Easter term through to the examinations in June, I revised with a group of other students from my tutorial group. I had prepared well and fully believed that my determination to pass this time would ensure my success.

However, my problems were continuing to mount. A week before the start of the examinations, after many sleepless nights, the anxiety and uncertainty became unbearable. I decided to ask my doctor to arrange for me to have my chest x-rayed at the hospital, even though I was afraid of what the results might reveal. Despite my apprehension, I decided that if I was dying it would be better to know how long I had to live than to continue living in fear.

I went to my doctor's surgery and this time saw his wife, who was a member of his practice. I asked her to examine my chest in the hope that she would find something that other doctors had missed. Using her stethoscope, she examined my chest and declared that there was nothing wrong with my lungs. Upon hearing of my request to have my chest x-rayed, she chuckled and again repeated that she could find nothing wrong with my breathing. Although relieved to hear her positive diagnosis, I realized that my doubts would still linger in my mind. I would not be satisfied until my chest had been x-rayed. She tried to change my mind, but I was resolute since it had taken great courage on my part to ask for such a thorough examination of my lungs. Much to her annoyance, she gave in and handed me the form for the hospital.

The next day I went to the hospital to have the my chest x-rayed. To my surprise, I was attended to straight away. Afterwards, the nurse told me to report to my doctor in a fortnight's time to get the results.

When I was walking out of the hospital, my feelings were mixed. I was glad to have done something positive, although I was apprehensive of the results. One way or the other I would discover if my illness was merely a figment of my imagination or whether I had been justified for repeatedly complaining to my doctor for many years.

Since I would soon be sitting the examinations again, I decided to do my utmost to forget my erratic breathing - if that was possible.

Chapter 22

A Breath of Fresh Air

A week before the results of the x-rays were due, the examinations at the Polytechnic began. I took the Politics exam on the Monday morning and then Economics on the following Wednesday. When I sat down in the examination room, my mind was suddenly filled with fear. I could feel myself beginning to panic, since my mind was dominated by my breathing problems. Consequently, I was unable to concentrate on the questions.

On the following Monday morning, as I was preparing to leave home to go to the Polytechnic, the telephone rang. I turned back and answered it. It was from my doctor. As soon as I heard his voice, I knew he was about to tell me that they had discovered an abnormality on the x-ray. He told me I would have to see a consultant immediately, who would arrange for me to undergo a number of tests in hospital. He did not go into great detail but mentioned that the hospital staff were concerned about a dark area in the region of my neck that had shown up on the x-ray. Surprisingly, I was not too worried at first, as I had long since prepared myself for the worst.

However, I suddenly realized that there were still the results of these tests to face, as well as the implications they held for my future. "Perhaps I do have a terminal illness!" I said to myself, while breaking out into a cold sweat. I tried immediately to dismiss the notion from my mind.

I felt relieved to remember that I had the Sociology examination to sit at the Polytechnic. It was a way of deferring my appointment with the Consultant. I asked my doctor if it was all right to sit the examination at the Polytechnic later that afternoon and to see the

Consultant the following day. He agreed but insisted I go in hospital early the next morning.

I felt justified in having persisted with my claims, even though I had wrongly assumed that there was something wrong with my lungs. Considering that I have no medical training, nor live in an ivory tower, it was only understandable that I was mistaken. "Now they will have to take notice of me," I said to myself, feeling as though a great burden had been lifted from my shoulders.

Later, I went to the Polytechnic to sit the written examination. The lecturers had granted me extra time, which entitled me to take a break mid-way through the exam. Having completed the first half of the examination, I went down to the refectory on the ground-floor for my break, escorted by a lecturer. Afterwards, we headed back up to the examination room on the fourth floor. The lecturer took it into his head to run up the stairs. Not wishing to allow him to get the better of me, I decided to run up after him.

Running up four flights of stairs would not have been too tiring to my legs, but by the time I reached the first floor landing I was breathing heavily, and upon reaching the second floor I was gasping desperately. I should have known better than to start running, but I did not want the lecturer to assume I was unfit. Halfway up the third flight, I could go no further and simply collapsed in a heap. I did not lose consciousness but merely lay on the stairs gasping for air. My mouth was wide open and my chest was expanding but not enough air was entering - the expansion was largely a muscular action. My mouth was gulping the air about me but I could barely inhale. It was a terrifying ordeal.

Suddenly, as if by instinct, I sat up and cupped my head in my hands, Moments later, I was amazed to find that my breathing had become easier. It certainly baffled me.

The lecturer asked me if I was all right, but, being embarrassed, I simply nodded my head. After a few minutes, I recovered and tried to act as though nothing had happened. He asked again if I was fit to continue, but I made light of the matter, since I was too proud to let him see that I was unfit.

I continued the examination but was unable to concentrate at all. My mind was too concerned with what had happened on the staircase and the phone call I had received from the doctor that morning.

Lying in bed that night, I was unable to sleep. I began wheezing very heavily and was convinced my life was about to end. In my desperation, I decided to go to Walton Hospital in the early hours of the morning. Luckily, I did not have to wait long before a nurse called my name. She escorted me to a cubicle and told me to lie on the examination bed, which had an adjustable back-rest. It was positioned so that I could lean back.

When the doctor came to see me, I was still wheezing badly. She went on to ask me many questions and then told me to sit up before giving me a breathing tube. She told me to take a deep breath and to blow into it. As I began to breath in, I realized immediately my wheezing had improved and that my breathing was almost normal. My face turned red with embarrassment as the doctor told me I should not be wasting her time. When she left the Sister and the nurse gave me a good lecture on the same lines. As I left the casualty department my head was bowed. I had never been made to feel so ashamed.

I walked home not knowing what to think. The whole affair was perplexing. I asked myself if I had been pretending to be breathing badly merely to get attention and wondered if my imagination was the culprit. What happened at the hospital truly baffled me. Then I remembered the telephone conversation with my doctor that morning telling me about the dark areas on my x-rays. I became totally confused.

The next day at the hospital, the consultant informed me I would have to undergo a series of tests on my chest. Apparently, the x-ray had revealed two dark patches around my throat. The tracheotomy scar could account for one of these areas, but the hospital staff were very concerned about the other one.

I was admitted into Broadgreen Hospital the following day. Most of the other patients had recently had a lung removed. The scar they bore started at the breast bone, continuing down to their side, around and up to the centre of their back - it was a gruesome sight. These particular patients certainly aroused my admiration. I felt guilty and ashamed of the way I had reacted to my breathing problems over recent years.

The next day, I had a bronchoscope - an inspection of the lungs, using a minute camera when the patient is anaesthetized. Apparently, the doctors realized that my breathing was abnormal during the operation. As a result, they gave me a supply of richly oxygenated air to breathe. Later, the anaesthetist came to see me and asked about the previous illnesses I had suffered. It suddenly reminded me of what had occurred in the same hospital five years earlier when I was undergoing the operation on my wrist. Nevertheless, although I told him about my breathlessness, he could not discover anything that could have caused my abnormal breathing. He and his colleagues remained puzzled.

All the other patients were very friendly, although they often had great difficulty in understanding my speech. Despite my babble, we had some lively debates on many topics.

My breathing continued to cause me great stress. By chance, I discovered that by raising my hands above my head I could cut off my breathing. The doctors were amazed when I showed them, since none of them had ever seen or heard of such a thing before.

One morning, after I had been in hospital for a week, another doctor came and asked me to demonstrate my ability to cut off my breathing by raising my hands. He was alarmed when I showed him and asked if I would mind giving a demonstration to a group of junior doctors during a lecture. I willingly agreed. When standing in front of them, I felt just as a celebrity must feel due to all the attention they were paying me. It was at this moment, I realized that I must have a rare condition.

I was discharged after a fortnight in hospital. The doctors did not tell me what was wrong with me, and I later found out they did not know. Apparently my condition was so rare that it baffled them.

During the following month, I continued to attend appointments with the consultant. In August, he decided that I should have a video x-ray made of the internal workings of the upper part of my body. The hospital had just acquired the video x-ray machine, and I was the first person on whom it was used. The staff were eager to see it in operation.

To my surprise, there seemed to be radiographers everywhere in the room - standing against the walls, huddled in the doorway and even crammed together outside, peering through the observation window.

It was a serious moment since my complaint certainly had the doctors baffled, not to mention my own apprehension. The room was in silence as a nurse strapped me to an inspection table. With the switch of a button, one end of the table was tilted so I was almost upright.

Despite the solemnity of the occasion, I decided to introduce a bit of humour onto the scene. "Now I know how Frankenstein must have felt!" I said aloud, as clearly as I could.

Suddenly, everybody present erupted into laughter.

A sombre silence soon befell the room as the doctors peered at a V.D.U. and discussed what they saw on the screen.

"I don't like the look of that," said one of them, as he pointed to the screen.

"Neither do I!" I said, out of the corner of my mouth, unable to resist the opportunity to be facetious - or to try to be.

Funny or not, laughter filled the room, once more.

After I had completed a series of tests in three hospitals, over a three-months period, the Consultant finally informed me that he had discovered the cause of my breathlessness. He told me that I was suffering from a very rare condition known as "tracheomalacia." It sounded very impressive, so I asked him to translate his jargon into language I could understand. According to his diagnosis, my windpipe would suddenly collapse for no apparent reason and not allow enough air to pass into my lungs. To remedy this he had decided to insert a wire frame into my windpipe to prevent it collapsing.

Although the thought of having a wire frame inserted into my throat alarmed me at first, I decided that if it worked, then why worry? However, after thinking it over, I realized that I normally had difficulty swallowing, especially tablets, since they would often get stuck in my throat and then dissolve - the taste was awful. I therefore decided to ask for a second opinion.

A few days later, I was admitted into hospital and underwent another bronchoscope. Later, I went to see another consultant.

I sat down in front of him, and, after asking a couple of questions, he leaned forward on his chair and examined the sides of my neck. He looked at me. "Hm, a goitre," he said. "You need a thyroid operation!"

I could barely believe what he had said to me, though I was very much relieved all the same.

Later, I discovered that the state of my breathing was dependent on the position of my head. When it was bent forward, the goitre - an enlarged thyroid gland - would press against my windpipe and thus restrict the air reaching my lungs. This explained the breathlessness when I was lying in bed, with my head supported by pillows. When I tilted my head back, my air-passage was again restricted.

"But why wasn't it discovered earlier?" I asked myself. To my mind, my doctor should have detected it when I had first complained to him years earlier, but nothing had been done. It was even more alarming to remember the arthrodesis operation on my wrist, five years ago. The state of my breathing had alarmed the anaesthetist, but he had failed to discover the reason then. However, I felt there was no justifiable reason why it had recently taken three months of tests to discover my problem, not to mention the eight years I had suffered with my breathing. "Hmph, so much for hi-tech," I said to myself.

I had the thyroid operation two weeks later. When I came around from the anaesthetic, the Sister asked me how I was feeling.

"A bit groggy but I'm not dead," I answered, before suddenly realizing the ease with which I could breathe. "Hey, it's easy for me to speak!" I was ecstatic.

Later, the doctor came to the ward to inform me that he had cut along my tracheotomy scar, so there would only be one scar on my neck. He also told me that he had weighed the diseased part of the thyroid gland after the operation. It was five times heavier than it should normally have been!

After arriving home from hospital the following week, I sat in the garden reflecting on my life. Foremost in my mind was the first time strangers had insulted me, assuming I was drunk or an idiot.. It had first happened while I was a patient at Delph, the annexe to Winwick, when I went alone into Warrington for the first time. My only wish at that moment was to have merely explained to the two women who had insulted me, that I never meant them any harm. The holiday in Lloret de Mar was also vivid in my mind, especially the numerous times the other holiday-makers ridiculed me because of the way I spoke.

However, only the paralysis affected my speech at that time. It was not until eight or nine years later that the thyroid had begun to restrict my breathing. It seemed ironic that at a time when I was beginning to master my speech, I should have the added burden of a goitre with which to contend. *C'est la vie*, I thought.

Enthusiasm was radiating from within me now that my health was no longer standing in my way. I felt as if I had another chance to start my life again. I was therefore all the more determined to build a new life for myself. I could barely wait to start working and was ready to try anything.

Chapter 23

Trying to Make a New Start

Now that I was breathing normally again, my zest for life had greatly increased. Although my speech was still impaired by the effects of the paralysis, it was significantly clearer than before the operation, not to mention the ease with which I could breathe and speak.

I was feeling on top of the world and was full of confidence - all I needed was to find a job. Whenever I went to the Job Centre, I would always try to be cheerful and positive, but I still remained without work. Due to the recession, it was difficult for most unemployed people to find work, but, since I was disabled, it was almost impossible. Eventually, it began to dawn on me that the prospect of my finding work was bleak, even though my speech had greatly improved.

Experience had taught me that it was no good simply waiting until something happened to change my situation. I had to take some initiative and make things work out for me.

I decided to become a social worker, since it was a fulfilling job and one where I felt I would be able to contribute much. In early May 1986, I wrote to Liverpool University to enquire about the social work courses they had to offer. To my annoyance, I received a reply stating that all the places for the forthcoming courses had been taken and I would have to wait until September before applying again.

During the weekdays, I would spend the mornings and afternoons in the city centre. I would visit the Job Centres, the library, or sit in coffee bars to perfect my much-improved speech.

Unable to obtain a permanent job, I tried to find work on a Community Programme. It would only last for a year, and I would be unemployed again when it finished, but at least it would be useful experience and keep me busy.

At the end of May, I was given an interview for the position of Welfare Officer for Spin - Services for People in Need. This was a Community Programme that provided help with gardening and decorating for people who were unable to do such tasks in their own homes.

At the interview I met Steve Foster, the Personnel Manager. Impressed by my recovery, he appeared genuinely interested in helping me. In the end, he employed somebody who was more experienced than me. I was extremely disappointed at first but later realized that he had given the vacancy to a more suitable candidate.

In early August 1986, I could barely believe my good fortune when the Job Centre gave me another interview for a job with a Community Programme. The position was for a part-time caseworker to work with the Vietnamese community in the Toxteth area of Liverpool. The successful candidate would work at the offices of a local neighbourhood council. The very thought of being accepted greatly encouraged me, since it was a position in which I felt I would certainly excel.

I attended the interview the same day, and discovered that, as a caseworker, I would be responsible for helping to solve the social problems of my Vietnamese clients. It would also be necessary to attend a weekly meeting of the Vietnamese Support Group. During the interview, I learned that Pat, the manageress, had recently graduated from Liverpool Polytechnic with an honours degree in Law. This immediately put me at ease, since we had something in common. The interview did not last long, and I fully expected to hear the reasons for my rejection. However, to my great delight Pat told me to start work on the following Monday.

It was wonderful news to hear, especially since I had the opportunity to work in the field I eventually intended to enter. I felt it was the chance for me to begin to repay the debt I felt I owed society. Even though most strangers had treated me unfairly for many years, I was still ready to accept society, if society accepted me. I was happy to be alive and extremely eager to get on with leading a "normal" life again. I intended to do my utmost to be successful as a caseworker.

I would have to complete a two weeks' training period before going around on my "patch" to help solve my clients' problems. I had spent the majority of the past sixteen years claiming either Unemployment or Sickness Benefit, so I was familiar with the benefit system.

The Southern Neighbourhood Council was an organisation that was totally independent of the Community Programme, even though both organisations shared the same building and provided similar services. Founded by local residents, the prime objective of the Neighbourhood Council was to assist those families living in the area that were least able to look after themselves. It provided home-helps for the disabled and ran a befriending service for those who were in need of it. In addition, it supplied expert advice on welfare rights. Each day, it would also provide cheap and affordable breakfasts and a three-course meal at lunch-time for visitors to the centre. It was mainly used by pensioners, the unemployed, the disabled, alcoholics and other low income groups.

On the first morning, Pat introduced me to Lan, the part-time Vietnamese interpreter, who would be working with me. Before leaving Vietnam, she had been a school teacher and spoke English well. She was well-liked by everybody who worked at the Centre.

Later, I went to the canteen and met May, where she worked for the Neighbourhood Council. She was in her late fifties and had worked as a part-time cook and caseworker for many years. Her language would have made any prison warder blush, but that did not worry me, since I believed that actions speak louder than words. She was rough and ready and had a heart of gold. Without doubt, she would always be the first to help anyone in need.

A Vietnamese client was waiting to see me when I returned to the office. His name was Dui Le Quoc and he was my age. He had been amongst one of the earliest groups of Vietnamese boat people to arrive in the U.K. Since he spoke Vietnamese, Chinese and English well, he had easily found work as a waiter in a Chinese restaurant in Toxteth.

In 1983, his parents, two younger brothers and two younger sisters were allowed to resettle in Liverpool from Vietnam. The family lived in two adjacent flats on the third floor of a tower block. Under the council's Urban Regeneration Strategy, the block of flats was soon to be demolished. The family was waiting to move into a new four-bedroomed house in the same area.

Dui had called into the Centre on his way to work to complain that nobody had visited his family for six months. His mother and two sisters were ill due to the dampness in their flat. He was pleased to hear that I would visit the family later that morning to see what help they needed.

Later, Lan went with me to visit the Le Quoc family. I had no idea what kind of reception I would receive, but was delighted to discover that the family were extremely friendly. They were all smiling broadly when I shook hands with the mother and daughters. I felt it was important to greet them warmly to let them see I wanted to be friendly and readily accepted them into our society. I had some idea how these unfortunate people must have felt. Like them, I knew what it was like to be discounted and detached from society.

No sooner had I sat down than Mrs. Le Quoc handed me a cup of tea and a plate of biscuits. None of the family were able to speak much English apart from Dui, who had gone to work, so Lan translated for me.

The poor condition of the flats surprised me, and it soon became apparent to me why Dui's mother and sisters were ill. The apartment was very damp due to poor ventilation, which became obvious when I examined each room. Mildew and other fungi were growing on the walls, a clear indication that the problem was condensation. I arranged for their doctor to attend to those who were ill and promised to help them in any way possible.

Later, I went with Lan to see the manager of the local Housing Department. She knew all the details of the Le Quocs' case, so I left it to her to ask the questions. I heard the manager telling her that the Le Quocs' new house would not be ready for at least three months.

We both returned to tell the Le Quocs the bad news. Distraught, the mother burst into tears.

Since my job was only a part-time position, I officially finished working at mid-day. As I walked to the bus stop to go home, I came across another Housing Department Office in the adjacent district. I did not want the manager of the housing office that was dealing with the Le Quocs' case to see that I was still wet behind the ears, so I decided to call at this office. I needed to find out the answers to some of the queries that had arisen over my first client's case.

I met the manager and we had a good conversation. Inevitably, I told him of my accident and that I wanted to become a social worker. He was very understanding and offered to help. I explained the difficulties facing the Le Quocs. After checking his books, he told me that they could move into a newly-built four-bedroomed house the following week. It was not far from their present home, which meant that they would not have to leave their new friends behind. I was very grateful to the housing manager.

On returning to the Le Quocs, I told them the good news. It was difficult for me to explain to Mrs. Le Quoc, so she telephoned Dui at work. When I told him the news, he was ecstatic and told me he would come straight home. When he arrived, I took the entire family to collect the key from the Housing Department, so I could show them around their new house.

The Le Quocs were delighted - I will always remember the look of gratitude on their faces. I have never seen a family so happy. I was doing a worthwhile job and hoped to be able to continue in the same way.

The next morning, I arrived at work and decided to update the files with details of the previous day's workload. To my surprise and disgust, I discovered that they had not been updated for six months. After recording the Le Quocs' particulars it became obvious to me that a full-time caseworker was needed.

When Pat arrived, she asked me to visit Chi, one of my clients. She had heard that his electricity supply has been disconnected and his meter removed. One of the other workers warned me that the previous caseworker had commented that Chi would rarely open the door to him when he had called. He had only spoken to Chi twice during his year of employment and had said that he was aggressive and sly-looking.

I checked Chi's file and discovered he had lived in the flat with another Vietnamese man who had left eighteen months earlier to live with his family in London. The records also mentioned that the friend could speak English well and had done all the shopping as well as personally paid all the bills. Chi was unemployed and receiving Social Security. The rest of his family were dead.

I went alone to call on him, as Lan had to attend a meeting elsewhere. I did not know if I was in any position to help him, but it was obvious that something had to be done.

When I knocked on the door there was no reply, so I shouted his name outside his flat. Chi eventually peered through the letter-box, so I showed him my identity card with my details printed in Vietnamese. He opened the door reluctantly and let me in. At first, he appeared terrified of me and continued to look down at the floor.

The flat reeked of mildew and was sparsely furnished. The wallpaper was peeling off the wall in places due to condensation. The curtains were drawn in the living room and the several candles scattered around the room only added to the gloominess of the place. Despite this, I found the flat was relatively clean and tidy.

I asked Chi if he had received any letters, but he was unable to understand me - not because my speech was unintelligible but because he simply did not speak English very well. I left the living room and signalled for him to follow me, as I walked to the front door. Taking a scrap of paper, I opened the door and posted it through the letter-box, saying the word "letter" as I did so. He looked puzzled at first but suddenly smiled as he realized what I meant. Indicating that I should follow him, he went into his bedroom and opened the top drawer of a dressing-table. I was amazed at what I saw. The drawer was almost overflowing with unopened letters. Amongst them were six electricity bills, the latest of which showed that £181.32p was outstanding. It also stated that to have a new meter and the electricity supply reconnected would cost another £20.

Using my own form of sign language, I attempted to tell Chi that he should save money out of his fortnightly Social Security giro to pay for his electricity bill. He must have understood my meaning, because he shook his head and walked out of the room. Moments later, he returned clutching £185 that he had obviously saved up.

I was surprised and began to wonder why he had not paid the account. I checked the dates of the outstanding bills and discovered they were all dated after his friend's departure to London.

Suddenly, it dawned on me that Chi genuinely did not know about the method of paying the bill. I realized that the muddle over the electricity account was not his fault, since there had clearly been a breakdown in communication. It did not seem right to me that he should have to pay to have the supply reconnected and a new meter installed.

Chi certainly had my sympathy. To some extent, his situation was comparable to my own, so I was determined to try to get the £20 waived and to do everything in my power to help him. I took the £185 and gave him a receipt.

That afternoon, I went to the electricity showroom. I explained to the Manager that Chi had saved the money but did not know how to pay the bill. He merely laughed in response and said he had never heard that excuse before. I told him about Chi's alienation from society and the conditions under which he was living. The Manager was not impressed. I stressed that if the electricity company were willing to waive the combined fee of £20, the bill would immediately be paid. He remained deaf to my pleas.

I did not pay the bill but went to the Head Office to protest. They too showed no interest, so I had no option but to pay the basic £181.32. I was disgusted and all the more determined to have Chi's electricity supply reconnected free of charge.

Although there had been a negative response from the Electricity Board, I was sure that the Electricity Consultative Council would be able to help Chi. The next morning, I called at their offices and explained the situation to their solicitor, who agreed to take up the case with the Electricity Board. It would take a few weeks, but he promised to telephone me to let me know the outcome.

From my own experience, I had a good idea of how Chi must have been feeling. After calling on him several times during the first week, I concluded that people had probably misinterpreted his mannerisms. I did not find him sly but timid and afraid of living in a world that appeared alien to him. When I saw him in the street, he would walk with his head down and his shoulders shrugged forward. He had the typical look of a man without hope - a man that was merely going through the motions of living.

I realized that Chi's situation would greatly improve if he had a job. It would mean that he would be in a much better position to look after himself and to integrate into society. I decided to call on Steve Foster, the Personnel Manager of Spin, the Community Programme where I had previously applied unsuccessfully for a position myself.

Steve was very pleased to hear that I had secured employment and was enjoying my work. After telling him that Chi was wasting away, living alone on the top floor of an isolated block of flats, I asked Steve if he would consider employing him as a gardener on the Community Programme. He liked the idea, until I told him that Chi did not speak English very well. However, I pointed out that his English would certainly improve if he mixed with English workers. Steve told me he was willing to interview him for a gardener's post, but added that he would not employ him if he was unsuitable. I arranged for Chi to attend an interview the following week.

Chi and I went along to the offices of Spin a week later. Steve conducted the interview with Peter, the Supervisor of the Community Programme in Bootle, where Chi would be working should he be successful at the interview. Both Steve and Peter stressed to me the many problems that would have to be overcome if they were to employ Chi. Although the situation began to look ominous for him, they finally agreed nevertheless to give him a trial period of a month.

For the first three days, I took Chi to work on the bus in my own time to ensure he knew how to get there. As he worked in Bootle, the other side of Liverpool from where he lived, it would take him an hour to get there by bus. I first had to travel across Liverpool to call for him and then travel back across to Bootle with him. Finally, I had to return to the other side of Liverpool to arrive at work for nine thirty in the morning. It meant having to get up two and a half hours earlier.

On the following Saturday morning, in my own time, I visited the Le Quocs after they had moved into their new home. I wanted to ensure that no problems had cropped up. I was happy to discover that, apart from a few minor problems, they were managing fine.

When returning home, I felt proud and realized that I was having considerable success as a caseworker. Although employed on a part-time basis, the time I worked amounted to many more hours than even a full-time caseworker would normally have worked. Nevertheless, I was enjoying it and was all the more determined to become a social worker or a probation officer.

A week later, the Electricity Consultative Council informed me that the Electricity Board had decided to waive the reconnection charge. However, they insisted that Chi would have to pay for the installation of the new meter. I arranged for the electricity men to call at his flat later that day. I was pleased with the outcome of my battle to get as fair a deal as possible for Chi.

At the beginning of September, I applied again to Liverpool University to study on a course leading to a C.Q.S.W., the recognized qualification in social work. However, they again informed me that all the places on the course for the following year had been taken. I was bitterly disappointed.

In the evenings, I decided to take a two-year university course in counselling, run by Compass - Counselling on Merseyside, Pastoral and Supportative Service. I attended the course once a week and found it extremely interesting. In addition, I took a voluntary job for two nights of the week as a librarian and receptionist for Compass.

I called regularly on the Le Quocs, since they were having a few teething problems with their new house. One day, I was talking to Le Quan, Dui's eldest sister, since her English had greatly improved in recent months. I discovered she had a major problem, which needed to be redressed urgently, since it was causing her great concern. I saw it as a challenge that I was eager to meet, even though it was certainly beyond the responsibility of a caseworker.

When Dui arrived in Britain in 1980 he had applied to Ockenden Venture, the organisation dealing with the resettlement of Vietnamese refugees in Britain, for his parents, two brothers and two sisters in Vietnam to join him. The immigration procedure was a lengthy process. It had taken over three years for the family in Vietnam to receive their authorization papers permitting them to come to England. During this period, Dui's sister, Le Quan, had married. She had duly notified the North Vietnamese authorities of the marriage and that she and her husband wished to emigrate to the U.K. Eventually, the family's emigration papers arrived but her husband's name was not on the list, so he had no option but to remain behind in Vietnam. When the Le Quoc family emigrated, the authorities assured Le Quan that they would allow her husband to follow her to Britain as soon as his papers had been processed.

She regularly received letters from him and longed for the day when they would be together again. However, she realized that the North Vietnamese authorities were reluctant to allow young men to leave their country. As the months slowly turned into years, she had begun to question if she would ever see him again. Three years after arriving in the U.K., Le Quan's husband was still in Vietnam.

My heart went out to Le Quan, but I was a lowly worker on a Community Programme and had no power in my own country, let alone North Vietnam. What could I do to help her? I brought the matter up at the next meeting of the Vietnamese Support Group. They were not familiar with the case and told me that they had enough problems to deal with as it was. I sought the help of Amnesty International, but they were powerless to do anything, since Le Quan's husband was not classed as a political refugee. I contacted other organisations, but none were willing or able to negotiate Le Quan's case.

However, I could not merely stand by and do nothing. I had to do something, even if it was only in protest. I decided to write to the authorities in North Vietnam. Aware that a communist regime was in power there, I hoped that they would take more notice of me, as a member of the working class, than they would of British Government officials from a mighty capitalist power. In my letter, I explained that Le Quan was suffering both physically and mentally, because of her enforced separation from her husband. I wrote another letter so she would be able to copy it after Dui had translated it into Vietnamese. I posted the two letters and hoped it would hasten the emigration process.

During the ensuing four months, I heard nothing from the Vietnamese authorities. Although not fully satisfied with what I had done, there was nothing more I could do. However, in March 1987, I received a letter from the North Vietnamese Embassy in London. They thanked me for my letter and informed me that Le Quan's husband would be emigrating later that year.

I did not have any friends with whom to go out in the evenings, so I always stayed at home. Sitting in my room one night, I suddenly had a notion to write an essay. This was surprising for me, since the writing of essays was my pet hate at the Polytechnic. I wrote six pages about a boy waking up on the beach of an island after being shipwrecked. When reading my work, it suddenly became clear that I had the beginning of a novel. My excitement grew as my mind devised the plot of the story. I became so involved with writing the manuscript that I continued writing in the evenings and at weekends, even though I was working on the Community Programme and still doing the counselling course as well as the voluntary work.

After spotting an advertisement in the "Guardian" for a one-week course in London on "The Counselling of A.I.D.S. Patients," I decided to enrol. Although I was interested in helping people with this virus, it also occurred to me that this qualification might help me to secure work in the field of social work. I had to borrow £350 from the bank to pay for the course and expenses, but I thought it would be a very good investment.

Upon my return to Liverpool after the course, I imagined I would be in great demand as an AIDS worker - no such luck! - the only organisations that wanted my services were voluntary groups! Nevertheless, I became a member of the Christian Action for Aids and the

Liverpool Aids Support Group. After a few months, I realized that the expenses involved in going to and from these various organisations were too high, since I only earned the wages of a part-time worker. I was also attending the counselling course once a week as well as working voluntarily for Compass on two evenings during the week. On top of all this, I was writing my novel. After four months, it became clear I was working too hard and not getting enough sleep. I decided to discontinue the voluntary work - I needed some rest.

I was still working on the Community Programme and enjoying my work as a caseworker. Fortunately, I was still continuing to help the Vietnamese Community effectively. My efforts were well rewarded when I heard that there would no longer be a need for my post after the completion of my twelve month employment period; apparently, I had solved most of the major problems.

The day I left will remain in my memory for a long time. On arriving home, I suddenly felt weak and broke out in a heavy sweat. I felt awful and began to shiver violently. I went to bed with a couple of hot water bottles but could not keep warm.

Later that evening, my fever had become so much worse that my mother phoned for an ambulance to rush me to Fazakerley Hospital. I had pneumonia! According to the doctors, I had been working too hard and my resistance was low. *"C'est la vie!"* I thought!

Chapter 24

Enterprise

Finally discharged from the hospital, I found myself unemployed again and living on nothing but my fortnightly payments of Income Support. Although aware that I would be entitled to many benefits,I decided against it; the occasion when the clerk at the D.H.S.S. office assumed I was drunk was still fresh in my mind. The humiliation was such that I had continued refusing to admit to myself that I was disabled, even though I was clearly unfit for work. I hoped and prayed I would eventually find some kind of employment and refused to be discriminated against. In addition, I would have another label and the prejudice of society with which to contend and felt I had endured enough stigmatization and did not want any more. Although I still spoke with a slight slur, my speech had improved greatly since the operation, and I felt sure that some employer would give me a job.

I continued to keep up my spirits while looking desperately for work. I would buy the "Guardian" on Wednesday mornings and spend many hours applying for suitable social or community work vacancies. On Thursday evenings, I would apply for any suitable positions advertised in the "Liverpool Echo." It was expensive considering the fortnightly pittance I received from the Social Security was my only source of income. I eagerly awaited the mail each morning in the hope of receiving an invitation for an interview. Alas my disappointments were many. Any reply that I did receive would always be a rejection.

It was depressing but I would soon get excited and build up my hopes, whenever I wrote after another vacancy. I would also visit the Job Centre, even though there were rarely any genuine vacancies on the boards. I do not know how I was able to remain enthusiastic for so long, but I did. I cherished life and knew that one day my chance would come, so my relentless quest to live a "normal" life continued.

Whenever I applied for employment, I always ensured my application form and C.V. were neatly written and well presented. I could not understand, therefore, why nobody would employ me, or at least invite me to attend an interview. I finally came to the conclusion that the gaps in my employment record had something to do with it. I suppose employers did not believe that anybody could have had as many injuries as I and recover to lead a "normal" life.

However, I realized that there were many people who were worse off than me. In particular, I felt sorry for the unemployed married men and women who had families to support. I was fortunate in this respect, for I was single and did not have anybody but myself to support financially. Fortunately, my mother, despite living on her pension, seemed to be able to perform miracles with the money she received. She was a great help, and I felt guilty about my inability to help support her financially in the way I felt she deserved.

Now that I was almost leading a "normal" life again, I wanted to have a wife, my own children and my own home. I also needed to receive the respect that I, as a human being, deserved. To have these things, it was necessary to have peace of mind - to have peace of mind, I needed a job. Clearly a Catch-22 situation.

Although at first I was putting most of my energy into looking for work, I found that I was spending an increasing amount of time writing my novel. It was very enjoyable and I was content to stay in my room writing every night. I became obsessed with the story, which I called "Exiled in Paradise," the tale of Mike, a young Cadet Officer, awaking on a beach after being shipwrecked.

In December 1987, I took part in the Enterprise Allowance Scheme as a writer. This was a government initiative to encourage those out of work to become self-employed and to use their entrepreneurial skills to set up a business. The scheme would last for a twelve-month period, during which time those participating would receive £40 per week and not have to register as unemployed every fortnight. To qualify, it was necessary to have £1,000 in a bank account. Fortunately, my bank manager agreed to give me an overdraft facility to cover that amount. He must have believed in me, because my current account was already overdrawn by almost £400. I also had to prove to the government officers that I was serious about my business, so I took along my manuscript to show them. They were impressed enough to allow me onto the Scheme.

Deciding to put all my energy into becoming a writer, I spent many hours in the library, reading books on the art of writing. It was my belief at first that, after having experienced so many unusual aspects of life, I could not fail to become a successful writer. It did not take me long to discover that there was much more to writing novels than simply having experiences. To begin with, I found that there was no correct or incorrect way to write, and that I had to learn many skills to make my writing more attractive and readable.

Although I did not realize it at the time, my first mistake was to use long sentences. I had deliberately written sentences using many conjunctions purely in the hope of giving the reader the impression that I had a good command of English. Many of my sentences were so complicated that most readers would have become lost amongst the many conjunctions I used in each sentence. Instead, it would have been better to have made each sentence short and direct, so that it would lead directly to the point. Another mistake I made was my use of long words. I suppose it was a way of trying to impress the reader with my vocabulary. In short, my main mistake was to write to impress and not to express.

I also realized that the ability to write sentences was not the sole qualification needed to write a novel. The fact that I had never received any formal instruction on the "do's" and "don'ts" of writing a novel only made me more determined. Fortunately, having studied French literature at Grenoble University as well as when studying A level French, I did have some knowledge of literature. However, it was certainly not extensive. I was well aware that writing a book would not be an easy task. However, the hardest and most frustrating part would probably be to find a publisher.

After I had written the manuscript in longhand, Brenda, my sister, offered to type it for me. It was my first real attempt to write a novel, and I made many mistakes and had to rewrite sections many times - not to mention the retyping Brenda had to do. I should have begun by sketching out my plot and organising myself properly. Mistakes or not, I have never worked so hard in my life. Sometimes I would be half asleep while writing, but that did nothing to dent my enthusiasm. Thoroughly enjoying it, I just carried on.

I continued to make changes, although these were purely to improve the plot and to make the story more intriguing. By the following summer, I had still not finished writing my first draft.

The elapse of time had made me much more confident when speaking to strangers. Although my speech had greatly improved in clarity, it would still sound slurred at times, especially when tired or suddenly asked an embarrassing question. I had reached the point where, once having explained about the crash, I would no longer feel ashamed of the way I spoke. At long last, I was finally beginning to feel that society would one day accept me.

In September 1988, I enrolled at Millbrook College of Further Education to learn how to type and word process. At first, it felt strange sitting behind a typewriter in the commerce class, since I was the only male in the class of sixteen students.

Fortunately, after having been at the College for two weeks, I met Sheena Ewing, the Vice Principal. I had known her from her lecturing days in North East Liverpool Technical College, when I took A levels. After I had spoken a few words to her, she remarked that my speech had greatly improved. I was pleased to hear it. When I told her I was writing a novel, she showed great interest and offered to help me in whatever way she could. After telling her I was learning to type and word process, she told me not to bother attending any more lessons and promised to arrange for me to have the daily use of a word processor. Delighted that someone believed in my potential, I gained a great amount of confidence.

The next day, I received a basic lesson on word-processing and a manual so I could teach myself. Fortunately, I was advised to ask one of the commercial members of staff if I needed help.

Word-processing was difficult for me to grasp at first. I was terrified of pressing the wrong key and breaking the machine. Fortunately, as soon as I had mastered the eight function keys, it was mainly a case of being able to type.

Typing at a high speed was not necessary, since I often had to stop and think hard and long about the right word or phrase to use. The first month was a struggle and my progress very slow. At the end of the first term, I had managed to master all the word-processing techniques, although I was only able to complete one of the twelve chapters of "Exiled in Paradise." Nevertheless, I was making progress.

Colin and his wife Carola came to stay with us over the Christmas period. When they heard that I could use a word processor they were delighted and asked me how I had managed it. When I told them they were amazed, although they were more impressed when my mother told them I was writing a novel.

Later, Colin told me that he and Carola had decided to buy a word processor to help them manage their respective businesses. They asked for my advice on the type of models that would be suitable for them to use. I willingly agreed to help them.

That night, I lay in bed, wondering whether to ask Colin to lend me £500 to buy a word processor of my own. I had never asked anyone to lend me anything but my hopes were suddenly dashed, when I remembered that Colin had recently bought a new house in Pinner. I decided to forget the idea.

The next morning, we went to the city centre to look at various word processors. I advised Colin and Carola on which word processor to buy - they took my advice and bought one.

After we had returned home, I offered to show Colin how to get started on his new machine. He told me not to bother, as he would read the manual. I thought it was odd as he had no experience, but I did not press him on the matter.

When they were preparing to leave, I put the word processor in the boot of their car. Carola asked me to go to a nearby shop for a magazine she wanted to read on their journey home. I did so and returned a few minutes later. After exchanging farewells with my mother and myself, they got into their car and waved as they drove off.

"I'm glad to see him doing well for himself," said my mother, as we walked into the house.

"Yes, so am I - he's a good lad is our Colin," I replied.

"They told me to tell you that they hope you enjoy it."

"Enjoy what?" I asked, wondering what she meant.

"They've left you another present on your bed."

" What is it?" I asked, excitedly.

"Go and have a look," she said.

I ran upstairs and rushed into my room. Guess what was on my bed? The word processor I had minutes earlier put into the boot of their car. I really felt indebted to them as it was a great boost. I now had the potential to become an author - I was certainly going to continue trying.

After the initial euphoria was over, I did nothing but word process from early evening through the night until five or six o'clock the next morning. After sleeping until midday, I would go to the Central Library in the afternoon to check details and to edit the work done the previous night. I had to make many changes to the plot of the story, as well as to correct my many typing mistakes, caused by my double-vision and the lack of co-ordination. Nevertheless, I was making slow but steady progress.

In September 1988, I enrolled for the Playwright's Workshop run by Dave Evans at the University. We had met the previous year and I had mentioned that I was writing a novel. On our second meeting, he asked me how "Exiled in Paradise" was coming along. He was not surprised when I told him I had not yet completed it.

I liked Dave on meeting him. Despite holding down a high status job, he treated everyone as an equal. He was South African by birth and had been a journalist in Natal and the Cape. As an active fighter against the South African regime, the police had often harassed him because of his stand against the apartheid system - he had even been imprisoned for five years because of his beliefs. Later, he came to Britain to study at Oxford University. After graduating he moved to Liverpool to lecture at the University. I admired both his convictions and determination.

I decided to enrol on his course as I wanted to learn the art of playwrighting. It also made a break from writing the novel, which seemed to be forever in my thoughts.

The playwright course was enlightening. During the course, Dave encouraged each student to write a short play. Most weeks, professional actors would perform the plays, so the class was able to constructively criticize each drama and suggest improvements.

In December 1988, my year on the Enterprise Allowance Scheme ended. I had still not finished my novel, and it would still be a few months before it was ready to submit to a publisher. Again, I registered as "unemployed."

Writing was now in my blood, and I was thoroughly enjoying the long hours. The problem was that I would need an income to support me until my work was published - if it was good enough. Since I had become proficient at using my word processor, I decided to go into business for myself.

My idea was to start on a part-time basis merely to provide me with an income while I was writing. I proposed to supply small businesses with various computer services, using my bookkeeping, advertising, and word processing skills.

In January 1989, still classed as "unemployed," I enrolled on a Business Enterprise Programme. This was another government course providing tuition and advice in small business management.

After completing the course, I arranged to provide a computerized bookkeeping service for two shopkeepers. My third client was a travel agent. I suggested that he provide me with the details of both his present and previous clients, so I could create a database for his business. I would then be able to send a personalised letter to each of his customers to advertise current holidays, for example. He was enthusiastic.

At the end of April 1989, I had my business cards printed. I was eagerly waiting for the first Monday in May, the day I was due to start trading my services. However, I hit a snag - the printer on my word processor broke. Red faced, I had to tell each of my clients that I would not be able to begin the service on the arranged date. They were not very happy when I asked them to wait a week for my printer to be repaired.

While waiting for the printer to be mended, I concentrated on my writing. Since completing the year on the Enterprise Allowance Scheme, I had not spent much time writing "Exiled in Paradise. I had been too busy acquiring bookkeeping and advertising skills at a local enterprise agency. Working day and night for a week and grabbing a few hours sleep when I was able, I managed to complete the second draft of the manuscript. It had taken me more than two long years, and the story-line had changed significantly in the process. I was pleased since I only needed to finally edit the script before sending it to a publisher. My excitement grew.

Chapter 25

A New Future

On the morning that the Giro for my Income Support arrived, I was about to take it to the post office, when I received a phone call from the "Liverpool Echo." They had heard I had written a book and wanted to interview me. I was stupefied when Larry Neild, the journalist, asked if he could interview me. I had never been so surprised in my life. Naturally, I readily agreed to meet him.

Larry arrived later to interview me along with a photographer. Unfortunately, he believed that I had written an autobiography and was disappointed to learn it was a novel I had written. Apparently, the "Echo" would have considered serializing my work, if it had been an autobiography.

"Blast," I said jokingly, "there goes my chance for fame and glory!"

"'Why, haven't you been in the 'Echo' before?'" asked Larry.

"'The only time I've been in the 'Echo' was nineteen years ago, when I had a serious car crash,'" I said, trying not to sound too disappointed. "I was unconscious for three weeks, so I knew nothing about it at the time - to make matters worse I'd lost my memory."

Larry's eyes seemed to grow in size. "Unconscious for three weeks?" he queried, almost in disbelief. "You lost your memory! Tell me all about it!"

I told him about my injuries and the operations I had undergone since the accident. I did not mention my having been a patient in Winwick Psychiatric Hospital, because I did not want any association with the stigma given to psychiatric patients. I had already put up with enough insults from people and did not want any more.

"I don't think we can help you much with your novel," he said, "but I've certainly got a better story here than what I had expected"

It was only at this moment I began to realize that some people might be interested in reading about some of the events in my life. It certainly came as a great surprise to me. The way people had treated me in the past meant that I had at times believed my life was something of which to be ashamed.

I knew better now if the look on Larry's face was anything to go by. He told me that the article would feature in the "Echo" the following evening. I was ecstatic. For over nineteen years, only my mother had known of my troubled life, although I had never gone into the details. I had never told any of my family about the insulting treatment I had endured, since I did not want them to think that I was ever down-hearted or humiliated. Having said that, I suppose they must have known how people would react to hearing my speech.

Larry and other "Echo" staff strongly advised me to write an autobiography. They told me to hold on to "Exiled in Paradise," until I had made a name for myself with the autobiography, which, according to them, "should sell like hot cakes." They said that after my life story had been published, my name would become well-known and I would have a wider readership for my novel.

I certainly had reservations about waiting until I had written an autobiography before sending "Exiled in Paradise" to a publisher. The novel had taken over two years to complete, and I was eager to see it on the bookshelves - that was assuming a publisher were to accept it. Finding a publisher might well be a long and costly business. Since I was only able to afford the essentials to live on, I realized that it was going to be difficult. After thinking it over, I decided to consider writing an autobiography and to hold on to my novel.

Early the following afternoon, I went to the city centre and bought a copy of the "Echo." Standing in the street, I quickly flicked through the paper until I found the article. I was mesmerized at first and found it difficult to believe that the large photograph of a man sitting at the word processor was me. I rushed into the nearest cafe to read it.

The article was moving. I felt embarrassed at the tone and some of the comments it made - its tribute to my "fighting spirit," for example. It was a rarity to receive a compliment, let alone such an accolade given by the "Echo." Although the article was a true account of my life since the crash, I had never realized how much I had accomplished, probably because people had treated me so disdainfully. Also, I had been too busy, at first, trying to achieve success of a different kind.

I felt that I was finally receiving recognition for my long and frustrating battle. It was as if all the heartache and worry had all been worth it, since I could now hold my head up high and never be ashamed of having had a serious car accident. It seemed as if my whole life was changing for the better.

The next day, the telephone never seemed to stop ringing. Most of the calls were from the "Echo" readers who were thoughtful enough to look for my telephone number in the directory to congratulate me on my "bravery" - their word not mine. Many of the callers advised me to write an autobiography and several calls were from journalists who wrote for various magazines. I was surprised that people found my story so amazing, simply because I had never enjoyed remembering my past.

At first, I dreaded the thought of writing my life story. I had no idea where to start or what to write about. All my mind seemed able to remember were my many failures in business and the operations I had undergone, not to mention the countless times strangers had been insulting towards me.

In the end, I decided to send Dave Evans a letter with a copy of the article and seek his advice. We arranged to meet in the University coffee bar a couple of days later. He told me that after he had read the article he too had been amazed. When we had first met, I had told him that I had been involved in a car accident and had difficulty with my speech, but had not given him any further details. He did not ask me *if* I was going to write an autobiography, but merely asked *when* I was going to begin writing it.

I was not totally convinced that I would be able to complete such an undertaking. I did not think I would be able to write an entire book about my life and make it interesting. Dave gave me a pep talk, which seemed to do the trick. Taking the plunge, I simply got on with writing it. My excitement grew and I seemed to find the inspiration to carry on until I had finished each chapter.

I began the first draft of my biography in July 1989. I wrote for at least ten hours every day starting in the evening and working through until the morning. After six hours sleep, I would then go to the city centre and visit the library, checking certain details for the manuscript. Later, I would always spend some time in a coffee bar talking to people before returning home to start writing again in the evening.

Since I was making good progress, I decided to do some market research to see how the public would react to a story like mine. On many occasions, I would sit in a coffee bar and show customers the article from the "Echo" while promoting the autobiography. Their response was tremendous, especially when compared to the reception I expected to receive.

Encouraged by their response, I decided to see how the University and Polytechnic students would react. Their enthusiasm was similar, and, after showing them various chapters of the manuscript, many of them would treat me as a celebrity.

In May 1990, Sue Lindon, a student, wrote a very moving article about me in the University's Gazette. The following month, a similar article written by Richard Hill also appeared in "Precinct," the University's official magazine for lecturers and students.

It did not take long to realize that I had achieved my most desired wish: to be treated as a human being again and to be able to speak coherently, while holding the attention of a crowd of people. I no longer felt that I had to justify myself. I was happy and completely satisfied with the way my life seemed to be heading.

A little over a year had passed since that article had appeared in the "Echo." During this time, my life had changed so much. Before the article was published, I always tried to be cheerful and to give people the impression that I did not have a care in the world. I had been far from happy in reality, although I had never stopped trying to be "successful."

Happy with life

People would often ask me how I managed to overcome so many traumas in my life. Embarrassed to answer at first, I would tell them I was only human. However, when I thought seriously about it, I suppose it was a combination of traits in my character.

I feel my childhood played a major role in moulding my character. My parents were reasonably strict when they needed to be while lenient most of the time. I was a robust child and often rebellious, and as a result I developed a strong constitution and a defiant will to succeed. My parents tried to keep me on the straight and narrow, so I had a good sense of direction and a stable character. This helped me to recover from my initial injuries and to continue my effort to get over the traumas I came across later in my life.

Before the car accident, I never had any difficulty in making friends and acquaintances. I had a naturally exuberant, extroverted, and gregarious temperament, which made my rejection by society all the more unbearable. My exclusion from society made me feel as if I was being betrayed - it times, it felt as if I was being stabbed in the back with my own knife. It was difficult not to become cynical or disillusioned, but I was fortunate in being able to maintain a feeling of inner security. I was able to hold the steadfast belief in my mind that, one day, people would respect me again. This made the rejections and insults not only easier to bear, but almost irrelevant. In the end, the insults would almost bounce off me. Despite the initial hurt I would understandably feel, I was able to take them lightly, secure in the knowledge that I would one day have all the things I dreamed of - acceptance, friendship, respect ...

The "Echo" article was excellent in a number of ways. It hit the nail on the head when describing my method of recovery as D.I.Y. After abandoning speech therapy in disgust, I consciously chose to set about rebuilding my own shattered life. I took an active part in my rehabilitation and whenever real trouble hit me, I would try to confront it head on and fight back. This was the way to avoid becoming embittered, warped, and self-pitying. There was little chance that I would take an escape route into a fantasy world and give up my quest altogether, because I would look at my situation squarely and not have any grand illusions about myself. My attempt to see things objectively, or as I thought they were, would leave me no alternative but to do something about my situation.

Although at times I felt completely overwhelmed by feelings of isolation, apathy and worthlessness, my pride would always come to the rescue. The instant I felt that I was brooding or that I might be labelled as someone with an inferiority complex, my pride would reassert itself to ensure I made another effort to repel such a notion. I was not going to have anyone label me as having any kind of psychological disorder.

Even the fact that I was marginalized and discriminated against had a beneficial effect on my character. In the end, it prevented me from becoming self-centred, selfish and egotistical. I knew what it was like to suffer and to be the underdog, so I was able to empathize with other disadvantaged people, such as Chi, my Vietnamese client. I became a more humane and compassionate person because of the accident..

More importantly, the feeling of being marginalized and discriminated against generated the desire to be accepted. Later, this desire grew into a firm resolution that, regardless of what obstacles stood in my way, I would overcome my circumstances altogether. Somehow, I knew my efforts would bring "success."

At one time, my desire to "succeed" was nothing more than a wish to live a "normal" life like most people. However, this hardened into a determination to succeed at something that would bring me respect from many people.

Even though I have achieved my most cherished wish to speak intelligibly, my desire for success is still alive and kicking. However, it has now been focused on a specific goal: to become an accomplished author and playwright.

I wrote this book in the hope that anyone who reads it will be better informed about the stigmatization that many disabled people have to endure daily. By making my story accessible to a wider audience, I trust that people will be able to draw some inspiration from it and be better able to deal with their own problems. If I can help or encourage just one other person to continue the struggle, everything I have had to endure in life will have been worth it.

Life is wonderful - do not waste it!

THE END

Notes